E-GOVERNANCE AND INDIAN SOCIETY

E-Governance and Indian Society

An Impact Study of Andhra Pradesh, Karnataka & Kerala

Y. Pardhasaradhi
with
Rakesh Chetal
Namita Gupta

KANISHKA PUBLISHERS, DISTRIBUTORS
NEW DELHI-110 002

KANISHKA PUBLISHERS, DISTRIBUTORS
4697/5-21A, Ansari Road, Daryaganj
New Delhi -110 002
Phones : 2327 0497, 2328 8285
Fax : 011-2328 8285
E-mail : kanishka_publishing@yahoo.co.in
kanishkabooks@gmail.com

E-Governance and Indian Society:
An Impact Study of Andhra Pradesh, Karnataka & Kerala

First Published-2009

Edition-2025

ISBN : 978-81-8457-108-0

Rs. 850

PRINTED IN INDIA

Published by Madan Sachdeva for Kanishka Publishers, Distributors, 4697/5-21A, Ansari Road, Daryaganj, New Delhi-110002, Typeset by Sunshine Graphics, Delhi, and Printed at G.S. Printers, Delhi.

Foreword

Combined strengths of satellite communications, fibre optics technologies, microelectronics, computing technologies and several other materials technologies have made the modern Information and Communication Technologies (ICT) accessible to a large majority of ordinary people, in almost every walk of their lives. At the same time, ICT are also in the forefront of most strategic sectors as well as globally competitive commercial fronts. ICT are also a part of the cause of the phenomenon called globalization. ICT also strengthen globalization.

Naturally ICT have a great role to play in the governance of a country at the central and various other intermediary levels. The ultimate beneficiaries of e-governance are the people. In a country like India where access to the administration had become very difficult to a common citizen even for legitimate day-to-day tasks like paying electricity bills or paying taxes, e-governance is a great boon. The efficiency obtained through e-governance helps also the economic growth by reducing transaction time and costs.

India had understood these potential benefits as early as 1970's when it started its satellite communication experiments. Later INSAT spurred other ICT technologies.

But the governance systems did not catch up with necessary changes with speeds equal to technological changes. It is understandable as social systems are slow. There were also powerful vested interests against such changes. Finally several bold starts were made by a few forward thinking political leaders and administrators, in some States of India. They included several sectors like education, health, water supply, shelter and agriculture.

There are now a minimum critical size of number of experiments. Some are acclaimed as great successes. Some are with mix results. There are failures too. It is in this context the National Science and Technology Management Information Systems (NSTMIS) programme of Department of Science and Technology, Government of India had initiated a project to assess some of the e-governance programmes in a systematic form.

The impact study of e-governance carried out in the South Indian states of Andhra Pradesh, Karnataka and Kerala by Prof. Y. Pardhasaradhi and his team brings out many facts. It records the experience of various stakeholders. Concepts like gender parity in access to ICTs and empowerment of rural dwellers along with issues like' digital divide and expansion of services have been dealt at length in the study. This book is one of the end result of an extensive study which was funded by NSTMIS.

No doubt other researches on e-governance are being undertaken by many public administrators, but with limited areas of focus. Most of the studies done so far have concentrated only on issues like institutional re-engineering, success or failure of e-governance projects, cost-benefit analysis and the general perceptions of the citizenry towards electronic delivery of public services. However, this book presents a well-researched study in the realms of technological impact on society equal access to ICTs on the part of men and women and several sections of different communities, ICTs in education, agriculture (marketing), health, land records administration, property registration and automation of district administration. It has also identified further areas of e-governance research like the institutional/personnel adaptation of technology in administration, technical competency among the staff, leadership in e-governance and the notion of ownership of e-governance systems. In view of the above, this book would be of immense help to administrators, policy makers, researchers, academia and students.

If the findings given in the book are taken seriously, newer implementation strategies will emerge. I think the book will also help those in the ICT Industry, as the insights derived from this book can help them to expand e-governance businesses in India.

(Y.S.Rajan)

1/10/08

Acknowledgements

We are thankful to a number of individuals and departments/ institutions who have helped us in bringing out this research study in the book form. As we write this acknowledgement, we recollect the gainful insights and thoughts of a great number of researchers and government officials in the states of Andhra Pradesh, Karnataka and Kerala as well as other parts of the country.

First and the foremost we are indebted to National Science & Technology Management Information System (NSTMIS), Department of Science & Technology (DST), Government of India, which sponsored this study.

Our heartfelt gratitude is due to Prof. D. Ravindra Prasad, Advisor, Urban Governance, Administrative Staff College of India (ASCI), Hyderabad, and Dr. P.K. Mohanthy, IAS, Former Director, Center for Good Governance (CGG), Hyderabad, for being a constant source of inspiration. Their rich and scholastic experience in the areas of governance was of immense help in conducting this study.

A study of such high technical proportions would not have been focused and precise without advice and guidance of experts in this area. We profusely thank Dr. A. N. Rai, Scientist 'E', NSTMIS, DST and Dr. Pradosh Nath, Scientist 'F', National Institute of Science, Technology and Development Studies, New Delhi for their valuable suggestions.

We wish to make a special mention of Prof. S. Bhoopathi Rao, Prof. Sofi Ali, Prof. Ravinder Kaur and Prof. R. Limbadri from Department of Public Administration, Dr. Sriram Venkatesh, Department of Mechanical Engineering and Mr. P. Vishnu Dev, Department of Sociology, Osmania University, for their benign cooperation.

We are grateful to Prof. Prabhath Dutta, Advisor, Local and Urban Governance, Government of West Bengal, Prof. G. Koteshwara Prasad, Madras University, Chennai and Prof. D. Jeevan Kumar,

University of Bangalore, Bangalore, for their critical inputs for making this study comprehensive.

Equally important had been the support of Officials of National Informatics Centers (NIC) in Andhra Pradesh, Karnataka and Kerala, in providing the vital information on e-Governance programmes in the respective states. In the same vein officials of e-Seva, CARD, VOICE and Saukaryam in Andhra Pradesh, Bangalore One, Bhoomi and KAVERI in Karnataka and Akshaya, E-Collectorate and FRIENDS in Kerala extended their cooperation in the course of collecting the valuable data from their offices.

Mr. Sunil Dutt, Publication Officer, Indian Institute of Public Administration (IIPA), New Delhi, has helped in bringing out this book in its present form. We thank him for his suggestions and effort.

The project team that worked on this study collectively shares the credit for successful completion of this assignment. We acknowledge the contribution of the team comprising Dr. J. Musalaiah, Co-Investigator, Department of Political Science, Osmania University, Hyderabad, ably assisted by Mr. T. Venkatamallu, Mr. B. Ramalingam and Mr. T. Lakshmaiah as Project Associates, and Mr. D. Sriram in Data Compilation.

We appreciate the assistance rendered by Mr. Safdar Ahmed, Freelance Journalist in improving the project report and the editorial assistance for this book.

Mr. Madan Sachdeva, proprietor of Kanishka Publishing readily agreed to publish this work under the banner of his publishing house and has brought out the study in this beautiful form. We abundantly acknowledge his endeavour.

AUTHORS

Preface

Information and Communication Technologies (ICTs) are reshaping and redefining the globe constantly. They served as a powerful media in propagating and promoting the concept and culture of globalization in the developing world. Globalization reflects competitiveness and stretches itself to restructure traditional administrative systems in tune with the requirements of market economy. That the adaptation of new technologies in governance can drastically change the way the public administration systems functioned was never in doubt; all that was needed was an innovative public policy and flexible collaboration patterns with the private sector, primarily technical vendors at the highest level and operators at the grassroots level. Delivery of public services through electronic means and incorporation of ICTs in administrative structures—which are commonly termed as *electronic governance*—not only ensure transparency, accountability and responsibility but also empower the citizens in ways more than one. The Right to Information (RTI) Act of 2005 provides citizens of the country with access to any information related to governance and such information can be obtained mostly through electronic mode.

Access to information alone does not empower the citizens in real terms. Public participation right through the stages of policy formulation and implementation holds key to success of any governmental intervention or programme, especially in case of rural and urban development and in sectors like education, health, water supply, shelter, agriculture, and above all the national economy. Application of information and communication technologies in the administration of development programmes has resulted in greater efficiency and more success.

Much has been said and written about e-governance programmes in the country. Academics and public administrators have undertaken a vast field of study, but with limited areas of focus.

Primarily, they laid emphasis on issues like institutional re-engineering, success or failure of e-governance projects, cost-benefit analysis and the general perceptions of the citizenry towards electronic delivery of public services. However, this book presents a well-researched study in the realms of technological impact on society, equal access to ICTs on the part of men and women, ICTs in education, agriculture (marketing), health, land records administration, property registration and automation of district administration in the South Indian States of Andhra Pradesh, Karnataka and Kerala. The research was undertaken during 2005-07, which was a decisive period for e-governance in India. The study also focuses on further areas of e-governance research like the institutional/personnel adaptation of technology in administration, technical competency among the staff, leadership in e-governance and the notion of ownership of e-governance systems. Given the ground covered, this work would be of immense help to administrators, policy makers, researchers, academia and students of public administration and management.

Y. PARDHASARADHI

Contents

Acronyms

ACA : Additional Central Assistance
AOEMA : Asia Oceania Electronic Marketplace Association
ATM : Automated Teller Machine
B1 : Bangalore One
B2B : Business-to-Business
B2C : Business-to-Citizen
BEL : Bharat Electronics Limited
BEML : Bharat Earth Movers Limited
BESCOM : Bangalore Electricity Supply Company
BHEL : Bharat Heavy Electricals Limited
BOO : Build-Operate-Own
BOOT : Build Operate Own Transfer
BOT : Build-Operate-Transfer
BSNL : Bharat Sanchar Nigam Limited
BWSSB : Bangalore Water Supply and Sewerage Board
C2C : Citizen-to-Citizen
CARD : Computer-Aided Administration of Registration
CCC : Citizen Care Centre
C-DAC : Centre for Development of Advanced Computing
C-DIT : Centre for Development of Imaging Technology
CLR : Computerisation of Land Records
CMLR : Comprehensive Modernisation of Land Records
CPU : Central Processing Unit
CRT : Cathode-Ray Tube
CTC : Community Technology Centre

DC*Suite	:	District Collectorate Suite
DMRS	:	Document Management and Retrieval Systems
DPAR	:	Department of Public Administration and Revenue
DRO	:	District Registrar Office
EAF	:	E-Governance Assessment Framework
ECIL	:	Electronics Corporation of India Ltd.
FIFO	:	First in First Out
FRIENDS	:	Fast, Reliable, Instant and Efficient Network for Disbursement of Services
FTP	:	File Transfer Protocol
G2B	:	Government-to-Business
G2C	:	Government-to-Citizen
G2G	:	Government-to-Government
GBD	:	Global Business Dialogue on Electronic Commerce
GDRC	:	Global Development Research Centre
GIS	:	Geographic Information Systems
HAL	:	Hindustan Aeronautics Limited
HMT	:	Hindustan Machine Tools
ICSC	:	Integrated Citizen Service Centres
ICT	:	Information and Communication Technology
ICT4D	:	ICT for Development
IIAS	:	International Institute of Administrative Sciences
INR	:	Indian National Rupee
IP	:	Internet Protocol
ISP	:	Internet Service Provider
ISRO	:	Indian Space Research Organization
IT	:	Information Technology
ITPB	:	International Technology Park Bangalore
ITU	:	International Telecommunication Union
KAVERI	:	Karnataka Valuation and e-Registration
KEeLAN	:	Key Elements for electronic Local Authorities' Networks

KSEB	:	Kerala State Electricity Board
LAN	:	Local Area Network
LSG	:	Local Self Government
MIS	:	Management Information System
MoU	:	Memorandum of Understanding
NAL	:	National Aerospace Laboratories
NCSTC	:	National Council for Science and Technology
NeGP	:	National e-Governance Plan
NGO	:	Non-Government Organization
NIC	:	National Informatics Centre
NISG	:	National Institute of Smart Government
NKC	:	National Knowledge Commission
NOIE	:	National Office for the Information Economy
OCED	:	Organization for Economic Cooperation and Development
PC	:	Personal Computer
PM	:	Project Manager
PPP	:	Public-Private Participation
PPP	:	Public-Private Partnership
PQLI	:	Physical Quality of Life Indicators
R&D	:	Research and Development
RI	:	Revenue Inspector
ROI	:	Return on Investment
RPO	:	Regional Passport Office
RTC	:	Right, Tenancy and Cultivation Certificates
RTI	:	Right to Information
RTO	:	Regional Transport Office
S&T	:	Science and Technology
SDC	:	State Data Centre
SDP	:	Service Delivery Project
SRO	:	Sub Registrar's Offices

STPI	:	Software Technology Parks of India
SWAN	:	State Wide Area Networks
TSK	:	Touch Screen Kiosk
TSP	:	Total Solutions Provider
TWINS	:	Twin Cities Integrated Network Systems
UNDP	:	United Nations Development Programme
UNPAN	:	United Nations' Public Administration Network
VA	:	Village Accountant
VMS	:	Vendor Management System
VOICE	:	Vijayawada Online Information Centre
WAN	:	Wide Area Network

Glossary

Accountability: It means creating standards to make public staff and private personnel accountable for their actions.

Effectiveness and Efficiency: It is the measured with the cost-benefit ratio for government and involvement of private players.

e-Governance: It can be simply defined as the application of ever evolving information and communication technologies in the processes of governance, thereby bringing in a profound institutional change in the delivery of government services to the citizens.

e-Government: It is referring to a transformation of the business of government (processes, operations, and transactions) driven primarily by the ICTs.

Good Governance: It is epitomized by predictable, open and enlightened policy making; a bureaucracy imbued with professional ethos; an executive arm of government accountable for its actions; and a strong civil society participating in public affairs, and all behaving under the rule of law.

Governance: Governance is the exercise of economic, political, and administrative authority to manage a country's affairs at all levels. It comprises mechanisms, processes, and institutions, through which citizens and groups articulate their interests, exercise their legal rights, meet their obligations, and mediate their differences.

Information and Communication Technologies for Development (ICT4D): It is an increasingly popular, general term referring to the application of Information and Communication Technologies (ICTs) within the field of socio-economic development. ICTs can be applied either in the direct sense, where their use directly benefits the disadvantaged population in some manner, or in an indirect sense, where the ICTs assist aid organizations or non-governmental organizations or governments in order to improve socio-economic conditions.

Information Technology (IT): It is "the study, design, development, implementation, support or management of computer-based information systems, particularly software applications and computer hardware." IT deals with the use of electronic computers and computer software to convert, store, protect, process, transmit and retrieve information, securely.

Janasevanakendram: It is a one-stop Service Centre where remittances can be done quickly and various other services received.

Phodi: It means Division of Land in Kannada.

Responsiveness: It can be achieved with the response and inclusion of bottom-up service demands and adaptability to citizens' needs.

Revenue Sherishtedars: Deputy Tahsildars of the revenue department is called as Revenue Sherishtedar in Karnataka.

Saukaryam: Saukaryam means Facility in Telugu language.

Transformation: Transformation is both external (through simplified, enhanced government-client interactions via online services, no longer limited by the traditional confines of fixed office hours and physical office space) and internal (through streamlined government administration processes for greater efficiency and effectiveness).

Transparency: Transparency in the work flow of electronic service delivery–no bureaucratic hassles and openness in delivery mechanisms.

Project Executive Summary

The dynamics of public administration in India have changed drastically with the introduction of e-governance as a guiding concept in the early 1990s. Citizens, the world over, have been demanding smaller, effective and responsive governments, obviously inspired by the unprecedented and rapid success of the finance capital in the global market. Consequently, policy makers began the search for smaller and efficient governments. Re-engineering of service systems, performance management, transparency in government operations, downsizing or right-sizing the government workforce, emphasis on delivery of reliable and quick public services and citizen satisfaction came to be considered as benchmarks by most of the administrators. Quick decision-making, data-based planning and effective implementation have been the hallmarks of good governance. The potential and scope for application of information and communication technologies in governance are enormous. E-government has the ability to transform traditional administrative systems through effective utilization of ICTs.

Research in e-Governance

Research can be done primarily on applications and impacts of Information and Communication Technologies (ICTs) in the government arena, spanning across diverse functions such as rationalization of administration, service innovation, democratic renewal and efficient governance in multi-level political systems. Thrust should be on introduction of e-government in the area of public administration (*e-administration*), especially regarding the interface between technology and organization. With the expansion of online service delivery new challenges are gaining importance, such as reorganizing service processes, co-operating across different tiers of government, guaranteeing access and secure communication for all as well as analyzing economic and social impacts of e-governance. With effective implementation of administrative modernization modules, the research focus can also be expanded towards the largely neglected role of ICTs in policy-making and governance. The current research project intends to advance the way research is carried out with respect to quality, efficiency, innovation and impact of e-governance programmes in India.

E-Governance in India

E-Governance practices in India emerged and evolved mainly from native intuition, but the range of success of e-Governance initiatives has not been uniform. The bottom-up demand for delivery of electronic services was bleak initially, but the change in public perception was for the better with the governments roping in private industry and service-oriented organizations gradually. This trend can be established definitely with a review of the success of path-breaking e-governance models in the states of Andhra Pradesh, Karnataka and Kerala. Time and costs for availing public services have come down drastically bringing in a positive change in peoples' perception of e-governance. This holds equally true for both the rural and urban populace. The result of all these radical changes in public administration systems is the enhanced satisfaction level of the citizenry on the delivery of public services.

Methodology of the Study

Nine e-Governance projects in three states—e-Seva, CARD, VOICE and Saukaryam in AP; Bhoomi, KAVERI, BangaloreOne in Karnataka; Akshaya, FRIENDS and e-Collectorate in Kerala—were selected for this study to gauge the impact of e-governance on society with relative emphasis on the satisfaction of electronic services availing citizens in terms of transparency, accountability, responsiveness and reduction in time and costs. Other factors like digital divide, gender divide, cultural and ethnic values were also factored in to probe the extent and depth of e-governance systems besides their overall impact on societal transformation. The study covered 30 districts in the three South Indian States of Andhra Pradesh, Karnataka and Kerala and the total sample size is 2,761 including users, bureaucrats, and Technology providers.

Major Findings of this Study

- There is an increasing bottom-up demand for more electronic delivery of public services in urban areas, particularly cities and towns. The success of e-Seva, FRIENDS and BangaloreOne illustrates this point.

- E-services can be implemented successfully even in the rural areas with innovative and productive modules. Projects like Akshaya, Bhoomi and CARD are shining examples in this context.
- Total networking of District Administration is in the realm of possibility. Effective coordination among various departments is crucial to set up an integrated network right from the village panchayat to the district level. E-Collectorate of Palakkad can be a model for the entire country.

Constraints

Though a slew of positive attributes/impacts of different e-governance projects have been observed at the grassroots level in the course of this study, a number of inhibiting factors or constraints too have come to the fore.

- Ideas from early experiments in e-governance have definitely contributed to technology development and to the improvement of government practices. There is a wealth of experience already at hand at the local, state and central levels which can be made good use of.
- From the citizen's perception, achievements in the field of e-governance have been access to government information, cross-departmental portals and government portals.
- Broadening electronic services is imperative. Issues like authenticity and protection of data, information management, and usability are the major hurdles.

Major Recommendations

The following are the major recommendations for effective implementation of e-governance projects at all levels in India:

- Replication of successful technology modules on a national scale can save precious public funds and pave way for funding of e-governance projects in unexplored avenues.
- Transparency, accountability, responsiveness and reduction in time and costs in electronic delivery of public services that collective enhance the satisfaction levels of the

citizens are the key factors that determine the success of any e-governance project.

- Adapting institutions and personnel so as to maximize their capabilities in concert with new technologies which are hard to implement in public administrative systems that do not want to forego traditional authority.
- Improving trustworthiness by providing broader access to government information and assuring information systems security and user privacy.
- Bridging considerable gaps between successful models of e-governance and ongoing projects.
- Making e-services more citizen-centric than government-centric.
- Ensuring comprehensive and effective public-private collaboration in conceptualizing, designing and implementing e-governance projects .
- Integration of State Wide Area Network (SWAN) up to the panchayat level and cross-networking of SWANs with the Union Government can ultimately establish an e-government.

1

Introduction

E-governance, as it is known today the world over, can be simply defined as the application of ever evolving information and communication technologies in the processes of governance, thereby bringing in a profound institutional change in the delivery of government services to the citizens. However, this process in itself is very complex and varies from one ethno-political culture to another. The nature of polity, public administration units, political culture, ethno-sociological divides, and to a big extent, the divides along economy, geography (urban-rural), gender, define and determine the conditions for good governance. In this respect, inherent resistance to technology in governance can be found in traditional administration, particularly in the developing world. India, a decade ago, was no exception to this rule, but is gradually trying to emerge out of the shell. The success of various e-governance projects in different parts of the country bear testimony to this changing situation.

Electronic governance or simply called e-governance has been playing an important role in reengineering and redesigning organizations by integrating information science and technology within the existing administrative and management systems. The evolution of governance over the years and in various phases has changed the ways in which the governments used to deal with their citizens. The very nature of the interactive processes and the relations between the citizens and the governments is changing rapidly on a par with new developments and innovations in the field of information and communication technologies.

E-governance basically aims at improving citizens' access to government information and services. It makes the citizen the focal centre of government in terms of service delivery. Though there is a broad agreement on the definition of e-government and what it encompasses, there are differences in scope, budget allocations, resources, availability of skills and technology and the government's vision as a whole.

Definitions

Many definitions are in the public domain, which have generally been formulated by global bodies like the World Bank, the United Nations, Global Business Dialogue on Electronic Commerce and Organization for Economic Cooperation and Development.

According to the World Bank definition,[1] e-government refers to the use of information technologies (like Wide Area Networks, the Internet and mobile computing) that have the ability to transform relations with citizens, businesses and others arms of government. These technologies can serve a variety of purposes: better delivery of public services to citizens, improved interactions with businesses, citizen empowerment, and more efficient government management.

The United Nations' Public Administration Network (UNPAN)[2] has defined e-government as utilizing the Internet and the world-wide-web for delivering government information and services to citizens.

The Global Business Dialogue on Electronic Commerce (GBD)[3] has defined e-government as referring to a situation in which administrative, legislative and judicial agencies digitize their internal and external operations and utilize networked systems efficiently to realize better quality in the provision of public services.

The Organization for Economic Cooperation and Development (OCED)[4] says e-government is more about government than about 'e' that improves efficiency, services, achieves specific outcomes and contributes to broad policy objectives. It can be a major contributor to reform and help build trust between governments and citizens by opening up the policy process and challenging existing ways of working.

A report to the US Congress on e-government (2003)[5] says the following:

> *"E-government means different things to different people. Some define e-government in terms of specific actions: using a government kiosk to receive job information, applying for social security benefits through a website or creating shared databases for multiple agencies, as examples. Others define e-government more generally as automating the delivery of government services. Some observers of e-government initiatives suggest service delivery could become more convenient, dependable and less costly."*

The Working Group on E-government in the Developing World[6] defined e-government broadly as the use of ICT to promote more efficient and effective government, facilitate more accessible government services, allow greater public access to information and make government more accountable to its citizens.

Classification of E-governance

E-government can be classified as the following each catering to a specific sector:

- G2C – government to citizen
- G2B – government to business
- G2E – government to employee
- G2G – government to government

Objectives of E-governance

The basic objectives of e-governance on a universal scale can be listed as follows:

- improves efficiency
- improves services
- help achieve specific policy outcomes
- contributes to economic policy objectives
- contributes to reform
- help build trust between governments and citizens
- better service – more convenient, lower cost, more reliable
- cost effectiveness and efficiency
- greater participation – by citizens in government
- radical improvement in the quality of services to customers
- major improvements in administrative efficiencies
- remote rural areas being empowered by high speed Internet access.

Since this study is confined to the assessment of the impact of e-governance on citizens and society at large, it will be apt to look at the following objectives in the sector of government to citizen (G2C):

- Providing one-stop online access to information and services to individuals. Citizens should be able to find what they need quickly and easily, and access information in minutes or seconds instead of days or hours.
- Providing services that are citizen, not government focused.
- Doing away with bureaucratic hassles in the delivery of public services and dissemination of information.
- Building and enhancing trust between government and citizens.

Evolution of E-government

Generally, information technology means all the technologies associated with gathering, processing, storing and dissemination of information. Of late, the term has acquired a different connotation. The modern term 'Information Technology' (IT) came into public domain only in the late 1970s and is now used generally to embrace both computer and communication technologies and their common basis—microelectronic technology and all the related software technology.

Up and until the 1970s, computer and telecommunication technologies were regarded as quite distinct, but after remarkable technological changes in microelectronics, software, optics and increased integration of telecommunications with computer technologies, the distinction became increasingly less meaningful. Microelectronic technology has been the common basis both for rapid development and convergence of computer and ICTs. The shift from analogical to digital technologies in telecommunications has led to switching and transmission systems increasingly resembling computers and embedding increasing amount of software. Many communications facilities are now more or less like computers with special uses.

With the development of networking technology, communications between computers expanded greatly since the early 1960s when on-line computer systems were first developed. Together, these developments have blurred the traditional distinctions between telecommunications and computer technologies and this led to the contemporary definition of information technology.

The evolution of information technology – over the past five decades – can be divided into three eras[7]: Mainframe, PC (personal computer) plus LAN (local area network) and the Internet computing. The first functioning electronic digital computer, ENIAC, was built in 1946 in the United States. The period up to 1970s was deemed as the era for organizational mainframe and minicomputer– the era of mainframe. The first microprocessor which was invented by M. E. Hoff, Jr. in 1971 at Intel, a semiconductor company of California, changed the historical trace of information technology development. The central processing unit (CPU) of a computer on a chip became known as a microprocessor. The first personal computer 'the Altair' was developed in 1975. Two years later, Radio Shack introduced first personal computer with keyboard and CRT (Cathode-Ray Tube) display. This was the first complete personal computer to be marketed to the general public. IBM announced the IBM Personal Computer and entered the market in 1981. The PC became an instant hit with the people and the *Times Magazine* chose the 'personal computer' as its 1982 Man of the Year. Then the local area network revolutionized the way offices functioned.

The 1980s marks the end of the first (traditional) era of computer systems and the beginning of the second (micro-based). The effort that laid the foundation for the Internet started in 1969, known as ARPANET,[8] aimed at building a computer network enabling researchers to share ideas. The initial plan was to link four sites. There were nearly two-dozen sites by the end of 1971 and more than 200 by 1981. However, it was not initially an Internet because it connected hosts rather than networks. It was phased out in 1990 in favour of the more advanced NSFNET, a network established by the National Science Foundation of the United States. NSFNET then served as a technical backbone of the Internet. Simply put, the Internet is a network of networks. It is a huge collection of networks throughout the world.

In the 1990s, the Internet became very popular and embraced by all the peoples with different culture and background. Users of the Internet communicate mainly via electronic mail (e-mail); via Telnet, a process that allows them to login to a remote host; and via implementations of the File Transfer Protocol (FTP), a protocol that allows them to transfer information from a remote host to their local site. Global internetworking and the information superhighway were thus put on the agenda and the concepts of national and global information infrastructures were formulated gradually. Overall, the Internet, as a fundamental framework of global and national information infrastructures, provides great opportunities for improving and reshaping interactions among the three constituents of society – government, citizens and businesses.[9]

Government Informatization

Government exists to serve its citizens. In fact, its primary activity is record keeping. The public administration process is, to a large extent, virtually a process of data/information processing. Government authorities collect and process various data and information – on individuals, families, organizations and companies, and then on the basis of these data and information, produce new information for the public, such as policies, strategies, plans, regulations and then provide various citizen services. Information technology is used to support information processing of governments, including data gathering, storing, processing, dissemination and utilization.

It has been recognized that governance and public administration cannot be productive, effective and qualitative without the support of modern information technology. The use of information technology has been an absolute requirement for public administration and management development.[10] At the most fundamental level, information technology is changing or even eliminating many distinctions between reports, publications, databases, records and the like. It now permits information dissemination on a decentralized basis that is cost-effective at low-levels of demand. Many types of public information such as administrative, managerial, technical, statistical, scientific and referential may best be stored and disseminated by electronic means. For instance, national census and statistical reports could be made available on optical disks and accessible through the Internet to anybody.

Recognizing and tapping the technological changes is very crucial for the leaders of governments to formulate their visions on e-Government and work out government policies and strategies on the development of e-Government.[11] For example, an integrated revenue information system will improve tax data available to collection employees in the field; and revenue officers will be able to receive cases more quickly and depose them sooner. A system using distributed computing architecture and the Internet to automate and modernize tax collection process will enable the treasury to collect tax more efficiently.

There are at least three reasons why government informatization is crucial for any government to reach its objectives of economic and social development. First, given the economic importance of the public sector in any country, enhanced productivity in the public sector would entail significant gains for the economy as a whole. The public sector accounts for a large per cent of total employment, final consumption expenditure, and gross domestic fixed capital formation. Second, the public sector usually is the biggest and most wide-ranging collector of public data and information. These data range from economic and social activities to natural and geographic resources. Third, in an increasingly information-intensive global economy, well-functioning state information systems can facilitate access to global knowledge and international databases and the creation of new options for mobilizing and using local knowledge and resources.

During the late 1980s and 1990s, the guiding principle and the most popular term in government informatization were 'reengineering'.[12] Many government agencies and enterprises were quick to restructure their organization so as to make them computer friendly and implement more appropriate procedures compatible with an IT environment. The main efforts included: eliminating layers of traditional management, compressing job categories, creating work teams, training employees in multilevel skills, shortening and simplifying various business processes and streamlining administration. The results were impressive. The success of business process reengineering greatly streamlined the organizational structure, improved management, raised effectiveness and efficiency, and boosted productivity. In fact, in the US, the success of business process reengineering laid the necessary conditions for the emergence of the new economy in the 1990s.

To meet the demands of the information age, governments took advantage of the advanced technology to reinvent the existing modality and organizational structure of government. This was the transformation of the government and to a large extent, a transformation by informatization. In other words, the task was to construct a government of the information age by means of modern information technology. Accordingly, the guiding principle and the most popular term in government in the 1990s was 'transformation'. The transformation process is, in fact, the process of development and formulation of e-Government.[13]

Clearly, government is more than simply a user of ICTs. Every government has to chart out policies and strategies to exploit its information resource, to develop its information infrastructure, and to promote the utilization of information systems for the purposes of achieving more effective growth of public services. Failure to initiate effective and timely action will have serious ramifications for the ability of the government to stimulate social and economic development and the formulation of an information society.

Types of Government Information Systems

There are two types of government information systems which have great potential in public administration. They are Document Management and Retrieval Systems (DMRS) and Geographic Information Systems (GIS).[14] DMRS have the potential to manage the vast majority of information handled by any organization. They have the ability to manage semi-structured or unstructured information, such as the running text in a word processing file or a bit-mapped pattern in a faxed or scanned drawing.

GIS started off along with remote sensing in the mid 1960s. It acquired a following only after 1980s when people found out that GIS was tools that can be used for the purpose of combining spatial data obtained from various sources and relating to different subjects. The power of GIS comes from its ability to look at entities in their geographic context and examine relationships between entities. It offers the possibility of visualizing events at a much more spatially detailed level. The rapid development of microcomputer and software technologies has greatly benefited the proliferation and popularization of GIS.

Genesis of e-Government

The rapid development of information technology in the last decades of the 20th century, particularly the Internet, greatly promoted the development of government online and e-Government. According to a study conducted by the UNESCO, by the turn of 2000, nearly 56 countries had developed e-Government in some form or the other. Early in 1992, when Bill Clinton was elected as the President of the US, he declared that his administration would be an e-Government. After four years of serious efforts, remarkable outcomes had been achieved: by the end of January 1996, the employees of the Federal Government were reduced by 240,000; more than 2,000 federal offices were closed; about 200 federal project and the executive bodies were removed; and the expenses of the Federal Government fell by 118 billion US dollars. More than 3,000 new standards of public services were established by 200 Federal Departments and Agencies; 16,000 pages or more with regard to administration regulations were nullified; 31,000 plus pages of government rules were simplified. The successful development of e-Government in the United States had a far reaching impact on the development of e-governance the world over.[15]

The development of e-Commerce and new economy is tremendously pressurizing the governments to opt for e-governance. People and businesses hope that e-government would remove bureaucratic delays, simplify and integrate business procedures so that it would be easier for them to deal with the government, make the government more transparent, honest and clean. In fact, the main supplication of business and citizens in the information age is to transform the existing multi-departmental, multi-hierarchic and control-oriented government into an intelligent, service-oriented and customer-centred government.[16]

Additionally, many governments hope to take advantage of e-government to catch up with the waves of new economy, attract enterprises associated with new economy to invest into local economy and reverse industrial decline and promote regeneration through the intelligent use of e-government and other ICT systems.

Conditions for E-government[17]

1. *Political conditions:* Good governance, as a condition for sustainable development, requires genuine commitment from political leaders, the private sector and organizations of civil society. The introduction of e-Government requires strong political will.
2. *Organizational conditions:* Experience shows that the introduction of e-Government demands and causes profound

changes in the public administrative systems. To guide this transformation process, appropriate management and coordination mechanisms are needed.

3. *Cultural and human resources conditions:* Positive attitudes, knowledge and skills need to be in place, especially within the public sector, to initiate, implement and sustain e-Government. Cultural aspects may cause general resistance to change and information-sharing. Inadequate human resources may lead to lack of customer-orientation and overall commitment.
4. *Financial conditions:* The initial costs related to implementing e-Government can be considerable and governments may have limited capacity to bridge the period between initial investments and returns. Proper resource planning and access to innovative financing mechanisms are critical to the success of e-Government.
5. *Technical infrastructure:* Lack of technologies is a major bottleneck for countries aiming to implement and maintain e-Government. Legacy systems may also represent considerable obstacles to change.
6. *Data and information systems:* Management systems, record and work processes must be in place to provide the necessary data to support the move towards e-Government.

E-Governance in India

The dynamics of public administration in India have changed drastically with the introduction of e-governance as a guiding concept in the early 1990s. Citizens have been demanding smaller, effective and responsive governments, obviously inspired by the unprecedented success of the finance capital in the global market. Consequently, policy makers began the search for smaller and efficient governments. Re-engineering of service systems, performance management, transparency in government operations, downsizing or right-sizing the government workforce, emphasis on delivery of reliable and quick public services and citizen satisfaction came to be considered as benchmarks by most of the administrators.

As discussed earlier, many countries have done much to leverage ICT to deploy e-government services, but much work needs to be done before the vision of e-government can be fully realized, whether through adoption of already-existing commercial technologies and practices or through targeted research efforts directed at helping government and its suppliers address emerging new requirements.

In India, the first steps toward modern governance were taken by establishing the National Informatics Centre (NIC) in the 1970s. The NIC has done a remarkable job of connecting thousands of government offices which are the repositories of a wealth of information required for planning and execution of numerous development schemes as also for governance. It has been assigned the task of computerizing work in different departments of the Union and the State Governments. In the process, NIC has developed varied and exhaustive skills for computerizing and networking government offices. The more than two decades long pioneering work and experience of NIC has enabled it to give a broad view of everything connected with e-governance, to those who are involved in and committed to this challenging task.[18]

The New Economic Policy of 1991 reduced the scope and role of the public sector. The focus was on creating conditions whereby the public sector could function in competition with the private sector. The government has been trying to achieve these objectives by deregulating industries and liberalizing foreign investment and technology imports. Only eight types of industries are with the public sector, which invest only in infrastructure and in the protection of the poorest.[19] The government has acquired a more promotional role to provide suitable environment for the public and the private sector.

Grassroots governance has been a major concern of the planning process in India since the introduction of the *panchayati raj* in 1959. While the introduction of the system was itself a landmark, the follow-up action in various states failed to provide it with positive direction, particularly, in the realm of development administration. This paved the way for a crucial national agenda on PR reforms, culminating in the 73rd Constitutional Amendment. Later, several initiatives were launched by non-governmental organizations to involve local communities in managing their own affairs. Many state governments have launched schemes and programmes to promote people's participation. The guidelines of several centrally-sponsored programmes helped community based organizations to formulate and implement development programmes. Among the central ministries, remarkable steps have been taken up by the Ministries of Rural Development, Environment and Forests,

Education and Water Resources. These experiences of utilizing the ICT tools at the grassroots level have increased the transparency and accountability of the state.[20]

The Information Technology Revolution Act, 2000, enables the application of information and communication technology in governance—political, economic and social. E-governance has facilitated computerization and networking of varied departments and also the delivery of public services. Computerization of internal administration has resulted in automation and improvement in record keeping and file movement.

E-governance practices in India emerged and evolved mainly from native intuition, but under prescription for a lesser and transparent government by the World Bank and the International Monetary Fund. However, the range of success of e-governance initiatives has not been uniform. The bottom-up demand for delivery of electronic services was bleak initially, but the change in public perception was for the better with the governments roping in private industry and service-oriented organizations gradually. This trend can be established definitely with a review of the success of path-breaking e-governance models in the states of Andhra Pradesh, Karnataka and Kerala. These projects not only caused a jump in the revenue collections of the three state governments, but also timely payment by the citizens. Time and costs for availing public services have come down drastically bringing in a positive change in peoples' perception of e-governance theory and practice. This holds equally true for both the rural and urban populace. The result of all these radical changes in public administration systems is the enhanced satisfaction level of the citizenry on the delivery of public services and simplification of governmental procedures.

Various state governments have come up with projects and programmes, enabling the online provision of services such as education, medical and health, police, agriculture and extension, employment, passport, registration of vehicles, birth and death certificates, filing of income tax returns and the like. The last couple of years have seen e-governance take deep roots in India. Almost every state has an IT policy in place with the aim of evolving itself from being an IT-aware to an IT-enabled government. State governments are fast recognizing the benefits of an IT-enabled working environment.

As of now, e-governance projects are being run only in certain departments. This approach will gradually be extended to all departments eventually, leveraging the power of IT to streamline administrative functions and increase transparency. The governments of Singapore, Canada and Switzerland have implemented many citizen-centric portals, and set the benchmarks in this regard. With the help of IT, the government can process citizen to government transactions such as the filing of tax returns, death and birth registration, land records, etc.[21] Agriculture, power and education are fields where the government makes use of IT to provide services to citizens. The revenue departments are in the process of using information technology for collecting taxes.

Government Initiatives

The national e-governance plan (2003-07) reflects the strategic intent of the central government in the right perspective. Many projects are earmarked under this plan, and it is trying to address the digital divide.

From a political perspective, after watching the performance of some IT-savvy states in the 2004 general elections, the system has woken up to the need to focus more on rural development. The political systems are keener to use IT to disseminate information faster to farmers, disburse loans, improve education and the health systems in villages, etc. There is a clear-cut incentive to do it as 60 per cent of the vote-bank still lives in rural India. E-governance has to be supported by the will and resources of those who are in power, be it at the central or state level.

In future, education, agriculture, state wide area networks (SWANs) and Community Information Centre projects will be rolled out backed by a strong public private participation model (PPP) to achieve long-term sustainability. Projects in PPP mode in these areas can revolutionize the governance processes. In the next couple of years the industry (PPP) is expected to grow by 22-25 per cent.[22]

Research in E-Governance

The conceptualization, design, development, testing, delivery and support of operational government IT systems for department-end users involve an extensive supply chain that includes system integrators, vertical suppliers, major vendors, small technology companies, consultants, architects, and lastly, researchers. Government-end users and IT researchers are in a sense at the extreme ends of this supply chain and appear to be unlikely allies. However, objective conditions ordain them to have a mutual interest in innovation and in meeting future needs. By collaboration, they can conceptualize new opportunities in the field of technology with minimum risk, which may not be the case when they work independent of each other.

Research can be done primarily on applications and impacts of Information and Communication Technologies (ICTs) in the government arena, spanning across diverse functions such as rationalization of administration, service innovation, democratic renewal and efficient governance in multi-level political systems. Thrust should be on introduction of e-government in the area of public administration (*e-administration*), especially regarding the interface between technology and organization. With the expansion of online service delivery new challenges are gaining importance, such as reorganizing service processes, co-operating across different tiers of government, guaranteeing access and secure communication for all as well as analyzing economic and social impacts of e-governance. With effective implementation of administrative modernization modules, the research focus can also be expanded towards the largely neglected role of ICTs in policy-making and governance. Research can include potential contributions to improved coordination and coherence, efficient selection of relevant information under conditions of growing information overload and cooperation between policy-makers and administrative staff.

Another focus area deals with potentials and constraints related to online participation of enlightened citizens in the realm of policy making and implementation. This can be done under the head of e-democracy. Against the backdrop of the claim of a socially accepted and balanced information society targeting the involvement of a wide range of societal factors, research in this area can be dedicated to the significance of online participation for political decision-making processes primarily undertaken at local and regional governance levels. In addition, technological innovations in the realm of elections and referenda (electronic voting) generate problems which challenge and question hitherto known and approved voting standards, mainly the principle of secret ballot. The current research project intends to advance the way research is carried out with respect to quality, efficiency, innovation and impact of e-governance programmes on Indian society.

Organisation of the Study

The present study is structured into four chapters. The first chapter deals with the introduction of the study, definitions and classifications of Governance, good governance, evolution of e-Governance, objectives of e-Governance, government informatisation, types of government information systems, genesis of e-Government, conditions of e-Government, e-Governance initiatives in India, research in e-Governance and organization of the study.

The second chapter is on the conceptual framework of the study and study methodology. In this chapter we discussed the different definitions of e-Governance and e-Government, concept of good governance, survey literature on e-Governance and different methodologies from national and international research works.

The third chapter explains the different case studies selected as part of the study. The case studies are e-Seva, CARD, VOICE and Saukaryam from Andhra Pradesh, Bhoomi, KAVERI and BangaloreOne from Karnataka and Akshaya, FRIENDS and e-Collectorate from Kerala. The case studies evaluate the various dimensions of e-Governance and their overall impact on society.

The last chapter analyses the findings of the study. It also offers major suggestions for future e-Governance initiatives and the areas for further research to promote e-Governance.

REFERENCES

1. World Bank's e-government website: http://web.worldbank.org/WBSITE/EXTERNAL/TOPICS/EXTINFORMATIONANDCOMMUNICATIONANDTECHNOLOGIES/EXTEGOVERNMENT/0, menuPK:702592~pagePK:149018~piPK:149093~theSite PK:702586,00.html
2. www.unpan.org/egovernment.asp
3. Practical steps for efficient government: e-government, 2006, http://www.gbde.org/
4. Launched in 2001, the OECD E-Government Project explores how governments can best exploit information and communication technologies (ICTs) to embed good governance principles and achieve public policy goals. Directorate of Public Governance and Territorial Development (Home), E-government, http://www.oecd.org/department/

5. FY 2003 Report to US Congress on implementation of the E-Government Act, Office of Management and Budget, Washington D.C., March 8, 2004, website: www.whitehouse.gov/omb/egov
6. The Working Group on E-Government in the Developing World, Pacific Council on International Policy, UNESCAP, Bangkok, April 2002, website: www.pacificcouncil.org
7. Rapid Development of ICT in 20th Century, http://www.unpan.org/training_egovform.asp/ (Accessed Wednesday, April 05, 2006).
8. Rapid Development of ICT in 20th Century, http://www.unpan.org/training_egovform.asp/ op.cit.
9. Rapid Development of ICT in 20th Century, http://www.unpan.org/training_egovform.asp/
10. Information Technology Security Training Requirements: A Role- and Performance-Based Model, US Department of Commerce, Washington D.C., April 1998.
11. The Working Group on E-Government in the Developing World, Pacific Council on International Policy, UNESCAP, Bangkok, April 2002.
12. Rapid Development of ICT in 20th Century, http://www.unpan.org/training_egovform.asp
13. unpan1.un.org/intradoc/groups/public/documents/UN/UNPAN012553.pdf
14. A GIS is a computer system capable of capturing, storing, analyzing, and displaying geographically referenced information; that is, data identified according to location. US Geological Survey, http://www.erg.usgs.gov/isb/pubs/gis_poster/index.html
15. "Leadership For The New Millennium: Delivering on Digital Progress and Prosperity," a policy paper by the Working Group on E-Commerce, documents more than 1,300 e-government initiatives undertaken since 1993 (Govexec.com, January 19, 2001).
16. E-Government: What a Leader Should Know? Government Online and e-government, UNPAN.
17. E-Government: What a Leader Should Know? E-Government Readiness Assessment, http://www.unpan.org/training_egovform.asp
18. Prabhu CSR, E-Governance: Concepts and Case Studies, Prentice-Hall India Pvt. Ltd., 2004.
19. *Ibid.*, pp. 1-10.
20. Vikas Kanungo, *Citizen-Centric Governance in India*, ASSOCHAM World Bank Vision document, 2004, http://www.egovindia.org/whitepapers.html (accessed June 5, 2006).
21. Sreekumar T.T., *Civil Society and State-led Initiatives in ICTs: The Case of Kerala*, Information Technology in Developing Countries, Vol. 12, No. 3, December 2002.
22. Vikas Kanungo, *Citizen-Centric Governance in India*, ASSOCHAM World Bank Vision document, 2004, http://www.egovindia.org/whitepapers.html (accessed June 5, 2006).

2

Conceptual Framework and Study Methodology

E-Governance—as the term used in this study—refers to the ability of the governments and its entities, citizens, businesses and other stakeholder agencies to forge a dynamic partnership in the overall process of socio-economic development, while simultaneously restructuring and streamlining the government processes. This interaction may be in the form of obtaining information, paying taxes, bills filings, submission of requests, making reservations etc. This will allow individual citizens a 'one-stop shop' to interact with the government and business organizations at their convenience and location—seven days per week and possibly more than the usual government office hours. Services must be brought online in a way that allows citizens to complete all their transactions under one roof and within less time. Today individual business in the state face not only the direct cost of taxes levied; but also the indirect cost of the labour necessary to file returns, declarations and forms to meet regulatory requirements. E-Governance will significantly reduce the indirect and hidden costs through avoiding the aggravation of standing in queues, thus allow citizen to be 'on-line' and not 'in-line.' The government also gains through the benefits accrued to the citizens in the form of improved 'citizen satisfaction' on the delivery of services.

Citizen–Government relations through e-governance significantly contribute to:

1. Simplifying procedures to demand and receive services;
2. Achieving equal opportunity for processing requests and delivery services;

3. Increasing transparency of administrative services;
4. Allowing on-line access to general information.

The fundamental approach of this study is to assess the impacts of e-government systems on citizens' every day life and on governance in general. This raises a series of research questions concerning the social impact and the technical feasibility of e-governance systems in India. They are:

(a) Good Governance.
(b) Users and Usage of e-Government services.
(c) Availability and access to services.

Governance –Good Governance

The concept of "Governance" has been found to have varying definitions. Among them the United Nations Development Programme (UNDP) provides a more elaborated definition. Governance is:[1]

> *"the exercise of economic, political, and administrative authority to manage a country's affairs at all levels. It comprises mechanisms, processes, and institutions, through which citizens and groups articulate their interests, exercise their legal rights, meet their obligations, and mediate their differences."*

This definition indicates that governance has two major components: a country and its citizens. Governance is how a political entity (i.e. state) organizes and administers its functions through exercising power via its various agencies. In addition, governance includes the sum of procedures, actions, and entities available to citizens in order to enable them to conduct numerous operations, such as communicating their concerns, exercising their rights, undertaking their responsibilities, and arbitrating their disputes.

The Global Development Research Centre (GDRC) (2004) gives a further definition for governance:[2]

> *"the concept of governance refers to the complex set of values, norms, processes, and institution by which society manages its development and resolves conflict, formally and informally. It involves not only the state, but also the civil society at the local, regional, national and global levels."*

This definition shows that GDRC considers governance as how a country manages its internal affairs. In addition, it identifies the actors in "governance" as including the state (as a political entity) and the different levels of the civil society.

As a way of defining governance, the International Institute of Administrative Sciences (IIAS) differentiates between "government" and "governance." Government is an institution that consists of a set of sub-institutions, namely "the Constitution, Legislature, Executive and Judiciary."[3] To further define "governance," the IIAS identifies a number of components of which the concept is comprised; thus: "the degree of legitimacy, representativeness, popular accountability and efficiency with which public affairs are conducted."[4]

This suggests that there are four elements by means of which "governance" may be assessed: the presence of mechanisms that legitimize a system's structures, processes, and actors; and the extent to which the system's institutions and their actions are representative and accountable to the general public.

Clearly, the definition of governance varies according to the institution. Each institution produces a definition of the term in question by highlighting one element or a set of elements that make up the nature of governance. Nevertheless, they have one element in common: governance is not synonymous with government. Rather, government is just one factor among several who's internal and external interactions with the other factors, such as the civil society, the private sector and the general public, shape governance.

Good Governance

As in the various understanding of the concept of governance, "good governance" has also been viewed differently with various definitions. For the World Bank, good governance is:[5]

> *"epitomized by predictable, open and enlightened policy making; a bureaucracy imbued with professional ethos; an executive arm of government accountable for its actions; and a strong civil society participating in public affairs, and all behaving under the rule of law."*

In this definition, the World Bank highlights four elements that make up the building blocks of good governance. These include

(a) Transparency and predictability in policy making
(b) Professionalism in bureaucracy

(c) Accountability of government
(d) Participation of the civil society which swears by the law

With regard to the UNDP, good governance is described as[6]

"being among other things participatory, transparent and accountable. It is also effective and equitable. And it promotes the rule of law fairly. Good governance ensures that the voices of the poorest and the most vulnerable are heard in decision-making in the allocation of development resources, and that political, social and economic priorities are based on broad consensus among the three stakeholders – the state, private sector and the civil society."

This definition identifies the attributes that comprise the concept of good governance, which are as follows:

(a) Adoption of a participatory approach;
(b) Transparency and openness;
(c) Accountability through assuming responsibilities for actions;
(d) Effectiveness;
(e) Equity and fairness;
(f) Endorsement of the rule of law;
(g) Openness in decision-making and concern towards vulnerable social groups;
(h) Formulation of the national agenda through a consensus between state, private sector, and civil society.

From another perspective, the UNDP lists nine underlying characteristics of good governance.[7] They are:

(a) Participation
(b) Rule of law
(c) Transparency
(d) Responsiveness
(e) Consensus/Orientation
(f) Equity
(g) Effectiveness and Efficiency
(h) Accountability
(i) Strategic Vision

Various institutions, international organizations and authors reported different indicators of good governance, but it is generally agreed that the quality of government institution can be evaluated by assessing the quality of governance. In this background, good governance calls for a more appropriate government with people's participation and their eventual satisfaction.

New Information Logic to Governance

Information is critical to understanding the structure, functions, processes, and policy making of a government. Flows of information establish relationships between government and citizen, executive branch and legislative, bureaucrat and politician. Information is the lifeblood of public governance; perhaps it is the most revolutionary aspect of the present day communication technologies. The industrial age is being superseded by an information age' in which 'knowledge workers' and 'information labour' are playing a key role not only in shaping people's lives, but also the global economy. Information and communication are at the centre of this new economic revolution, bringing in new flexibilities into the work place, pushing aside the numerous functions associated with bureaucratic forms of organization. The interpretation of changes in contemporary societies has been mirrored by analyses of the emerging 'information society.'[8] Although there are numerous references to the 'information society', little has been said or written on the information age from the perspective of governance.

The ICT revolution has changed the world like never before. Information superhighways are bringing about profound changes in the way people work, learn and live. According to *The Economist,* "after e-commerce and e-business, the next big thing will be e-governance."[9] A new terminology emerged in the academics and society viz., 'IT & administration', 'e-government', 'e-governance', 'e-citizen' and lastly e-society. Advances in ICT offer potential benefits to governance. For instance, the increased performance and availability at reduced cost of microelectronics, fiber optics, voice and video compression, fast-packet switching and high—density storage technology could be utilized to make public administration more efficient.

Technology convergence on account of digitalization, wide bandwidth transmission, and compression technologies offer public services to the citizens at a reduced cost and in a less time. Real democratic governance could be fostered when a country has access to a much greater diversity of communication sources and network designs. ICT promotes good governance in three basic ways[10]: *(a)* By increasing transparency, information, and accountability *(b)* By facilitating accurate decision-making and public participation and *(c)* By enhancing efficiency in the delivery of public goods and services. Ultimately, governance through the means of ICTs can pave the path for 'good governance.'

E-Governance and E-Government

The terms "e-governance" and "e-Government" are not used interchangeably in this study. Of the two, e-government is a narrower term, referring to a transformation of the business of government (processes, operations, and transactions) driven primarily by the ICTs. Transformation is both external (through simplified, enhanced government-client interactions via online services, no longer limited by the traditional confines of fixed office hours and physical office space) and internal (through streamlined government administration processes for greater efficiency and effectiveness).[11]

E-Governance, however, is a broader term that includes transformation at least four levels.[12] First, it involves the transformation of the business of government. Second, it involves a transformation in the operational definitions of the principles upon which governance is founded, shifting towards increased participation, openness, transparency and communication. Third, it involves a transformation in the interactions between government and its (internal and external) clients, classified as government-to-citizen (G2C), government-to-business (G2B), government to its internal employee clients (G2E), government to other government institutional clients (G2G), and citizen-to-citizen (C2C). Finally, it involves a transformation of society itself, through the emergence of 'e-societies', made up of networks of relationships between communities and citizens at the individual level, besides networking various non-government organizations (NGOs).

In the above discussed background, the main research goal of this study is to assess the impact of e-governance systems on Indian society and on governance in general. For this, we have utilized various indicators and surveyed different methodologies from various studies. The following section of the study describes at first the literature related to the research problem and the different methodologies that went into the study.

SURVEY OF LITERATURE ON E-GOVERNANCE

The Impacts of Internet on the Public Administration – Citizen Relationship: A Study at Bahia's Tax Authority

In this research paper, Moysés de Oliveira Andrade Júnior aims at understanding the impacts on the Tax Authority and taxpayer relationship with the emergence of the Internet as a communications channel, particularly, in the case of Bahia's Tax Authority. (Bahia is one of the 26 States of Brazil, and is located in the northeastern part of the country on the Atlantic coast. It is the fourth most populous Brazilian State.) This study also aims to make a brief comparison between Bahia's experience and the reality of rendering services by the United States Public Administration, concerning its implications on relationship between government and citizens, technological requirements of the Internet environment for the provision of tax services as well as the automation of the checking routines.[13]

Globalization and the State

This two-part UN World Public Sector Report (2001) argues that globalization, although not a new phenomenon, is unquestionably of paramount significance for all countries, developed or developing, rich or poor, large or small. Part one of this report deals with globalization and the State. Despite the great opportunities that globalization presents, not all countries have been able to take full advantage of it. Experience has shown that some countries have fared much better than others, while some have not benefited at all, mainly due to uneven distribution of resources. Part two of the report presents data on public sector, measurement tools and relevant statistical information. It provides a meaningful indication on how quantitatively the public sector changes over the years and tries to make some connection between those changes and its functioning.[14]

Good Governance, Globalization and Civil Society

This compilation of articles primarily deals with reformist concepts like civil society, good governance, globalization and participatory development. These concepts have been defined variously by different theorists the world over, but when it comes India, an evolving modern society, they acquire a quite a different connotation. 'Civil' society is yet to become inclusive whereas we are still catching up with globalization and good governance simultaneously.[15]

Globalization and Good Governance—Pressures for Constructive Reforms

This compendium is the outcome of the papers presented at the 19th Congress of the International Political Science Association at Durban in July 2003. It attempts at analyzing a wide spectrum of the basic issues and problems involved for constructive reforms in securing good governance, and discuss the strategies to overcome them in the context of the experiences of some select countries. The authors seek to reflect some of the pertinent issues with a view to discern and evaluate some viable alternative packages of constructive reforms towards good governance in a globalized world polity.[16]

Decentralized Governance and Participatory Development

This well-researched book critically evaluates the mass movement launched by the Left Democratic Front Government of Kerala to ensure people's participation in development process through the local-self government set-up. It analyzed the constraints and possibilities in participatory planning and democratic decentralization with special reference to Kerala. It also tried to assess the role of civil society organizations in the development process as well as the constant opposition to the people's plan from the then opposition, the UDF, led by the Congress.[17]

The Role of Information and Communication Technology in Building Trust in Governance: Towards Effectiveness and Results

The basic premise of this research study is that ICT has the potential to contribute to good governance. If effectively deployed, ICT may become an important means of breaking the vicious circle of bureaucracy and lead to the achievement of the Millennium Development Goals, especially, the objective of alleviating poverty. This study assumes that ICT has the potential to improve governance by strengthening the level of trustworthiness of government services and, as a consequence, citizens' trust to government.[18]

E-Government at the Crossroads

The three main conclusions of the UN Global E-government Survey 2003 are: (1) No country or group of countries in the world owns the monopoly on imagination, wisdom and commitment or political will for use of e-government for the delivery of the public value of human development. Original, advanced content of e-government applications finds a home in the geographic and developmental South, as it does in the North. (2) Only very few governments have opted to use e-government applications for transactional services or for networking. (3) Even fewer governments use it to support the genuine participation of citizens in politics. Those who do, in most cases, apply it at a very rudimentary level.[19]

Enabling ICT for Rural India

In this research study done by Rafiq Dosani and others from Stanford University, there is an elaborate discussion on the experiences of India in the application of ICTs for rural development. This report explains the problems facing rural use of ICT and to make recommendations to improve usage. Over three months, from September to December 2004, this research team visited nine ICT projects. As a generalization, it concluded that all the projects are still experimenting with how best to serve rural users through ICT. There are successes and failures, good and bad practices and local demand to learn from in order to help frame the recommendations.[20]

Government on the Web 1 (PPG)

This is a research project done at the London School of Economics in 1999 by the UK National Audit Office on how new information and communications systems (ICTs) restructure the public administration. The research team involved Prof. Dunleavy, Dr. Margetts, Dr. Matt Mulford, Dr. Klaus Goetz, Steve John and Don McCarthy from the Department of Government, and several other members from elsewhere in LSE. It conducted a major investigation involving: survey of all UK Government Websites; surveys of government influentials; overviews of developments in the USA, Germany and Australia; interviews with leading private sector comparators; and extended case studies in the areas of social security policy, and trade and industry.[21]

Government on the Web 2 (PPG)

This 2001-02 study was lead by Professor Dunleavy and Professor Helen Margetts (School of Public Policy, University College London) and carried out by a team including Simon Bastow Ruth Callaghan from PPG and Hala Yared (UCL). The study covered two new Whitehall Ministries, HM Customs and Excise and the Department of Transport, Local Government and the Regions. The methods used included a census of all Central Government Websites and comparison of progress since 1999; a census of all Local Government Websites; case studies in the two departments and detailed analysis of policy-making in the Office of the e-Envoy; and research overseas in Australia, New Zealand, United States and Netherlands.[22]

Advancing Return on Investment Analysis for Government IT: *A Public Value Framework*

This research study done by Anthony M. Cresswell and others at the Centre for Technology in Government, New York, deals with the complex issues related to investments on e-government projects and the returns they accrue. The report says the returns, may be large or small, obvious or obscure, and can run from a few minutes saved in a routine transaction to improving the trust and legitimacy of an entire government. Assessing returns remains a core problem in IT planning and decision making. That problem results from shortcomings in the available methods and models for assessing public returns, what we call public return on investment (ROI). Three significant shortcomings have been highlighted in this report. They are: (1) incomplete analysis of public value, resulting in too narrow a scope of what can be considered returns to the public, (2) lack of systematic attention to how government IT investments generate results of value from the point of view of the public and (3) weak or absent methods for tailoring a public ROI assessment to the specific context and goals of a government IT investment.[23]

E-Government for Development

This module prepared by Richard Heeks helps a researcher in fine-tuning his research methodology. Besides it could be of great help to learners' as it spells out various definitions of e-government besides giving a complete glossary of words related with it. It gives an analytical framework to identify the causes of failure of e-government project and also sets up quantifying standards to evaluate the success of a specific scheme/programme.[24]

A Multi-Disciplinary Analysis of E-governance: Where Do We Start?

Zelinna D. Pablo and Shan L. Pan in this seminar paper tells us how to understand and manage e-governance, which draws from multiple and diverse disciplines. E-government has to be managed and its potentials harnessed, if government is to fulfill its mission and remain responsive within the context of a rapidly changing society. This paper proposes a starting point for the deliberate, systematic and holistic development of e-governance. It analyses the multi-disciplinary nature of e-governance from six perspectives, provides a framework that facilitates the systematizing of current and future materials into an organized body of knowledge.[25]

Information Technology Research, Innovation and E-Government

This seminal work done by the Committee on Computing and Communication Research to Enable Better Use of IT in Government, Computer Science and Telecommunications Board, Division on Engineering and Physical Sciences, National Research Council, has identified various challenges ahead in implementing various e-government initiatives in the United States of America. It says to realize the potential of e-government that has been demonstrated in early efforts will require addressing implementation issues, resolving shorter term technology issues, and conducting research on longer-term challenges. While government can in many cases build on technology developed for the commercial sector, targeted computer science research is needed where government leads demand or has special requirements. For a sound foundation for e-government and other applications of information technology throughout society, it is imperative to have a continuing, broad federal computer science research programme.[26]

The Deepening Divide – ***Inequality in the Information Society***

This book argues that digital divide in some of the most important regions of the world—North America, Europe, East Asia and the Third World—is a comprehensive social problem. Information inequality is both an old and a new problem. It is old since people have always had to be motivated to adopt a particular medium, had to make an effort to obtain it and improve their operating skills. It is an old problem because an unequal distribution of resources and positions in society has always been the primary cause behind these differences to access. The digital divide is a new type of inequality for two primary reasons: the first is the character of the new media and the second is related to new inequalities and the development of new types of society.[27]

E-Governance – A Change Management Tool

This book by P. Panneervel primarily illustrates six e-government projects undertaken by the author during the course of his career as a bureaucrat. It helps a wide range of people, particularly those working in public administration, universities, non-governmental organizations and professionals. By extension, it is a narration of personal experience of the author which gives an indication to the possibility of the problems likely to be faced in future implementation by practitioners, project managers, government officers, voluntary agencies, etc. A specific focus has been given to the emerging e-governance experts from the students' community.[28]

Civil Society and State-led Initiatives in ICTs: The Case of Kerala

T. Sreekumar, in this article, says that India began to design and execute rural development program with a relatively visible ICT content in the 1970s. The Dharampur Sub-District Infrastructure Planning for Development (1977) is an early example of attempts to use computer applications for cost optimization and decision-making. By the late 1980s India had developed networks such as NICNET connecting government users. The study is based on the reflections on two major ICT initiatives promoted by the State Government in Kerala—FRIENDS and IT@School Project.[29]

Empowering the Poor: *Information and Communications Technology for Governance and Poverty Reduction—A Study of Rural Development Projects in India*

This annual report of the United Nations Development Programme (2006) sets out to examine the application of large-scale approaches to the use of Information and Communications Technology (ICT) for electronic governance and poverty reduction. The study argues that ICTs are effective tools in the fight against poverty, when used appropriately. If ICTs can be used to reduce poverty, why in India are they not being used more extensively to do so? The study examined 18 development projects in India that make use of ICTs in the form of community telecentres for the benefit of the poor. It says that several projects have failed to understand the importance of cultivating close relationships with their beneficiary community, either by employing inappropriate staff within telecentres or by failing to supply incentives for those staff to ensure that they are sensitive to the needs of the community. As a result, the quality of the services of the projects has suffered.[30]

Global e-Government

In this report, Darell M. West, from the Centre for Public Policy, Brown University, presents the annual update on global e-government. He says that there are technological issues that frustrate citizens. They include: pages not loading correctly (e.g. Zimbabwe), links not functioning properly (e.g. Venezuela), pages taking an extremely long time to upload (e.g. Vanuatu), sites with overly sophisticated language (e.g. Vatican), websites of very small countries designed for tourists/investors rather than its own citizens (e.g. Vanuatu), extremely small font size (e.g. Uruguay Agriculture and Switzerland Foreign Affairs), web pages designed for investors/ tourists being of much higher quality than those designed for a country's own citizens, and websites with disclaimers to protect government agencies, but no privacy/security.

Time for a Big Push

Ibrahim Ahmad, in this article, says that the issue of connectivity is at the top of mind among all champions of e-governance. Many believe that as long as telecom and Internet connectivity is poor, any meaningful e-Governance will not be achieved. Systems uptime is another key challenge. There is a big gap between what customer support vendors promise and what they deliver. Bureaucrats and e-Governance project leaders have not been able to overcome this problem. Data security is another factor. Most users in the government are not very sure how safe and tamper proof is all the information that will be stored on computers and will be exchanged over networks. E-Governance itself has to move into next generation which demands faster and better training. Standardization of technologies has to be achieved at the earliest.[31]

METHODOLOGY

Survey of Methodologies

In keeping with the true tradition of research, we made a literal survey of the methodologies adopted by various researchers in their study of e-governance and the related issues. Many have adopted different benchmarks and parameters besides taking unique perspectives and approaches to the study of e-governance not only in India, but also the world over. This part presents a review of various e-governance methodologies so as to provide a basis to the methodology that we adopted for our study on impact of e-governance projects on Indian society.

1. e-Government Benefits Study[32] sponsored by the National Office for the Information Economy's (NOIE), Australia is one among the important studies on e-Government benefits. This study concentrated on demand, benefits, benefit-to-cost ratio for government, managing e-government, etc. The framework developed for the study was meant to capture evidence on the past, present and future expectations of demand and benefits from three major stakeholder groups viz., GOL (Government on line service users representing 1586 consumers), Non-GOL (Citizens, Business and Intermediaries who are not users of government online services but may be users of the Internet representing 305 people); and (Commonwealth government agency representatives supplying government online services-agencies representing 60 people of six focus groups). The data was collected by the external research agencies mainly through online surveys and interviews. The study concludes that people not making sue of e-government services have expressed their interest in e-governance services, in contrast to what the e-governance users said. Regular users cited barriers such as the usability of websites-navigation, incomplete information, visibility and discoverability-finding government services, poor search capability; and online security and privacy.
2. How to Evaluate E-Government / Different Methodologies and Methods by Marcin Sakowicz[33] is one of the best in reviewing various methodologies on e-governance. This chapter reviewed ten different e-governance projects methodology viz., e-Europe, EU, UNPAN, e-Government Benchmarking Electronic Service Delivery, KeeLAN, Eforum, Momentum Research Group, The Government Online Study (GO), Taylor Nelson Sofres, E-Public Services in Poland, Balanced E-Government and Infoville and presented appropriate methodology to the Central and East European countries. The pertinent conclusion drawn by the researcher is that e-government evaluation methods adopted in advanced countries like USA and European Union may not be useful for countries that are trying to implement e-governance.

Moreover, they may limit the researcher's understanding of the evaluation methodology of e-Governance.

3. A Framework to assess the impact of e-Government systems on governance by Driss Kettani[34] *et. al.* presented a novel model of methodological framework and presented different indicators and illustrate its application to the Fez e-Government Project. This consists of assessing the impact of e-Government on each constituent of Government taken individually. These authors identified five major outcome categories that need to be assessed. These include: technology, organization, citizen, regulation, and good governance related outcomes.
4. This well-drafted report on 'Key Elements for electronic Local Authorities' Networks' (KEeLAN)[35] presented an excellent e-governance model of the EU. Fifty case studies have been selected out of 100 best-practice websites based on front-office performance of service delivery, identified after scanning 700 e-Government websites of European Union local authorities. As per the study the important bench markings in e-governance are *(a)* Leadership; *(b)* Policy and Strategy; *(c)* People; *(d)* Resources; *(e)* Processes; *(f)* Regional Context.
5. An article titled 'Assessing the impact of E-Government on local governance based on real settings of developing countries'[36] by Driss Kettani *et. al.*, reviewed the current range of understanding with respect of certain of the concepts of particular significance to the Local E-Government project including the notions of governance, e-governance, and good governance. It mainly attempted to identify means to operationalize certain concepts as a way to systematically assess the significance and value of the outcomes being produced. At the end the study, they presented a method of assessing the outcomes of the Fez e-Government project, specifically on its contribution to enhance good governance.
6. 'PC Kiosk Trends in Rural India'[37] by Kentaro Toyama *et. al.*, presented a study based on questionnaires presented to Kiosk operators and customers of kiosks operated by Drishtee (providing e-government services to rural villages in India) and n-Logue (Enhance quality of life of every rural Indian by driving the digital revolution profitably). The data was collected by implementing the three sets of questionnaires,

one is a baseline questionnaire for each kiosk village and kiosk operators, second one is a recurring questionnaire for kiosk operators and third one is recurring questionnaire for kiosk customers. Total questionnaires implemented are 225 questionnaires for kiosk operators and 1125 for Kiosk customers. The study concluded that most kiosk operations are running below the expected revenue and operators are happy as they have not depended upon this income primarily.

7. An important study by the IIM, Ahmedabad on 'Gyandoot: Rural Cyber Cafes on internet'[38], located in the Dhar District of Madhya Pradesh, presented a detailed picture of cost-benefit analysis of ICT implementation for rural masses. The study collected the data from Citizen Users:32; Government Officials:10; Sochaks:18; Citizens–Non Users:41 and Gyandoot Project Staff: 04 and broadly concluded that among the twelve services provided by the Gyandoot, the respondents are satisfied with only two services in terms of savings in cost, reduction in time, improvement in accessibility, convenience and reliability.
8. 'e-Governance Initiatives in Bangladesh: An Analysis of Strategy formulation for re-inventing Good Governance'[39] presented by Department of Business Administration, Jahangirnagar University, Bangladesh, is useful to measure the success of e-governance. The report presented an eight factor model of e-governance, which can be categorized into *internal interface* and *external interface*. Internal interface by increasing organizational capacity depends on four areas viz., Leadership, Management, Skill and Technology. External interface includes Information, Interaction, Transaction and Integration is key areas in increasing transparency/accountability. These factors increasing value to the citizen in e-governance and promote participation.

The above discussion on Governance and e-Governance and survey of literature and the diverse methodologies presents a multitude of factors useful in understanding or assessing the impact on e-governance on governance systems, and by extension, societies. Obviously, the above studies present a different list of indicators as per their project environment and the objectives. However, the study we carried out is based fundamentally on indicators that sum up the broad perspective of the citizen on e-governance in Indian society.

Study Indicators

- Impact of e-Governance on overall Quality of Life of people (as perceived by the people, leaders, bureaucrats etc.)
- Peoples acceptance and adaptability of e- Governance
- Users responce on transparency in electronic services
- Peoples perception of financial integrity and authenticity
- Levels of accountability
- Reduction in time and costs in availing electronic services
- Innovation in Public Private Partnership modules
- Overall satisfaction of the people on the processes of e-governance.

Impact Measurement

Indicator	*UNDP Definition*	*Project Working Definition*	*Outcome Measurement Indicators*
Transparency	Transparency is built on the free flow of information. Processes, institutions and information are directly accessible to those concerned with them, and enough information is provided to under-stand and monitor them.	Transparency in the work flow of electronic service delivery – no bureaucratic hassles and openness in delivery mechanisms.	1. Citizens' perception on the functioning of administrative structures. 2. Online availability of relevant public services.
Accountability	Decision-makers in government, private sector and civil society organizations are accountable to the public, as well as to institutional stake holders. This accountability differs depending on the organization and whether the decision is internal or external to an organization.	Creating standards to make public staff and private personnel accountable for their actions.	1. Citizens' access to relevant information on administrative processes. 2. The role of public and private personnel.

Contd...

Indicator	*UNDP Definition*	*Project Working Definition*	*Outcome Measurement Indicators*
Responsiveness	Institutions and processes try to serve all stake-holders.	Response and inclusion of bottom-up service demands and adaptability to citizens' needs.	1. Curbs on middle-men and corruption. 2. Change in the behaviour of government staff.
Effectiveness and Efficiency	Process and institutions produce results that meet needs while making the best use of resources.	Cost-benefit ratio for government and involvement of private players.	1. Access and availability of electronic services. 2. Reduction in time, costs and efforts for citizens.
Overall Satisfaction		Satisfaction related to the outcomes of above indicators.	Overall levels of citizens' satisfaction on the delivery of e-services.

OBJECTIVES OF THE STUDY

- To understand the nature and extent of e-governance in Andhra Pradesh, Karnataka and Kerala.
- To assess the role of e-governance in improving citizen services.
- To trace the method of restructuring the government for transformation to e-governance.
- To check out the method of training and acclimatization of the personnel.
- To know the awareness of citizens on e-governance projects.
- To gauge the satisfaction of people on the delivery of services through electronic means.
- To point out the fundamental obstacles and hurdles in the implementation of e-governance programmes.
- To understand the socio-political implications of e-governance.

Framework of the Present Study

The framework for the study was designed to asses the impact of e-governance programmes on society to a maximum extent with a sample size, of which a majority is the stakeholders (users and government officials). All efforts were made to capture evidence on past, current and future expectation of demand and benefits from the users of electronic services. The respondents include:

- Direct users of electronic services, non-users (a negligible minority), entrepreneurs (kiosk managers), intermediaries (kiosk operators).
- Government officials, government agency representatives, consultants.

A field survey was undertaken to gather opinion and feedback on benefits from a citizen perspective through a structured questionnaire. Opinion and feedback from government officials, agency representatives and others was gathered through informal discussion with an unstructured questionnaire. The views and perspectives of non-users was also elicited, though their number is small, in order to arrive at a broader assessment of the impact of online services on all sections of society.

However, the two major groups of the sample size (2,761) include:

- 2173 citizens who are direct users of online government services, cutting across age, gender, literacy, technology, geographical (rural, urban) divides.
- 588 government officials, government agency representatives who are tasked with the implementation of e-governance programmes.

The study was undertaken in 30 districts—10 districts each in the states of AP, Karnataka and Kerala—with emphasis on equitable geographical distribution and covered the following nine e-governance projects:

- e-Seva
- CARD
- VOICE & Saukaryam
- Bhoomi
- KAVERI
- BangaloreOne
- Akshaya
- FRIENDS
- e-Collectorate

A brief description of the projects covered under the study:

1. *e-Seva – Hyderabad, Andhra Pradesh*

The project was started as a pilot in the twin cities of Hyderabad and Secunderabad, and was thus called TWINS (Twin Cities Integrated Network Systems). It was started at the cost of Rs. 10 million, fully funded by the Government of Andhra Pradesh. In Hyderabad, through e-Seva, citizens can view and pay bills for water, electricity and telephones, besides municipal taxes. They can also avail of birth/death registration certificates, passport applications, permits/licenses, transport department services, reservations, Internet and B2C services, among other things.

2. *Computer-Aided Administration of Registration Department (CARD) – Hyderabad, Andhra Pradesh*

In this project, 214 registration offices have been computerized since 1998. This project provides services such as encumbrance certificates, valuation certificates, market value search, etc., on user charge basis. The time taken for registration of documents has been reduced from one day to 15 minutes. More than 4 million documents have been registered, and 2.16 million encumbrance certificates and 3.73 million registration check slips have been issued since 1999.

3. *VOICE and Saukaryam, Andhra Pradesh*

The Vijayawada Online Information Centre (VOICE) was launched in June 1998 and implementation was completed in December 1999 to deliver municipal services such as building approvals, and birth and death certificates, to the people of Vijayawada. It also handles the collection of property, water and sewerage taxes. The VOICE system uses five kiosks located close to the citizens. These are linked to the back end processes in the municipal offices through a wide area network. The application has helped reduce corruption, made access to services more convenient, and has improved the finances of the municipal corporation.

Project Saukaryam (meaning facility) was completed in January 2001 in Visakhapatnam Municipal Corporation for delivering all the civic services online. It was taken up in a PPP mode without much additional costs to the corporation. A Metro Area Network covering 120 Sq.Kms. using broadband / leased circuits. It covers all the civic services ranging from online payment of dues to allowing lodging of grievances online or filing building plan application and offers their status online.

These two projects have been subsequently merged into e-Seva which is now a common portal for offering online services both in the urban and rural areas across the State of Andhra Pradesh.

4. *Bhoomi – Bangalore, Karnataka*

The Karnataka government's 'Bhoomi' project has led to the computerisation of the centuries-old system of handwritten rural land records. Through it, the revenue department has done away with the corruption-ridden system that involved bribing village accountants to procure land records; records of right, tenancy and cultivation certificates (RTCs). The Department of Revenue, Government of Karnataka, has computerized 20 million land ownership records of 6.7 million farmers in the state. Each record is available online from 177 taluka kiosks. A farmer can walk into the nearest taluk office and ask for a computer printout of his land record certificate for Rs. 15. He can also check details of land records on a touch-screen kiosk by inserting a two-rupee coin. These kiosks, installed at the taluk office, will provide the public with a convenient interface to the land records centre.

5. *Karnataka Valuation and e-Registration (KAVERI)*

KAVERI is a comprehensive computerization project aimed at automating the entire registration process and speedy delivery of registered documents to the citizens of Karnataka. Initially meant only for property registration, KAVERI's scope has been extended to the registration of firms and societies and marriages. Efforts are on to successfully link it with the Bhoomi Project so that land records can also be accessed from the SRO (Sub-Registrars Office) instead of having to go to the taluk offices. The KAVERI project won the best e-Governance Project award for the year 2004 at the 40th annual conference of the Computer Society of India (CSI). Similar initiatives that have been successfully implemented in other states are CARD in Andhra Pradesh, HIMRIS in Himachal Pradesh, and PEARL in Kerala.

6. *BangaloreOne*

The Government of Karnataka is keen to provide integrated services to the citizens deploying the tools of Information and Communication

Technology (ICT) so as to enhance Speed, Convenience, Certainty and Accountability in providing such services through the concept of a 'One-Stop-Shop' facility. Accordingly, the state government decided to implement an e-Governance project called the Bangalore One or B1 Project on the lines of similar projects implemented elsewhere in India, especially e-Seva that was successful in Hyderabad and other major towns of Andhra Pradesh. The Bangalore One project has been successfully launched on 2 April, 2005 with 14 service centres providing 24 different services (18 government and 6 private) to citizens of Bangalore.

7. *Akshaya – Malappuram Kerala*

In 2001, a joint project between local bodies (gram panchayats) in rural areas, municipalities in urban areas and private entrepreneurs in Malappuram District of Kerala was started to bridge the digital divide by providing community access to computers and the Internet. Five hundred and sixty-five Community Technology Centres (CTCs) have been implemented in the district. Akshaya operates PPPs in establishing the CTC in remote villages.

8. *Fast, Reliable, Instant and Efficient Network for Disbursement of Services (FRIENDS), Kerala*

This one-stop service centre uses computers to provide public services such as payments of electricity bills, examination fees, motor vehicle tax, building tax, property tax, water bills and telephone bills. This project is operational in all 15 district headquarters of the state. The services are provided on a user-charge basis and government officials operate the counters at the FRIENDS centres.

9. *e-Collectorate, Palakkad, Kerala*

DC*Suite (District Collectorate Suite) or simply e-Collectorate is an integrated suite of applications for the Collectorate based on an integrated solution architecture covering all functional areas and activities of the Collectorate in Palakkad District of Kerala. There are twenty functional areas identified including Workflow based File Management System, Public Grievances Monitoring System, and Revenue Recovery Management etc. for computerisation. In addition, there will be add-on optional modules for knowledge management, district portals etc. Public access, transparent administration and service delivery are the key features of the project that was launched on the 26th of October 2004. The project will gradually be extended to all the districts in Kerala, but as of now there are to plans to implement it in Malappuram, Kannur and Pathanamthitta Districts.

Method of Data Collection

The present study is basically a comparative analysis of e-governance programmes in the three States of Andhra Pradesh, Kerala and Karnataka. The data has been collected through net, official documents, discussions, questionnaires and interview schedules besides regular field notes. The areas of comparison and impact of e-Governance are:

(i) Citizen Services
(ii) Restructuring of Administration
(iii) Government On-line
(iv) ICT penetration to rural areas

Reference Period of the Data to be Covered

1998–2000: pre-e-governance and transition phase.
2004–2007: post–e–governance phase.

Break-up of Data Collection

Sl. No.	*State*	*Programme*	*Districts Covered*	*Officials*	*Public*	*Total*
1.	ANDHRA PRADESH	CARD (Sample: 306)	1. Hyderabad	8	25	33
			2. Nizamabad	3	21	24
			3. Mahabubnagar	5	21	26
			4. Vishakapatnam	6	22	28
			5. E. Godavari	5	29	34
			6. W. Godavari	6	26	32
			7. Krishna	7	24	31
			8. Kurnool	6	24	30
			9. Chittoor	7	28	35
			10. Ananthapur	6	27	33
			TOTAL	**59**	**247**	**306**
		E-SEVA (Sample: 312)	1. Hyderabad	12	27	39
			2. Nizamabad	5	21	26
			3. Mahabubnagar	4	24	28
			4. Vishakapatnam	6	27	33
			5. E. Godavari	5	26	31

Contd...

Sl. No.	State	Programme	Districts Covered	Officials	Public	Total
			6. W. Godavari	4	24	28
			7. Krishna	5	26	31
			8. Kurnool	7	22	29
			9. Chittoor	6	28	34
			10. Ananthapur	6	27	33
			TOTAL	**60**	**252**	**312**
		SAUKARYAM & VOICE (Sample: 304)	Saukaryam Vishakapatnam	20	121	141
			Voice Vijayawada	33	130	163
			TOTAL	**53**	**251**	**304**
2.	KARNATAKA	BHOOMI (Sample: 302)	1. Bangalore	10	25	35
			2. Mysore	7	21	28
			3. Madikeri	5	21	26
			4. Mandya	6	28	34
			5. Shimoga	7	23	30
			6. South Canara	6	23	29
			7. Gulbarga	6	21	27
			8. Raichur	7	25	32
			9. Bidar	8	25	33
			10. Bijapur	4	24	28
			TOTAL	**66**	**236**	**302**
		KAVERI (Sample: 302)	1. Bangalore	5	23	28
			2. Mysore	8	28	36
			3. Madikeri	7	24	31
			4. Mandya	6	29	35
			5. Shimoga	7	22	29
			6. South Canara	5	22	27
			7. Gulbarga	7	24	31
			8. Raichur	6	23	29
			9. Bidar	7	20	27
			10. Bijapur	8	24	32
			TOTAL	**66**	**239**	**305**
		BANGALORE ONE (Sample: 312)	Bangalore City	70	242	312
3.	KERALA	FRIENDS (Sample: 301)	1. Thiruvananthapuram	10	25	35
			2. Kottayam	8	23	31

Contd...

Sl. No.	*State*	*Programme*	*Districts Covered*	*Officials*	*Public*	*Total*
			3. Ernakulam	8	25	33
			4. Thrissur	5	22	27
			5. Kollam	7	21	28
			6. Palghat	8	28	36
			7. Malappuram	6	26	32
			8. Kozikode	6	25	31
			9. Wayanad	4	16	20
			10. Kasargode	7	21	28
			TOTAL	**69**	**232**	**301**
		AKSHAYA (Sample: 304)	Malappuram	69	235	304
		E-COLLEC-TORATE (Sample: 315)	Palakkad	76	239	315
			TOTAL	**588**	**2173**	**2761**

Limitations of the Study

Any major research study is bound to face several limitations or obstacles which are inevitable for reasons of time and space. The study area is so vast geographically as well as demographically. The study covered a population of 172 million (2006 estimates) in a geographical area of 505,722 km.[2] The actual area of study comprised 30 districts in the three states with a sample size of 2761 of which 588 are officials and technical staff associated with the implementation of the e-governance programmes and 2,173 are citizens utilizing electronic public services. Then, there are linguistic barriers coupled with different regional accents. Translators did help us a lot, but there was a problem in putting across our queries to rural and uneducated citizens. Users in urban centres, particularly cities had little time to spare for sharing their experiences with the research team.

As part of the study, we selected three programmes from each state which are entirely different in terms of services, software modules and institutional arrangements. The delivery processes too are different from each other. Therefore, it was very difficult at drawing generalities, measure the impact of the e-governance programmes, and finally arriving at definitive conclusions.

The socio-economic needs of the respondents/ users were varied and their use of electronic services was limited to a few areas. For instance, all the users of Bhoomi are either farmers or land owing citizens and their need is confined only to get an electronic Record of Tenancy and Cultivation (RTC) certificate. Of these users, only a half or so had the use of KAVERI which caters to the property registration services. Barring these two services, the select respondents had no use of other electronic services.

The research team faced immense problems in the collection of primary data for reasons of access and availability of the officials concerned as also the attention span of the respondents. There was also a problem in understanding the various software modules and the back-end processes of the select e-governance programmes.

REFERENCES

1. Asia Oceania Electronic Marketplace Association (AOEMA) (2004) *E-Government from a User's Perspective: E-Government: Définitions and Objectives,* [Online], Available: http://www.aoema.org/E-Government/Definitions_and_Objectives.htm (Access on 15 February, 2007).
2. The Global Development Research Centre (GDRC 2004) 'Understanding the Concept of Governance', [Online], Available: http://www.gdrc.org/u-gov/governance-understand.html (Access on 15 February, 2007).
3. The Global Development Research Centre (GDRC 2004) 'Governance: A Working Definition', [Online], Available: http://www.gdrc.org/u-gov/work-def.html Accessed on 16 February, 2007.
4. *Ibid.,*
5. The World Bank: 'What is Governance?', [Online], Available: http://www1.worldbank.org/mena/governance/Issues-KeyQuestion.htm Accessed on 19th January, 2007.
6. The Global Development Research Centre (GDRC (e)) 'Towards a Set of Urban Governance Indicators', [Online], Available: http://www.gdrc.org/u-gov/indicators.html Accessed on 19th Janruary, 2007.
7. The Urban Governance Initiative, Good Governance issues Report Card: Solid Waste, 2003; http://www.tugi.org/reportcards/solidwaste.PDF. Accessed on 20th January, 2007.
8. Christine Bellamy and John A.Taylor, '*Governing in the Information Age*', Buckingham, Open University Press, 1998, pp. 3-6.
9. "The Next Revolution — A Survey of Government and the Internet", The Economist, June 24, 2000, p. 3.
10. For a full length discussion on these areas See: Francisco Magno and Ramonette Scrafica, Research Study on IT and Good Governance, Asia Foundation, Manila, 2003.

11. IADB (Inter-American Development Bank). "E-governance, E-government: ICT for Development". http://www.iadb.org/ict4dev/governance.htm (Accessed on 11th December 2006).
12. Zelinna D. Pablo, A Multi- Disciplinary Analysis of E-governance: Where do we Start, Pacific Asia Conference on Information Systems 2002 and IADB, *op. cit.*
13. *Moysés de Oliveira Andrade Júnior, 2003* www.gwu.edu/~ibi/minerva/Fall2003/Final%20papers/Moyses_Andrade.pdf (accessed 11 February 2004).
14. UN's World Public Sector Report, 2001.
15. Sharma B. M. & Roop Singh Bareth (eds.), Rawat Publications, 2004.
16. Jain R. B. (eds.) Deep & Deep Publications Pvt. Ltd., 2005.
17. Mohanan B., Concept Publishing Company, 2005.
18. Chrisanti Avgerou (*et. al.*), Inter-American Development Bank, Washington, 2005 (website: www.iadb.org/sds/ict).
19. World Public Sector Report-2003, Department of Economic and Social Affairs, United Nations, New York, 2003.
20. Rafiq Dosani, *et. al*, Stanford University, National Informatics Centre, 2004.
21. Research project at the London School of Economics -1999.
22. Research project at the London School of Economics–2003.
23. Anthony M. Cresswell and Others, Centre for Technology in Government, New York, September 2006.
24. Heeks, Richards, IDPM, University of Manchester, UK, 2004.
25. Zelinna D. Pablo and Shan L. Pan, 2004, *op.cit.*
26. National Academy Press, Washington DC, 2004.
27. Van Dijk, Jan, Sage Publications, 2005.
28. Panneervel P., Rawat Publications, 2005.
29. Sreekumar T.T., *Information Technology in Developing Countries*, Vol. 12, No. 3, December 2002, CGG, IIM, Ahmedabad, www.iimahd. ernet. in (Accessed 12.01.2007).
30. Harris, Roger and Rajesh Rajora, UNDP-APDIP ICT4D Series, 2006.
31. Ahmad, Ibrahim, *Dataquest*, Vol. XXV No. 5, March 15, 2007.
32. E-Government Benefit Study, Commonwealth of Australia, 2003.
33. Marcin Sakowicz, "How to Evaluate E-Government? Different Methodologies and Methods", Warsaw School of Economics, Department of Public Administration, E-mail: maskow@sgh.waw.pl.
34. Driss Kettani, Bernard Moulin and Asmae Elmahdi, "A Framework to assess the impact of E-Government Systems on Governance," School of Engineers, Alakhawayan University, Morocco, Article received through e-mail.
35. Key Elements for Electronic Local Authorities' Networks (KEeLAN), Benchmark Report www.keelan.ie/uploads/documents/egovernment/Benchmark.Report.pdf (Accessed 21.12.2006).

36. Driss Kettani, Michael Gurstein and Asmae El Mahdi, "Assessing the impact of E-Government on local governance based on real settings of developing countries" School of Engineers, Alakhawayan University, Morocco and Vancouver, CANADA. Article received through e-mail.
37. Kentaro Toyama, *et. al.* 'PC Kiosk Trends in Rural India' by, Microsoft Research, Bangalore, India, presented a Paper in International Seminar on "Policy and Options and Models for Bridging Digital Divides" March 13-14, 2005, Tampere, Finland. Contact: kentoy@microsoft.com
38. Centre for Electronic Governance, IIM, Ahmedabad study on 'Gyandoot: Rural Cyber Cafes on internet', Dhar, Madhya Pradesh, Draft Report, October 2002.
39. 'e-Governance Initiatives in Bangladesh: An Analysis of Strategy formulation for re-inventing Good Governance' Department of Business Administration, Jahamgirnagar University, Bangladesh, www.egovaspac.apdip.net (Accessed 22 November 2006).

3

Case Studies

e-SEVA, ANDHRA PRADESH

Background

The project was started as a pilot in the twin cities of Hyderabad and Secunderabad, and was thus called TWINS (Twin Cities Integrated Network Systems) initially. It was started at a cost of Rs. 1 crore, fully funded by the Government of Andhra Pradesh in December 1999. The project provided services such as registration of birth and death certificates, registration of vehicles and learners' driving licenses. After a successful pilot, 10 centres were started on 25 August 2001 and then the project was renamed as e-Seva. On 10 October 2001, a portal—http://www.esevaonline.com - was launched. Currently, 250 centres are in operation across the state.

About Andhra Pradesh

Andhra Pradesh was formed on 1st November, 1956 under the States' reorganisation scheme. It is the fifth largest State with an area of 2,76,754 sq. km, accounting for 8.4 per cent of India's territory. The State has the longest coastline (972 km) among all the States in India. It lies between 12°41' and 22°N latitude and 77° and 84°40'E longitude, and is bordered by Maharashtra, Chhattisgarh and Orissa in the north, the Bay of Bengal in the East, Tamil Nadu to the south and Karnataka to the west. Andhra Pradesh is the fifth largest state in India by area and population. It is the largest and most populous state in South India. The state is crossed by two major rivers, the Godavari and the Krishna. Unofficially, the state can be divided into Telangana, Rayalaseema, Coastal Andhra, North Coastal regions.

The state capital Hyderabad is the fifth largest city both in terms of geographical spread and population in India. It is spread in over 260 square kilometers and has a population of 8.1 million (greater Hyderabad). Hyderabad and Secunderabad are twin cities separated by Hussain Sagar—bound by Tank Bund. This manmade lake was carved out during the time of Ibrahim Qutb Shah in 1562. The Charminar (Four Minars) built in the centre of the city by Muhammad Quli Qutb Shah in 1591 was in commemoration of the eradication of a plague in the region.

When India gained Independence in 1947, Hyderabad ruler Nizam demanded a dominion status within the country. Later, on September 17, 1948 the Nizam signed the Instrument of Accession to the Indian Union. On November 1, 1956, the states of India were reorganized on linguistic grounds. Hyderabad and the surrounding areas were added to Andhra Pradesh. Thus, Hyderabad became the capital city of the new state.

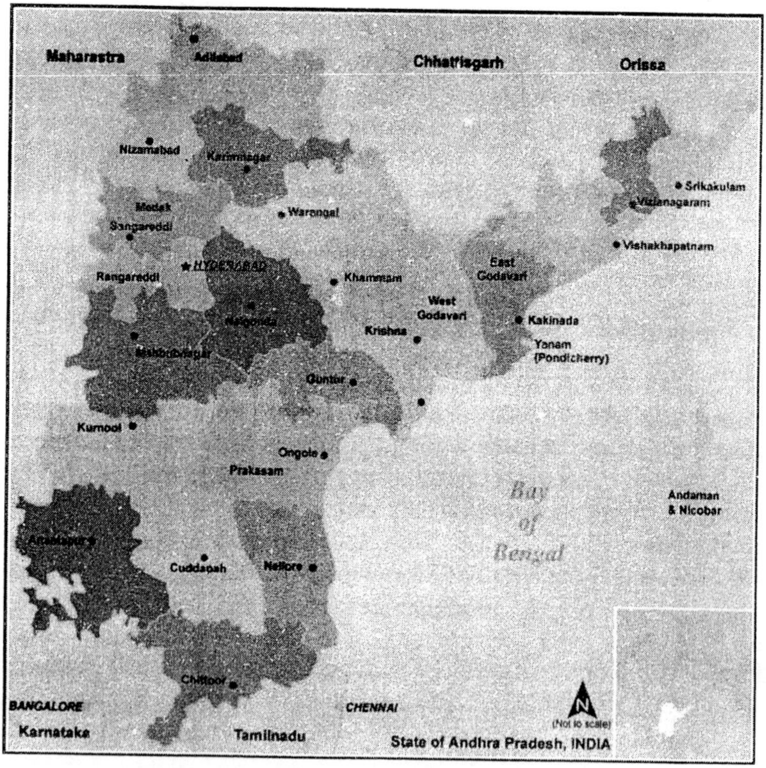

State of Andhra Pradesh, INDIA

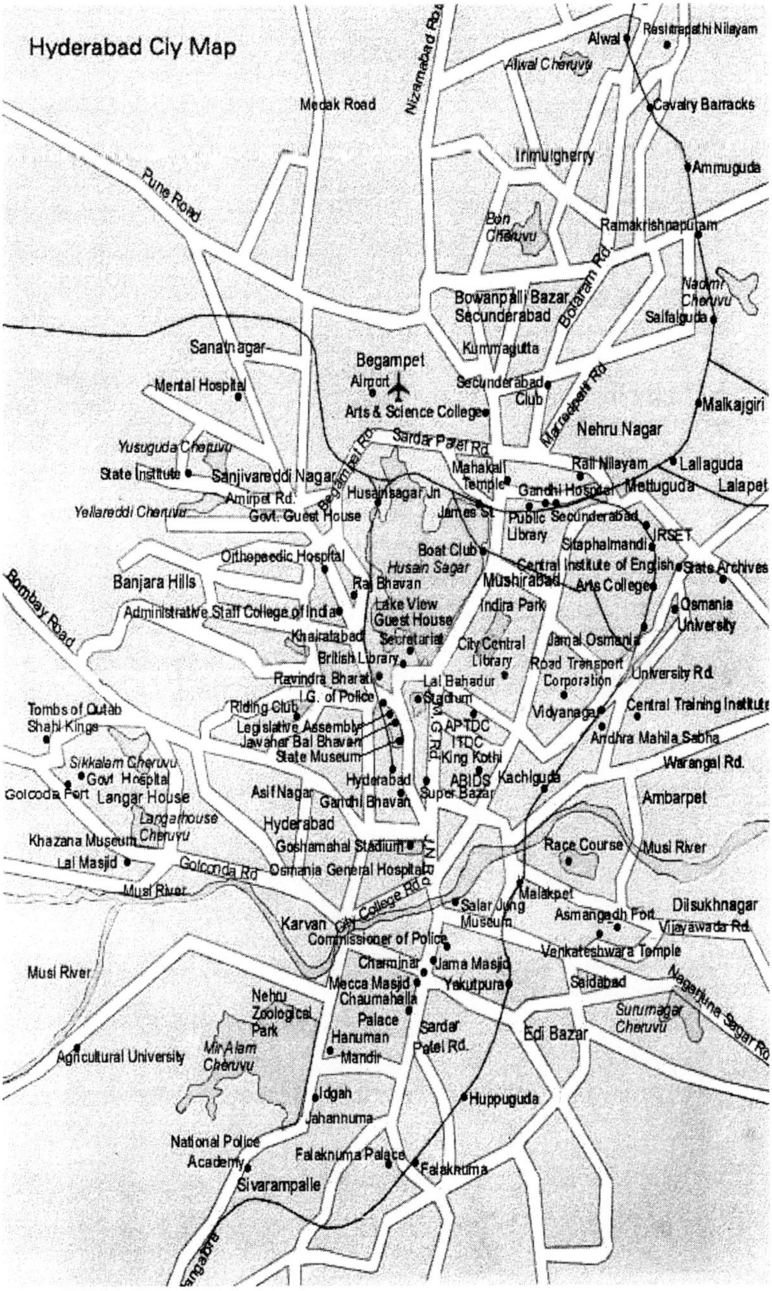
Hyderabad Ciy Map
Alwal
Rashtrapathi Nilayam
Alwal Cheruvu
Medak Road
Cavalry Barracks
Trimulgherry
Ammuguda
Pune Road
Bon Cheruvu
Ramakrishnapuram
Nadimi Cheruvu
Bowanpalli Bazar
Secunderabad
Botaram Rd.
Safilguda
Sanatnagar
Kummagutta
Begampet
Airport
Mental Hospital
Secunderabad Club
Arts & Science College
Malkajgiri
Nehru Nagar
Sardar Patel Rd.
Yusuguda Cheruvu
Rail Nilayam
Lallaguda
State Institute
Sanjivareddi Nagar
Mahakali Temple
Gandhi Hospital
Mettuguda
Lalapet
Amirpet Rd.
Husainsagar Jn
Yellareddi Cheruvu
Govt. Guest House
James St.
Public Library
Secunderabad
IRSET
Boat Club
Sitaphalmandi
Orthopaedic Hospital
Husain Sagar
Central Institute of English
State Archives
Bombay Road
Banjara Hills
Raj Bhavan
Mushirabad
Arts College
Lake View Guest House
Indira Park
Osmania University
Administrative Staff College of India
Khairatabad
Secretariat
City Central Library
Jamai Osmania
British Library
Road Transport Corporation
University Rd.
Ravindra Bharati
Lal Bahadur
I.G. of Police
Stadium
Tombs of Qutab Shahi Kings
Riding Club
Vidyanagar
Central Training Institute
Legislative Assembly
APTDC
Jawahar Bal Bhavan
ITDC
Andhra Mahila Sabha
State Museum
King Kothi
Sikkalam Cheruvu
Warangal Rd.
Govt Hospital
Hyderabad
ABIDS
Kachiguda
Golconda Fort
Langar House
Asif Nagar
Gandhi Bhavan
Super Bazar
Ambarpet
Langarhouse Cheruvu
Hyderabad
Khazana Museum
Goshamahal Stadium
Race Course
Musi River
Lal Masjid
Golconda Rd
Osmania General Hospital
Musi River
Malakpet
City College Rd.
Salar Jung Museum
Dilsukhnagar
Asmangadh Fort
Karvan
Vijayawada Rd.
Commissioner of Police
Venkateshwara Temple
Charminar
Jama Masjid
Musi River
Mecca Masjid
Yakutpura
Saidabad
Nehru Zoological Park
Chaumahalla Palace
Nagarjuna Sagar Rd.
Surunagar Cheruvu
Hanuman Mandir
Sardar Patel Rd.
Edi Bazar
Agricultural University
Mir Alam Cheruvu
Idgah
Huppuguda
Jahannuma
National Police Academy
Falaknuma Palace
Falaknuma
Sivarampalle

AP at a Glance

- Geographical Area: 275,000 sq. km.
- Forest Area (Sq. Km): 63814
- Districts: 23
- Mandals: 1123
- Villages: 26586
- Towns: 264
- Population: 7.65 crore
- Literacy Rate: 61.11 per cent
- Sex Ratio: 978
- Density of Population: 275/sq.km.
- Per Capita Income: Rs. 10,590
- State Income: Rs. 78,705 crore
- Zilla Parishads: 22
- Panchayats: 21,934
- Municipalities: 121
- Municipal Corporations: 13[2]

Objectives and Goals of e-Seva

- To provide real-time online transactions.
- To improve government-customer interface at all levels.
- To improve service quality and innovation.
- To improve operational efficiency.
- To provide cost-effective services.

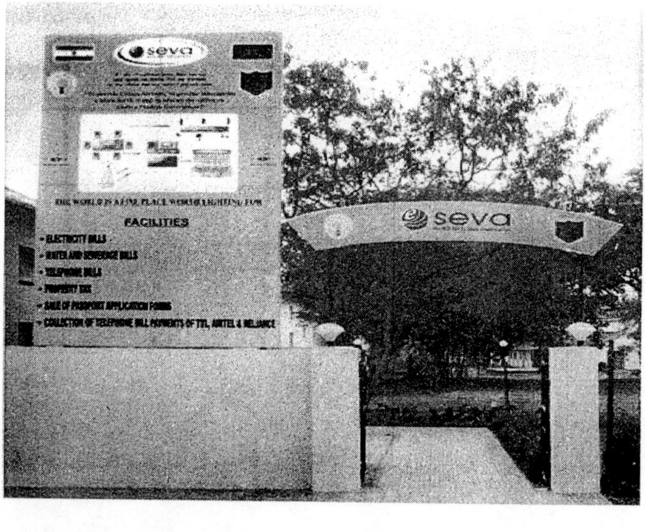

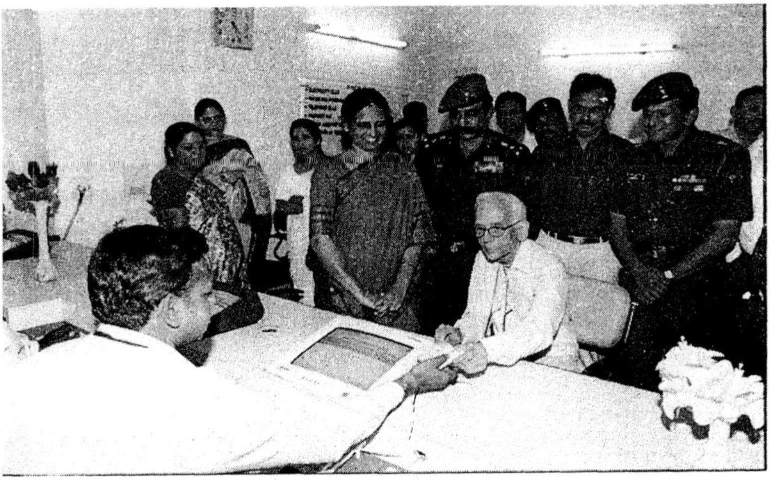

Planning

It was planned on the lines of Singapore Online,[4] a well-known web portal that provides all the information that users want to know. E-Seva is one of the major IT project undertaken by the government of Andhra Pradesh as a part of e-governance. E-Seva is the first kind of service in the country, providing a wide spectrum of citizen friendly services that will save citizens running around various departments. E-Seva is built on the success of TWINS (Twin Cities Network Services) pilot project, which was launched in December 1999 in Hyderabad, the state capital. It was designed to provide citizens of Hyderabad and Secunderabad to handle integrated 19 services pertaining to six departments for delivery on a one-stop mode.

Services Provided

Presently, the e-Seva centres provide around 55 services such as payment of water and sewerage bills, property taxes, commercial taxes, income taxes, phone bills, registration of vehicles, issue of learner driving licenses, transfer of ownership of vehicles, registration of new trade licenses, renewal of trade licenses, registration of birth and death, birth and death certificates, filing of passport applications, collection of examination fees, registration of documents and stamps (non-judicial), sale of bus tickets, sale of non-judicial stamps, collection of small savings etc. The services are provided within 60 seconds to 120 seconds. The centres operate on working days from 8 am to 8 pm and on public holidays from 9 am to 3 pm. Citizens are not charged for any utility payments. Services like the payment of electricity/water/telephone bills and transport/property taxes are available on a 24 ×7 basis on the Web portal.

Public-Private Partnership

E-Seva is a government organization build on public-private partnership model. Infrastructure and building are provided by the government. Staff is provided by government as well as by the private. Government recruits the staff through deputation and the respective departments pay salaries. Private hire the staff through tenders and they are protected by minimum wage act.

Salient Features of e-Seva

- All services can be availed at any centre
- All services can be availed at any counter within the centre, i.e., a consumer need not visit one counter for one service and another for another service
- There are no jurisdictional limits. A resident of Secunderabad can pay his bills at the old city of Hyderabad and vice-versa
- Services can be availed on holidays as well

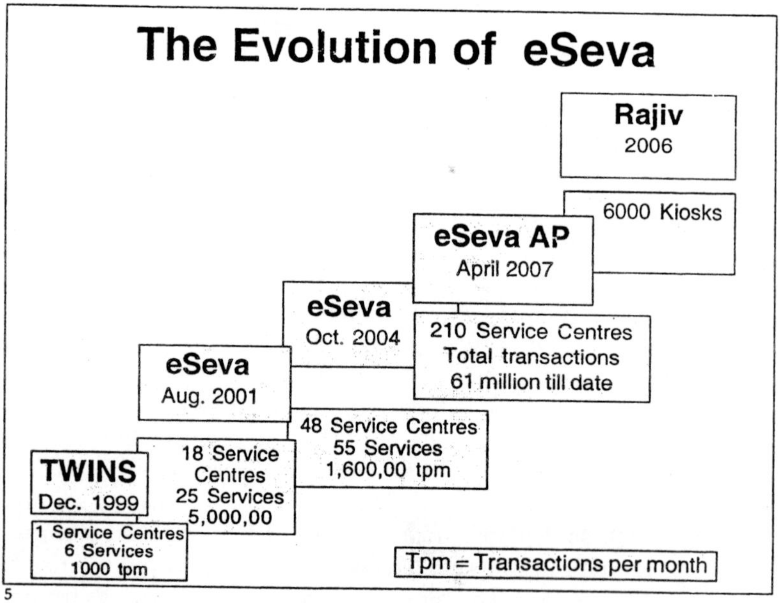

- Bill payment can be made over the Internet
- Online service: e-forms, e filing, and e-payments.

About Rural E-Seva

The rural e-Seva project was launched on the 25th of August 2001 in the district West Godavari. The project is a tool to bridge the digital divide in the rural areas and has used Information Technology for providing access to various B2C and C2G services to the people living in rural areas. Under this project web enabled rural kiosks termed e-Seva centres have been established at the mandal (a sub district unit of administration) level. The unique thing about these centres is that they are run and managed by the women self help groups and have been able to position the rural women as information leaders to help bridge the gender divide. This is an attempt to replace the traditional form of governance and its accompanying deficiencies with a modern, more open, transparent and responsive service delivery system. The project is based on BOOT (Build Operate Own Transfer) model.[6]

Target Group and Intended Beneficiaries

Citizens of the twin cities of Hyderabad and Secunderabad and also the major towns (municipalities) in districts are the target group and intended beneficiaries. As of now, over 250 centres are servicing the various needs of the users.[7]

Institutional Arrangements

The Directorate of e-Seva is headed by a director and has two deputy directors, one assistant director (technical), one assistant director (promotion), three senior assistants, one grievance officer and two helpers. Almost all the hardware and software services have been outsourced. A PPP was envisaged at the outset, in 2001. Global tenders were called for entrepreneurs to take up e-Seva centres. CMS Computers Ltd. got the tender for managing the centres. Software was designed at a cost of Rs. 2.5 million by another company called RAM Informatics. The Government provided the premises and the managerial staff. The managing company provided the hardware, networking solutions, operators (with salary paid by the Government), engineering staff, help-desk staff and security staff at all the centres. The Government provided updated databases concerning the services while the company paid all telecom/leased line bills and electricity dues. A Memorandum of Understanding (MoU) was signed between the Government and the company for five years. On each transaction, Rs. 5 as a user charge is collected from the concerned department out of which 75-80 per cent is paid back to the private partners. Earlier, four new-generation banks – Global Trust Bank, ICICI, HDFC and UTI – were selected to facilitate net-transactions of the payments. Later, two more banks, IDBI and Centurion Bank, also joined. A 4 per cent surcharged was charged on every credit card transaction, which has been reduced to 1.5 per cent.[8]

Technologies

The network architecture is designed as an internet on a Wide Area Network (WAN). The network is designed in three tiers. The first tier for the client-end is located at the e-Seva centres. The front end is Java-based. All the centres are on 64 kbps dedicated leased lines, with ISDN backup. The second tier has two Sun E250 model and two Compaq ML530 model data servers. The second tier also consists of Application Servers (using Oracle GiAS and running on Sun Solaris 8 Operating System), Database Servers (using Oracle 8i R3 and running on MS Windows 2000 Operating System), Network Monitoring Servers (using Cisco Works and WhatsupGold on MS Windows 2000 Operating Systems), Management Servers (using MS putin), Firewall (using Cheuqn) and Web Servers (using Apache). All the machines used in this tier are Intel machines, along with Cisco switches and routers. The third tier is made of Departmental servers with an Oracle database as the backend in the concerned departments (Electricity, Municipality, Passport Office, Transport Department, Registration, Commercial Tax, etc.). These servers keep consolidated databases. They are linked with 64 Kbps DB link (except the Electricity Department server which has a 2 Mbps pipeline). The network architecture provides dedicated leased lines, with ISDN backup.

Technical Details of e-Seva

Department/Agency

Information Technology and Communications Department.

Year of Launch

Pilot: TWINS, December 1999.
Seva: 25 August 2001.

Project Cost

TWINS Pilot site Rs. 1.0 crore.

Site preparation by Government @Rs. 3.0 crores.

Hardware, software, networking at Hyderabad by M/s. RAM Informatics & M/s. CMS Computers @Rs.5.0 crores.

CERTIFICATE OF COMPLIANCE

This is to certify that the
QUALITY MANAGEMENT SYSTEM of

eSeva

Head Office : Road No.7, Banjara Hills, Hyderabad – 500 034, Andhra Pradesh, India.
Sites : 27 Sites (Details Of Sites As Per Annexure 'A').

has been assessed by International Certification Services (Asia) Pvt. Ltd. and registered as complying with the requirements of the following International Standard:

ISO 9001 : 2000

The Quality Management System applicable to:

Scope: Providing Realtime Online Integrated Citizen Services (eSeva) Pertaining To Central, State, Local Governments And Private Corporate Enterprises Through Its 27 Centres.

Registration No.	:	[illegible]
Registered Date	:	14th March, 2003.
Valid for	:	3 years
Expiry Date	:	13th March, 2006.

IAS-ANZ

Managing Director
International Certifications Services.

Accredited by Joint Accreditation System of Australia and New Zealand

[illegible]

International Certification Services (Asia) Pvt. Ltd. [illegible]

The cost for establishing e-Seva centres at districts @ Rs. 27 Crores.

Technology Used

* 3-tier architecture.
* Oracle 9iAS Application server on Sun Solaris.
* Servers of different departments are connected to the e-Seva Data Centre, which is in turn connected to different ICSCs.
* The connectivity is point-to-point leased line connectivity, with ISDN as backup.

System Developed/Implemented by: M/s. Comvision and M/s. Ram Informatics Ltd.

E-Seva, Hyderabad: M/s. CMS Computers Ltd. and Ram Informatics Ltd.

E-Seva at Districts:

Software: M/s. Ram Informatics Ltd.

Hardware and Networking Equipment

Zone -I:	M/s. CMS Computers Ltd.
Zone -II:	M/s. United Telecom Ltd.
Zone -III:	M/s. CCS Infotech and Data Management Corp. Ltd.
Zone -IV:	M/s. CMS Computers Ltd.
Zone -V:	M/s. CMS Computers Ltd.
Zone -VI:	M/s. CMS Computers[10]

Primary Access Points

Primary access points for e-Seva services are the e-Seva centres, which are established on spacious premises. Each centre has a waiting foyer, help desk, token counter and eight to 15 operator counters. Six of the e-Seva centres have ATMs (two each of State Bank of Hyderabad, State Bank of India and Andhra Bank). Citizens can excess the portal from their households as well to avail of the services online.

Capacity Building

All the operators are given four-day operational training on the operator terminal. Some efforts have been made in providing IT training in the concerned departments. The Government and its numerous departments have paid little attention towards creating an e-workforce. There is an over-dependence on private technological partners, CMS Computers Ltd. and RAM Informatics Ltd., for all technological solutions. The dependence on RAM Informatics Ltd. and Jyothy Computers to provide all e-worker needs to be rectified by building the capacity and skills of redundant government employees. This becomes important in the context of a proposed expansion of 237 new e-SEVA centres and the fact that the Government has to pay monthly salaries to all the operators engaged in these 237 centres.

Project Outcomes

Until now e-Seva has facilitated more than 61 million transactions that include e-payments. The project is set to roll in all the 127 municipalities by the end of 2007-08. The service delivery centres are adding new G2C and B2C services on public demand. It is an ISO9001:2000 certificate holder which can handle many services. Regrettably, that has not happened. The scaling up of services is definitely not progressing as was indicated in the beginning. Also, there is definitely a lack of security to the money deposited in cash. In the first-ever case of embezzlement of funds in urban e-Seva centres in Krishna District, an accountant fled with Rs. 10 lakh from Chuttugunta e-Seva centre.

G. Srinivas Rao on deputation from the VMC to e-Seva is reported missing since June 6 and a case has been registered with Machavaram police after due process of inquiry and verification of the accounts by e-Seva authorities on June 10, 2007. Such loopholes have to be plugged in with institutional arrangements and definitive working module. Credible franchises have to be selected to build up on the public trust that e-Seva already enjoys.

Sustainability

This project is financially sustainable. The government, private entrepreneur and users, are all winners in this project. The huge acceptance by the public of e-Seva counters also confirms its future sustainability. The organizational re-engineering and management practices adopted are also favourable for its sustainable existence.

Replication and Scaling Up

It is very unfortunate that the country's most successful e-governance project has not been seriously replicated in any other parts of India.

This project was scaled-up with the installation of 237 new e-Seva centres (including all 117 municipalities) in the rest of the 23 districts in the State of Andhra Pradesh. These new centres fall in six zones (four zones are taken up by CMS Technologies, one zone by United Telecom Limited, and one by CCS Technologies). Each district will be a separate internet to start with, which will eventually be integrated into the Internet.

Survey on the Impact of e-Governance on Society: A Case Study of e-Seva

We carried out the present study at e-Seva centres in the twin cities of Hyderabad and Secunderabad as well in nine other districts of the State of Andhra Pradesh. The districts that have been covered under the study include Mahaboobnagar, Nizamabad, Kurnool, Anantapur, Chittoor, Nellore, Krishna, East Godavari and Visakhapatnam. Responses were elicited from a total of 252 users – 184 male and 68 female—falling in the age groups of under 20, 21-30, 31-40, 41-50 and 51 and above.

A majority of the people surveyed has studied at least matriculation (secondary school certificate) which is 30.2 per cent, while 13.9 per cent of the respondents are illiterates. Over 21 per cent of the respondents have finished Plus Two and nearly 28 per cent are graduates. Only 5 per cent said they hold a PG degree.[11]

The State of Andhra Pradesh is a medley of urban as well as rural peoples. There is a constant growth in the number of dwellers on account of migration from the countryside following the expansion of economic and livelihood opportunities in tune with the globalized economy.[12] As per the latest figures, urban dwellers form nearly 30 per cent of the total population of Andhra Pradesh. Naturally, one can see a huge mix of families with a peasant background in the urban areas. Over 37 per cent of the respondents said they are either peasants or farm labourers (26.2% peasants and 11.1% labourers). Nearly 25 per cent of the respondents are pursuing an independent occupation while 19 per cent are into government service. Whereas 13.5 per cent of those surveyed said they have 'other' occupation—34 out of 252—while the remaining 5.2 per cent said they are non-agricultural labourers.

Despite the varied nature of the occupations of the respondents, it has emerged that on the broader plane a majority of them are equally comfortable and adaptable to the new technologies by the state government in the delivery of citizen services.

Sex

	No. of Respondents	*Per cent*
Male	184	73.0
Female	68	27.0
Total	252	100.0

Age

	No. of Respondents	*Per cent*
Below 20	24	9.5
21-20	66	26.2
31-40	69	27.4
41-50	63	25.0
51 and Above	30	11.9
Total	252	100.0

Education

		No. of Respondents	*Per cent*
Valid	Upto SSC	76	30.2
	Intermediate	54	21.4
	Degree	69	27.4
	Post Graduation	13	5.2
	Other	5	2.0
	Illiterate	35	13.9
	Total	252	100.0

Occupation

	No. of Respondents	*Per cent*
Agriculture	66	26.2
Agriculture Labour	28	11.1
Non-Agriculture Labour	13	5.2
Government Service	48	19.0
Independent Occupation	63	25.0
Other	34	13.5
Total	252	100.0

Awareness

	No. of Respondents	Per cent
Heard	25	9.9
Not Heard	13	5.2
Heard and User	214	84.9
Total	252	100.0

There has been a tremendous response in the case of awareness on the e-Seva though 15 per cent of those surveyed were illiterates. Nearly 85 per cent of the respondents said they have heard about e-Seva and are regular users. Among the non-users — who form 15 per cent of the respondents — 10 per cent are in the know of the e-services while only 5.2 per cent have not heard anything on the e-Seva programme. Though only 5.2 per cent of the respondents claimed of not being aware of the e-services, we can safely conclude that they are very popular among the masses even in rural areas.[13]

The Transparency Factor

Transparency in dealings or transactions between the government and the citizens is a vital benchmark to define the success scale of any e-governance project. E-Seva has scored big over other such e-projects in the country enjoying a robust 94 per cent trust with the study respondents. Only 6 per cent of those surveyed expressed second thoughts over the key variable of transparency. The transfer of moneys paid and the technology utilized to provide back office support are compatible with the expectations of a public that has overwhelmingly accepted the new information and communication technologies in governance. The table below shows the perception of the respondents on the question of transparency.

Transparency

	No. of Respondents	Per cent
Yes	236	93.7
No	16	6.3
Total	252	100.0

Accountability

While nearly 94 per cent of the respondents believed there was transparency in the transactions done at e-Seva centres, only 87 per cent of them were assured of accountability. This is almost a 7 percentage points dip in the respondents trust over the maintenance of accountability in the delivery of e-services. Also, is the case with no-sayers. Whereas only 6 per cent said there was no transparency in the deals struck at e-Seva centres, over 13 per cent expressed themselves negatively on the question of accountability. This comparison shows that a significant section of the users still have doubts–after six and a half years of implementation of e-Seva, including the pilot stage – on the scale of accountability maintained in e-services. Such a negative perception notwithstanding, nearly 87 per cent of the respondents said there was accountability in the functioning of the e-service delivery centres and this by any standards reflect the opinion of the majority. However, there is a need to scale up the accountability levels of the project from the lessons learnt over the past six years.

Accountability

	No. of Respondents	*Per cent*
Yes	219	86.9
No	33	13.1
Total	252	100.0

Responsiveness

We have already discussed in the previous case studies that responsiveness is a crucial factor that elevates the overall popularity of an e-governance project. Partly, responsiveness has to seen than perceived and partly to be delivered voluntarily than on demand. Such an approach may change the public perception of a project to the positive side. There are many inherent and institutionalized hurdles for implementing such good practices of governance in the Indian context. As far as e-Seva is concerned, more than 90 per cent of the respondents said the project is receptive towards their suggestions and needs – in terms of scaling up service delivery and addition of new services that are basic in nature – while more than 9 per cent of them replied in the negative. Those saying 'nay' are a significant component in that they constitute almost 10 per cent of the total respondents. A very receptive and sensitive front office management is required to address the demands and needs of the e-services users. There is definitely a help desk, but a separate counter can be installed to hear oral or written submissions with regard to the quality of services, addition of new services and simplifying the transactional procedures.

Responsiveness

	No. of Respondents	*Per cent*
Yes	228	90.5
No	24	9.5
Total	252	100.0

Availability of Services

Services that are viable have been made available to the citizens, right from the pilot state of TWINS project. Many new and basic services were added when the e-Seva rolled out in August 2001 as a regular e-governance model. Services are available all through 12 hours a day and for 6 hours on public holidays and Sundays. Most of the users are satisfied on this particular aspect which has reflected in a major way in the present study.

Availability of Services

	Frequency	*Per cent*
Yes	246	97.6
No	6	2.4
Total	252	100.0

Nearly 98 per cent of the users covered under the study said basic services are available to them at all times. Those not happy with the availability of services at e-Seva centres are very miniscule in number and represent a mere 2.4 per cent of the total respondents– 6 out of 252. New services are being added once their feasibility has been established and new centres and frachise centres are coming up to cover the entire urban population in the state. At the urban and rural levels, scaling of services has to be taken up on a priority basis and in a time-bound manner.

Utility of Services

Whereas the availability of services has never been in question in the case of e-Seva, there has not been a full replication in terms of utility of the services. From the table below, it is clear that comparatively the utility of services has not been on a par with availability of services. Of the total respondents, 88.5 per cent said the services that are on offer at the centres do have utility value while 11.5 per cent claimed there was not utility for e-services. This has primarily to do with the complex nature of the services. A few of them are being utilized exclusively by particular sections like traders, businessmen, transport operators, four wheeler dealers, insurance officers, etc. These services may or may not have a utility quotient for the larger sections of the users. However, in the long term these specialized services too would have become normal services with a larger clientele.

Utility of Services

	No. of Respondents	*Per cent*
Yes	223	88.5
No	29	11.5
Total	252	100.0

Use of the Programme

E-Seva project, on a broader plane, has a widespread use for the denizens of cities and major towns – where it is operational – in Andhra Pradesh. The usability factor of this project has only strengthened over the years with more and more sections of urban society accepting it as an indispensable means to avail services and dispose of their utility bills at one go under a common roof. The table below reflects this upward trend in the acceptance of e-services by people at large.

Use of the Programme

	No. of Respondents	*Per cent*
Yes	245	97.2
No	7	2.8
Total	252	100.0

Over 97 per cent of the users surveyed said the programme has been very useful to them while less than 3 per cent of the respondents expressed the opposite view. From these figures it is clearly evident that the usability factor of e-Seva is acquiring more of a positive image than reflecting a negative side. On one plane, the programme seems to have reached a saturation level in terms of usability but on the other it appears there is a need to scale up the utility levels of the services provided at the e-Seva centres.

The Time Factor

Several studies by governance experts and academicians have unambiguously accepted the fact that e-Seva is a trendsetter in India in the key aspects of reduction in time and costs for the citizens in securing services from the governmental departments. It has been declared the model e-governance project for the entire country.

Time Taken for Services Before e-Governance Programme

	No. of Respondents	*Per cent*
1/2 Day	135	53.6
1 Day	77	30.6
2 Days	40	15.9
Total	252	100.0

Whereas a majority of the citizens—more than 84 per cent of the respondents concurred with this view—used to spend half day to a day for availing governmental services, the implementation of the e-service delivery scheme has limited this time frame to a mere 10 minutes or less than that. Over 97 per cent of the study respondents echoed this opinion. And, less than 3 per cent of the user respondents claimed it takes 30 minutes for them to complete the transaction at the e-Seva centre.

Time Taken for Services Before e-Governance Programme

	No. of Respondents	*Per cent*
Within 10 Min	245	97.2
Within 30 Min	7	2.8
Total	252	100.0

It is to be noted that at least 16 per cent of the respondents themselves claimed to have spent over 2 days to complete a deal with certain departments or governmental agencies. There have been no such prolonged delays in the case of e-Seva where the maximum time taken to conclude a complex deal has come down to less than 30 minutes. This has been pursued as a revolutionary change by many a user who subscribe to the notion that time is money.

The Cost Factor

Time is almost equivalent to cost when it comes to getting things done or worked up in a short period. In matters of governance the cost factor was never given a prominence before the era of good governance or e-governance dawned on the country. Previously, a majority of the people used to spend anywhere between Rs. 50 and Rs. 100 for governmental transaction. Of the total respondents, nearly 58 per cent said they used to incur an expenditure of Rs. 50 for availing service and nearly 30 per cent put the cost at Rs. 100. Only 12.7 per cent pegged their previous expenditure at Rs. 25.

Money Spend Before e-Governance Programme

	No. of Respondents	*Per cent*
Rs. 25	32	12.7
Rs. 50	146	57.9
Rs. 100	74	29.4
Total	252	100.0

With the implementation of e-governance models or programmes, the costs involved in securing services from the government departments and agencies have become very modest. Nearly 85 per cent of the respondents they are incurring costs up to Rs.15 under the e-Seva programme while 15 per cent of them claimed to be spending Rs. 25 for e-transactions.

Money Spend Under e-Governance Programme

	No. of Respondents	*Per cent*
Rs. 15	214	84.9
Rs. 25	38	15.1
Total	252	100.0

Overall Satisfaction

From the analysis of the above variables, we can safely conclude that the overall levels of satisfaction among the users are very high. Nearly 80 per cent of the respondents said they are highly satisfied while more than 20 per cent said they are satisfied, though on a moderate scale. Those claiming to be not at all satisfied are very negligible and make no difference to the overall perception of the respondents.

Satisfaction

	No. of Respondents	*Per cent*
Highly Satisfied	200	79.4
Moderately Satisfied	51	20.2
Lowly Satisfied	1	.4
Total	252	100.0

REFERENCES

1. Maps of Andhra Pradesh and Hyderbad City (right).
2. www.aponline.gov.in (accessed 2nd March 2006).
3. E-seva centre at Secunderabad Cantonment (left), military officials at the centre (right).
4. Visit http://www.singaporeonline.com.
5. The graphical illustration shows the evolution of e-seva.
6. www.esevaonline com. (accessed 12th January 2007).
7. www.aponline.com. (accessed 8th March 2007).
8. ICTD Case Sudies, 2006, Asia-Pacific Development Information Programme, UNDP Regional Centre, Bangkok.
9. ISO 9001: 2000 centification for e-seva project for providing real time online integrated citizen services.
10. www.esevaonline com. (accessed 12th May 2006).
11. The literary rate of Andhra Pradesh is 61.11 per cent–70.85 per cent male and 51.17 per cent female.
12. Ramachandrudu G. and Prasada Rao M. (eds.) 2004, Census 2001 and Human Development in India, Vedam Books, New Delhi.
13. Rural literacy in AP is nearly 20 per cent less than urban literacy (70%) and this can be cited as a major reason for lack of awareness on e-seva programme.

COMPUTER-AIDED ADMINISTRATION OF REVENUE DEPARTMENT (CARD), ANDHRA PRADESH

CARD was one of the earliest projects of e-governance implemented in India. It was more of a computerized project rather than an e-government project, as it had no such grand agenda of transforming the government. Land registration offices throughout Andhra Pradesh operate computerized counters to help citizens to complete registration requirements within an hour instead of several days, as was necessary under the traditional manual system. The lack of transparency in property valuation under the old system resulted in a flourishing business of brokers and middlemen leading to corruption. The project has been designed to change the antiquated procedures that have governed the registration system, affecting sales of urban and agricultural properties. Under the CARD programme, citizens can complete registration formalities within an hour.

Application Context

Registration to document changes in ownership and transactions involving immovable property is governed by the Indian Stamp Act of 1899. Deeds of various kinds are required by law to be written on stamp paper of prescribed value. Certain transactions require a fixed duty. Registration is carried out at an office. In Andhra Pradesh, there are more than a million documents per year that need registration. The process of registration is a very complex procedure that requires 11 steps and thus is very time consuming. Moreover a hierarchy of officers is required for the same.

This manual registration system generated a number of important drawbacks. Most importantly:

- *Lack of transparency in valuation:* The basic value registers usually were not accessible to the public, and even if they were, it was difficult for a common citizen to read them and calculate the amount of various transaction fees during the registration. All this results in a host of corrupt practices and a flourishing business of brokers and middlemen who exploit the confusion surrounding the registration process.

- *Tedious back office functions:* Conventional manual methods of copying, indexing and retrieving documents are laborious, time consuming, and prone to errors and manipulations. Thus, a premium is often paid for speedy delivery of services.
- *Difficulties in preserving documents:* The registers occupy a lot of physical space, usually in ill-maintained backrooms. They also deteriorate with age and repeated handling.

New Approach

The Computer Aided Administration of Registration Department (CARD) is designed to eliminate the maladies affecting the conventional registration system by introducing electronic delivery of all registration services. CARD was initiated to meet the following key objectives:

- Demystify the registration process.
- Bring speed, efficiency, consistency and reliability.
- Substantially improve the citizen interface.

These goals were to be achieved by:

- Introducing a transparent system of valuation of properties, easily accessible to citizens.
- Replacing the manual system of copying and filing of documents with a sophisticated document management system using imaging technology.
- Replacing the manual system of indexing, accounting and reporting through the introduction of electronic document writing.

Since 60 per cent of the documents and certified copies relate to agricultural properties, the success of the CARD project would greatly benefit the rural farming community. Agriculturists would also benefit from a possible link-up of the CARD network with the rural bank network, which would enhance the efficiencies of the rural credit services by eliminating the need for paper-based procedures.

Table–1
Difference Between the Time Taken in Manual and CARD Service

Service	*Manual*	*CARD*
Valuation of Properties	1 hour	10 minutes
Sale of Stamp Paper	30 minutes	10 minutes
Document Writing	Not Available	30 minutes
Registration of the Land Deed	1-7 days	1 hour
Encumbrance Certificate	1-5 days	10 minutes
Title Search	3 days	15 minutes
Certified Copies of Documents	1-3 days	30 minutes

Source: "Computer-aided Registration of Deeds and Stamp Duties," posted on www.worldbank.org and www.ap-it.com

Background

The Registration Department of the Government of Andhra Pradesh has 387 Sub-Registrar's Offices (SRO) in 23 districts of the state. The gross revenue earned by the department is Rs. 12 billion. The manual systems in all the activities caused long delays, red-tape and corrupt practices. The Computer Aided Administration of Registration Department (CARD) project was conceptualized to computerize all activities and procedures of the Registration Department. A pilot

Figure 3 : The CARD Process

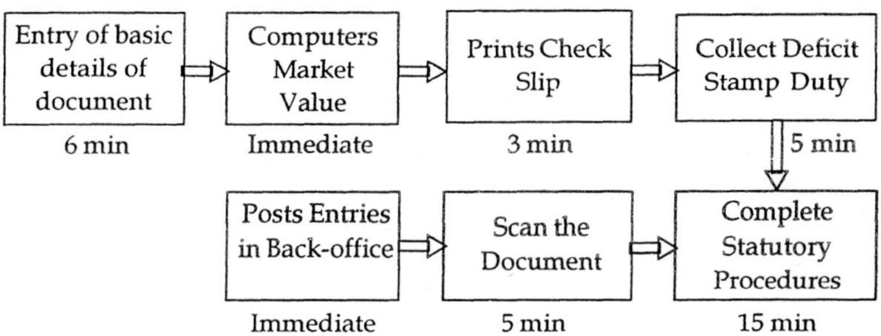

Source: Challenges of E-Government Two Success Stories from India, by Satyanarayana, www.ap-it.com

was conducted at two SROs in August-September, 1997. The project was started on 4 November 1998. Presently, the project covers the whole State of Andhra Pradesh.

Goals and Objectives

- To simplify the registration procedure
- To enhance the speed, reliability and consistency of the system
- To provide transparency in valuation
- To replace copying/filing systems with imaging
- To preserve documents on CDs
- To automate all back-office functions
- To enable a system that enables setting time and quality standards
- To smoothen the government-citizen interface

Planning

After the success of the two pilots, the project was scaled up in two phases. In 2000, the first phase was extended to 181 SROs. In 2001, the second phase was extended to 249 SROs. By the end of 2005-06, all the 387 SROs were covered under the CARD project.

Services Provided

All the services of the Registration Department are provided to citizens for nominal user charges. The most popular services are registration of deeds, issue of encumbrance certificates and market value searches. The prevalent user charges are: Rs. 95 for registration of documents (maximum of 10 pages with Rs. 5 for every additional page), Rs. 10 for motor vehicle search certificates, Rs. 20 for encumbrance certificates and Rs. 20 for certified copies of the documents.

Target Group and Intended Beneficiaries

The intended beneficiaries are all the citizens who want to register their deeds, get a valuation of their immovable property, certified copies of documents, encumbrance certificates and to register societies, firms, marriages, etc.

Institutional Arrangements

The Inspector General of Registration and Stamps heads the project, and is supported by the Technical Director (NIC), Chief Information

Officer and Deputy Inspector General (IGRAS). Each District Registrar is responsible for the functioning of CARD in the SROs under the district. One official from each District Registrar Office (DRO), at the rank of a senior clerk, takes up the task of the Data Processing Officer for two to five SROs, after intensive training. Each SRO has at least two data entry operators (one clerk and one section writer). All the hardware and maintenance of the LAN is handled by WIPRO, a private IT company, which has been awarded a maintenance contract for five years. All the software upgrades are done by NIC.

Technologies

The project works on a LAN. On every 387 SRO CARD office centre, there is provision for one server and four computers (three for B category SRO centres, two for C, D, E category SRO centres and one for F category centres). Each centre is provided with a scanner, a laser printer, a dot matrix printer and a UPS. The server uses Linux as the Operating System along with Oracle 8i for databases. The client end uses Developer 2000 whereas the front end is Windows 98/95 as well as Windows 98 for scanning.

The uptime of the system is more than 98 per cent, owing to an effective maintenance contract. Each district office is linked through a network, through dial-up connectivity to the Inspector General of Registration and Stamps office server. The software takes care of security through a username and password and maintains an audit for all activities.

- Client/Server
- Oracle database
- Linux platform
- Windows 98 in client

Primary Access Points

Primary access points for the citizens are the 387 SROs in the state.

Capacity Building

The project is implemented and managed by in-house staff. There are two clerks in each SRO. In all, 1,400 clerks/section writers have been given two-week training to take up the job of data entry operators; 76 senior clerks have been given 10-week training to take up the job of data processing operator job; 67 Assistant

District Registrars have been given three-week training; and 40 District Registrars have been given one-week training. Roughly, 3,811 man weeks (76 man years) of training have been imparted so far. Technical staff has also been given training on the CARD software. User manuals on CARD and the imaging software have also been issued.

Benefits and Costs

Six months following the launch of the CARD project, about 80 per cent of all land registration transactions in AP were carried out electronically.

The time required for services such as valuation of property and provision of certified copies of registered documents now takes 10 minutes instead of a few days as under the earlier system. ECs are now issued to citizens in a span of 5 minutes, using a system that searches through more than 15 years of records from over 50 offices. Land registration can be completed in a few hours, whereas earlier it took 7-15 days. After factoring out the natural upward trend in nominal revenues, the CARD system has generated a modest increase in revenue. The growth rate in net revenue collected has gone up by almost 20 per cent.

The main advantage of this system has been the awareness in rural public towards the benefits of ICT in important activities and so the public is demanding for more such projects at the rural level. The main disadvantage of the system has been the decrease in employment due to the loss in enforcement power.

Constraints and Implementation Challenges

Some legislation such as the Registration and Stamps Act, Urban Land Ceiling Act, Surplus Agriculture Land Act, Endowment Property Act, and the Property Act needed a change to accommodate the new procedure. The Government of Andhra Pradesh issued a circular to provide legal sanction for the scanned documents. All registered documents and deeds of the previous 13 years had to be coded and digitized to ensure encumbrance certificates were valid. Properties change names, categories, size and utility over time and there are discrepancies in different departmental documents. The codification of all property types was a huge task. Similarly, guidelines for the costs of land and buildings as well as for the different purposes and areas covered had to be digitized. The guidelines for the market rates for municipal corporations, municipalities, other urban areas, major gram panchayats, minor gram panchayats, and cantonment boards were decided differently for 80 land types (such as residential, commercial, industrial, agriculture, dry land, etc.). The documents and deeds registered since 1983 have already been scanned and stored on CDs.

The problem of shifting from the manual system to the new system was solved by computerizing all processes and procedures required at all the steps from acknowledgement of receipt to issue of a registered document. More than 5,000 government employees were trained in the new system. Maintenance of hardware, especially in remote rural areas, was arranged for by signing a contract with WIPRO. Power cuts of more than 12 hours were mitigated by installing UPSs at all the offices.

Project Outcomes

The project has increased the speed of registering property and producing related documents. Previously, citizens had to wait for three to seven days to obtain encumbrance certificates. After the CARD system was implemented, they receive such certificates in just 10 minutes. Similarly, certified copies of the documents were issued after seven days, while through the CARD citizens can now get them in only 15 minutes. The time taken to register a deed or a document has been reduced from three to seven days to one day. The CARD project registers 1.18 million documents and serves 5 million citizens in a year. Since the inception of the project, 4 million documents have been registered, 2.16 million encumbrance certificates have been issued, 3.73 million registration check slips have been issued and 75,907 certified copies have been provided to the public.

Sustainability

The project has improved the government-citizen interface. Around Rs. 300 million has been spent on the project, but no impact assessment had been carried out by the time of the study. The increase in revenue collection through CARD has still not been proven, but the project has generated more than it has invested since 1999. Rs. 380 million have been generated from the registration of documents, Rs. 37 million from the issuance of registration check slips, Rs. 43

million from encumbrance certificates and Rs. 1 million from certified copies. Up to the time of the study, the project had earned Rs. 475 million against a one-time investment of Rs. 300 million. The project will become further sustainable if all the services could be successfully made available online.

Replication and Scaling Up

The project has already been implemented in all the SRO centres in the state. Now, it is planned to network all SRO centres to the DROs through 64 Kbps dedicated leased lines and all DROs with state servers through 128 Kbps dedicated leased lines. It is also planned to install network-monitoring software in the system as well as to introduce storage of scanned documents in the form of microfilms.

Similarly, the department aims to upload record of documents on the web. The long-term vision is to provide all the services of the Registration Departments through the web.

The project has been replicated in the states of Maharashtra and Punjab with a few modifications. In Maharashtra, the entire project is implemented in an innovative PPP, in which government provides data, premises and service operators whereas the private partner takes care of the hardware, software, and network support and management of the facility.

Impact of e-Governance on Society: A Case Study of CARD Project, Andhra Pradesh

We carried out the present study at Sub-Registrar Offices in the twin cities of Hyderabad and Secunderabad as well in nine other districts of the State of Andhra Pradesh. The districts that have been covered under the study include Mahaboobnagar, Nizamabad, Kurnool, Anantapur, Chittoor, Nellore, Krishna, East Godavari and Visakhapatnam. Responses were elicited from a total of 247 users—219 male and 28 female. The sample size reflects the age old tradition in Indian society where all the decisions regarding sale and purchase of property are taken by the heads of the family—majority of them men.

Property sale, registration and other related things fall within the ambit of those having a family or those who have accrued ancestral property. This is seen in the age pattern where almost 90 per cent of the respondent is above 31 years of age. In this again, those in the age groups of 41-50 and 51 and above dominate.

Sex

	No. of Respondents	Per cent
Male	219	88.7
Female	28	11.3
Total	247	100.0

The CARD project encompasses the whole of Andhra Pradesh and is well entrenched even at the rural level with a vast network of automated registration services, generally provided at the Sub-Registrar Offices. The survey sample has thrown up quite a large percentage of illiterates, mostly farmers and those pursuing traditional occupations in villages. Over 18 per cent of the respondents are illiterate with no formal education. At least 55 per cent of the respondents—54.7 per cent to the precise—have either completed matriculation or Intermediate.[2] Those who have completed graduation or post-graduation represent 27 per cent of the respondents.

Age

	No. of Respondents	Per cent
21-30	21	8.5
31-40	80	32.4
41-50	106	42.9
51 and Above	40	16.2
Total	247	100.0

The State of Andhra Pradesh is a medley of urban as well as rural peoples. As per the latest figures, urban dwellers form nearly 30 per cent of the total population of Andhra Pradesh and the rural

Education

	No. of Respondents	Per cent
Upto SSC	100	40.5
Intermediate	35	14.2
Degree	50	20.2
Post Graduation	17	6.9
Illiterate	45	18.2
Total	247	100.0

folk follow varied occupations. Nearly 63 per cent of the respondents have agriculture as the main preoccupation. Nearly 12 per cent of the respondents are into government service while over 15 per cent follow independent occupation. Over 10 per cent of those surveyed have named occupations different from the above.

Though literacy levels and occupational status confirm the rural predominance in Andhra Pradesh, it is not surprising to note the high levels of awareness among the masses on the implementation of e-governance programmes particularly that cater to their basic needs. There is a high level of awareness on the CARD project in the state with nearly 88 per cent of the respondents claiming to be aware or have used electronic registration services. Those who have not used, but have heard about the services are over 11 per cent of the sample size.

Occupation

	No. of Respondents	Per cent
Agriculture	155	62.8
Government Service	29	11.7
Independent Occupation	38	15.4
Other	25	10.1
Total	247	100.0

Awareness

	No. of Respondents	Per cent
Heard	28	11.3
Heard and User	219	88.7
Total	247	100.0

The number of documents that are getting registered online is increasing by the year in Andhra Pradesh, especially after 2004 when the real estate and other property dealings reached the pinnacle. Normally, there is a bit of suspicion in the minds of people while going for registration of property. This has to do with the corrupt practices that officials and middlemen resort to. However, electronic registration has brought a new era of transparency in the registration department and SROs at the operational level. Over 96 per cent of the respondents see transparency in the programme while those holding the negative opinion form only 3.6 per cent of the sample size.

Transparency

	No. of Respondents	*Per cent*
Yes	238	96.4
No	9	3.6
Total	247	100.0

The perception of accountability in CARD is on the high side with over 92 per cent of the respondent coming out positively. Less than 8 per cent of the respondents do not see or perceive accountability in the registration process.

Accountability

	No. of Respondents	*Per cent*
Yes	228	92.3
No	19	7.7
Total	247	100.0

Complete automation of the registration process in the registration and stamps department in Andhra Pradesh beginning in 1998 has brought in a positive change in the outlook of the personnel. Creative innovations on the part of the personnel have turned around the department which now leaves all the steps of registration to the computer. The main outcome of this being increased responsiveness on their part. Nearly 90 per cent of those surveyed believe there is responsiveness in the programme while less 10 per cent of them replied in the negative on this aspect.

Responsivenss

	No. of Respondents	*Per cent*
Yes	221	89.5
No	26	10.5
Total	247	100.0

CARD services have spread to all the SROs in the state and are available to the masses on all working days. There is an effective automated network on ground linked with the state registration department portal. This is reflected in citizens' perception on the availability of electronic registration of property services. Nearly 94 per cent of the respondents claimed that services are available while only 6 per cent of them complained of non-availability of services.

Availability of Services

	No. of Respondents	*Per cent*
Yes	232	93.9
No	15	6.1
Total	247	100.0

Registration of property is a must at all levels and citizens utilize these services at the SROs. Therefore, there is high utility of electronic registration services in AP. Over 93 per cent of the respondents are utilizing the CARD services while less than 7 per cent have not or yet to utilize them.

Utility of Services

	No. of Respondents	*Per cent*
Yes	230	93.1
No	17	6.9
Total	247	100.0

E-governance programmes have struck a chord with the people in Andhra Pradesh, including the rural areas. Even those who have no use for them appreciate the quality of services provided by such projects. Over 97 per cent of the respondents say the programme is very useful or can be of use to them in future while less then 3 per cent suggest CARD is of no use to them. On the usefulness front, CARD scores high of all the projects we covered under the study and matches with that of e-Seva and Bhoomi.

Use of the Programme

	No. of Respondents	*Per cent*
Yes	240	97.2
No	7	2.8
Total	247	100.0

Barring the preliminary documentation work, the registration process takes less time in the case of CARD. Prior to 1998, the minimum time for property registration was three days to one week. This was the opinion of nearly 59 per cent of the respondents. Those who said the timeframe ranged from 2 to 1 days form 41 per cent of the respondents.

Time Taken for Services Before e-Governance Programme

	No. of Respondents	Per cent
1 Day	21	8.5
2 Days	80	32.4
3 Days	106	42.9
1 Week	40	16.2
Total	247	100.0

There has been a drastic change on the time front with the implementation of the CARD services. Now, the process of registration hardly takes 10 minutes and the maximum timeframe is less than 30 minutes. Over 76 per cent of the respondents claimed they are getting their registration work done in less than 10 minutes while the remainder 23.5 per cent pegged the timeframe as less than 30 minutes.

Time Taken for Services Under e-Governance Programme

	No. of Respondents	Per cent
Within 10 Min	189	76.5
Within 30 Min	58	23.5
Total	247	100.0

The Cost Factor

With regard to the costs involved in the registration process, there is marked reduction. This involves travel and the documentation costs. In the case of CARD, user charges are levied to the range of Rs. 15 to Rs. 25. Over 87 per cent of the respondents claimed to have spent anywhere between Rs. 100 and Rs. 500 prior to the implementation of the programme.

Money Spend Before e-Governance Programme

	No. of Respondents	Per cent
Rs. 50	32	13.0
Rs. 100	138	55.9
Rs. 500	77	31.2
Total	247	100.0

Money Spend Under e-Governance Programme

	No. of Respondents	*Per cent*
Rs. 15	209	84.6
Rs. 25	38	15.4
Total	247	100.0

However, the costs have come down drastically after CARD was rolled out at all the 387 SROs in the state. Nearly 85 per cent of the respondents now spend only Rs. 15 to get their property or title deeds registered while the remaining 15 per cent users put the cost at Rs. 25.

Satisfaction

	No. of Respondents	*Per cent*
High	181	73.3
Moderate	54	21.9
Low	12	4.9
Total	247	100.0

Reduction in time and costs for citizens availing registration services is the key outcome of CARD project. Normally, satisfaction levels on this count should be high for a programme like CARD and this reflects in the opinion of the respondents. Over 73 per cent of those surveyed have high levels of satisfaction on CARD and nearly 22 per cent claim they are satisfied, though moderately. Less than 5 per cent of the users said their satisfaction on CARD services is on the low side.

Overview

CARD is being implemented successfully and at a minimum cost. It shows that e-government solutions can be implemented in a span of three to four years, even with innumerable complications and procedures. The project proves that e-government could be implemented by just training the existing staff, without adding new technical staff. Another lesson is that in the absence of PPP, public finances can be mobilized to get projects implemented.

Presently, besides photocopies, four copies of a CD of the registered documents are stored (two for the SRO, one for the DRO and one for the IGRAS). It is recommended that the triplication of storage and archiving of documents be eliminated. There seems to be an extra computer at each SRO: offices with four computers have three operators, those with three computers have two operators and those with two computers have one operator. The reason for the provision of one extra computer at all 387 SRO centres is not clear. It is recommended that this proportion be rationalized according to the workload. All the hardware provided to 103 SROs in the year 2000 needs to be changed or urgently upgraded. Software should be upgraded so that scanned/digitized photographs of the people involved in the registration process could be electronically pasted onto the original and stored documents. There is no monitoring of MIS in the SRO offices on a daily or weekly basis. The MIS monitoring system needs to be improved at DRO and IGRAS levels.

REFERENCES

1. CARD process.
2. The average literacy rate in Andhra Pradesh 61.11 per cent as per the 2001 Census.

VIJAYAWADA ONLINE INFORMATION CENTRE (VOICE), ANDHRA PRADESH

Background

The Vijayawada Online Information Centre (VOICE) was launched in June 1998 and implementation was completed in December 1999 to deliver municipal services such as building approvals, and birth and death certificates, to the people of Vijayawada. It also handles the collection of property, water and sewerage taxes. The VOICE system uses five kiosks located close to the citizens. These are linked to the back end processes in the municipal offices through a wide area network. The application has helped reduce corruption, made access to services more convenient, and has improved the finances of the municipal government.

The Vijayawada Online Information Centre – in short VOICE – delivers municipal services such as building approvals and birth and death certificates. It also handles the collection of property, water and sewerage taxes. The VOICE system uses five kiosks located close to the citizens. These were linked to the back end processes in the municipal offices through a wide area network. The application has reduced corruption, made access to services more convenient, and has improved the finances of the municipal government (known as municipal corporations in India). Subsequently, the e-government scheme was merged with the mainstream e-Seva programme in 2005.

Application Context

Vijayawada is a city of one million (70% literate) spread over 57 square kms in eastern Andhra Pradesh in India. It is a major agricultural trading centre serving domestic as well as export markets. The local government had an annual budget of approximately Rs. 1.5 billion in 1999, of which 70 per cent came from taxes and rest through loans and grants. Nearly 50 per cent of the budget was used for capital expenditures.

Citizens have faced many difficulties in dealing with the municipal government, including bribery and harassment as well as the need to make frequent trips. Several trips to municipal government offices were needed to obtain a building permit or death and birth certificates. The issuance of certificates often was delayed with the intent to extract a bribe. However, complaints could not be filed easily and officers were inaccessible.

In paying taxes/rentals/charges for advertisements in public places, a citizen had to visit the appropriate municipal department to get a demand note and then go to the bank to make the payment. Meanwhile, the municipality lost revenue as a result of collusion between staff and the payee to lower the demand, and due to the inability to send notices to defaulters for follow up.

A New Approach

With funding from the Federal Ministry of IT (48%), the Andhra Pradesh State Government (32%) and the municipality (20%), the VOICE project was launched in June 1998 and implementation was completed in December 1999. There are two components of the VOICE system: (1) work stations distributed in key departments where the work of the department has been automated, and (2) the citizen's interface.

Citizens can go to any of the five kiosks set up in different parts of the city. Some information can be accessed from an Interactive Voice Response System. Those with an Internet connection also can connect to the Web server and retrieve information.

The hardware components include four servers located in the municipal office and 18 clients distributed amongst various departments networked in a LAN. Each kiosk has two terminals with multilingual software. Application, software such as Lotus Notes for grievance work flow and a Geographic Information System are used actively. CMC Ltd., a public sector software company, developed the entire application as a product which can be customized for other municipal governments in India.

The following departments have been automated: town planning, taxation, public health, estate, and engineering. Citizens can see the municipal budget allocations online. The status of tax payment, grievance registration, and birth/death certificates also is available online. Business people can inquire about their tax status, advertising space available for lease, and register complaints.

Modules

VOICE community empowerment through a community network includes:

- Grievances and Suggestions
- Property Tax
- Water and Sewerage Tax
- Births and Deaths
- D and O Trades
- Development Projects
- Building Approvals
- Commercial Complexes
- Advertisements
- Health Programmes
- Commissioner's access to Information
- Citizens' access to the Commissioner

Implementation Challenges

Implementation took place over the course of 18 months. There was considerable resistance to these changes from revenue earning departments, which stood to loose the income received from bribes. Preceding implementation of the project, performance review meetings were held to make officers accountable. The departments later saw the new system as a way of coping with the pressure to perform.

Minimizing the gap between the requirements of the officers and the features that were planned for the system by the developers was a constant challenge. Several meetings had to be organized during the development phase to close this gap. The implementation of the VOICE system was regularly monitored by the commissioner and CMC Ltd., the system developer.

Data entry to create the data bases was a huge task. Nearly 1.5 million records from various departments had to be entered. It was found that the internal staff was unable to cope with this load. A large part of the work was outsourced, but progress had to be monitored closely.

When the system was implemented, training was provided to 220 staff that would interact with separate modules of the system. Sixty officers were given a basic course by professional IT training institutes. A core team of 8 officers was trained in systems administration to manage an internal support desk.

There was nevertheless a tendency to bypass the system and do paper work outside it. The commissioner interacted with departments through the system and did not allow anyone to bypass the system. For example, tender monitoring, issue of work orders, and work progress monitoring was done only through VOICE screens.

Benefits and Costs

The cost of the project paid to the developer was Rs. 18.7 million ($0.4 million) of which 48 per cent was spent on hardware and system software and 52 per cent on application development. This is about 9 per cent of the yearly expenditure on establishment.

The benefits have accrued to the citizens and the municipal government. Corruption has been reduced, services are quicker, and the municipality has become more responsive. In just under a year, the system issued 15,000 birth/death certificates, 2,100 building approvals and 224,000 demand notices for taxes. Nearly 7,700 grievances were registered, of which 97 per cent were resolved. The commissioner can view these statistics by wards and departments, making monitoring more effective. Nearly 700 suggestions have been sent by citizens.

All internal processing of applications is now screen-based, generating greater efficiency. For example, the rent calculation for the bill boards is automatic and transparent; the system tracks advertising agencies that have not renewed contracts; and outstanding collections are sent timely notices. The impact on revenue should become known after June 2001.

Key Factors

This application is significantly different from other service delivery applications, as one of its goals was reform of the municipal government. Reforms of this kind need a champion within the organization, and in the case of VOICE, success was largely a result of the involvement of the commissioner. Identification of key staff to form a core team, constant monitoring, and marketing of the concept to citizens also contributed to the success of the project.

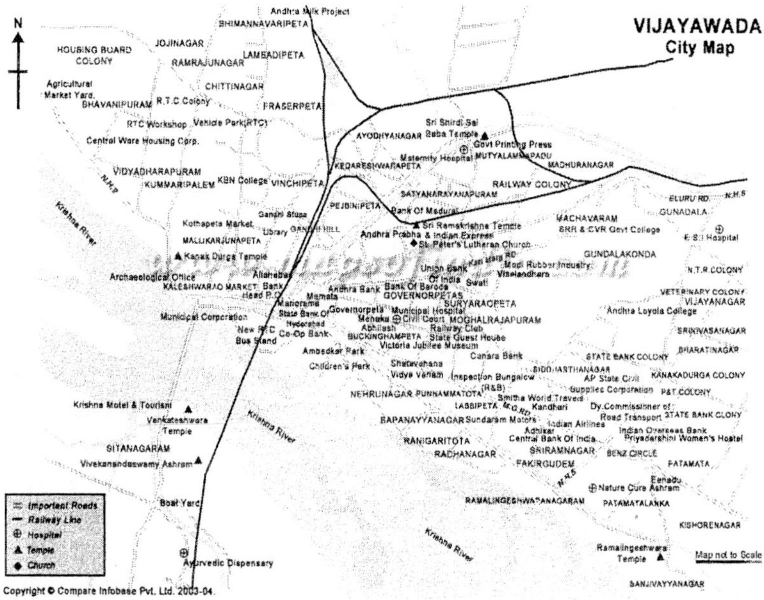

The application is an example of a partnership between federal and state government agencies, the municipal government, and a software development company. Contrary to the pattern in many government departments where new software applications have been custom developed in-house, this product was developed by a private company. The application will be quicker to implement and robust, but likely will be seen as more expensive than in-house software development (which, while relatively inexpensive, may be of poorer quality and reliability).

VOICE was a local initiative, not part of a grand design in the state's e-government effort. In fact, VOICE competes with an application, TWINS, developed by the State Government to deliver some services in the city of Hyderabad.

The utility of VOICE could be enhanced by offering information and services from other government departments like police, road transport, railways, and registration. This would require a high degree of coordination at the state level. In the interim, many local initiatives undoubtedly will sprout, and later a solution to link and integrate these different applications will have to emerge.

About Vijayawada

Vijayawada literally translates to *The Place of Victory*. It is also known as Bezawada in the local slang. (It is also known as Blazewada due to its scorching summers!). It is the third largest city in Andhra Pradesh, India and is located on the banks of the Krishna River to the south, bounded by the Indrakeeladri Hills on the west and the budameru stream on the north. The fertile Krishna delta extends from Vijayawada towards Bay of Bengal to the east. There are plenty of canals that go through Vijayawada and irrigate the farm land throughout the delta. Vijayawada is situated along the Madras-Howrah, and Madras-Delhi rail route, and is famous as being both the largest railway junction in South India and the most important station of the South Central Railway. National highways 5 and 9 pass through the city.

History

The discovery of pre-historic remains belonging to the stone-age man all along the banks of the Krishna River from Machilipatnam to Nagarjuna Sagar provides evidence that this part of the river valley was inhabited by the Stone Age man. Besides being an important religious centre for Buddhists and Hindus, Vijayawada is also a centre of Andhra culture. The Chalukyas of Kalyan and the great king Sri Krishna Devaraya once conquered this place, and the famous Chinese traveller Xuanzang (Hsuan-Tsang) visited this place in 639 AD when Buddhism was at its zenith in the region.

During the British Raj, the city experienced significant growth. In particular, the completion of the Prakasam Barrage in 1959, and the railway bridge on the Krishna River connecting Guntur City and its District helped in expanding the agricultural and commercial base of this region.

Geography

Vijayawada is a teeming city with over 1.2 million population located at 16.52° N 80.62° E. It has an average elevation of 11.88 meters (39 feet). The topology of Vijayawada is plain lands in between small to medium sized hills. Krishna River runs through the city. These hills are part of the Eastern Ghats chain cut through by the mighty Krishna

River. They also have very low elevation compared to the average elevation of the ghats. Three canals originating from the north side of the Prakasham barrage reservoir namely Eluru, Bandar and Ryves run through the city. Another canal Buckingham canal originates from the south side of the reservoir. With Krishna River flowing through the land, the soil around here is very fertile and cultivated intensively.

The climate is hot in summers touching 46 degree Celsius. Winters are mild and pleasant with temperatures from 10°C to 30°C. Vijayawada gets it rainfall from both the south-west monsoon and north-east monsoon. It is also prone to many cyclones that originate in Bay of Bengal.

City Administration

The city is run by the Vijayawada Municipal Corporation and is divided into 59 divisions. The commissioner, normally an IAS cadre official, is appointed by the state government. The city police is headed by a Police Commissioner, who is an IPS officer.

Growth in IT

The city has a very good educational background and historical importance but still is not really up to expectations in the IT and Internet fields. There are 20 units of IT in Vijayawada, generating revenues of approximately Rs. 42 crores (Rs. 42, 00, 00,000) in 2006-07. The APIIC is also setting up an IT park SEZ at Gannavaram, 20km from the city, to facilitate the growth of IT in this region. Construction major L&T got the contract for developing this IT Park with a budget of Rs 300 crores and employment for 10,000 IT professionals. Latest news is that due to restrictions at the Gannavaram area due to airport, the IT Park will now be set up in Mangalagiri area.

Survey on the Impact of e-Governance on Society: A Case Study of VOICE

We carried out the present study to gauge the impact of e-governance on society as part of which the e-services project of VOICE in Vijayawada, AP, was selected as a case study. The total sample size is 130 of which men are 103 and women 27–80 and 20 per cent respectively.

Sex

		Frequency	Per cent
Valid	Male	103	79.2
	Female	27	20.8
	Total	130	100.0

The respondents fall in the age groups of below 20, 21-30, 31-40, 41-50 and 51 and above. Those above 31 years of age to the maximum limit are a majority among the users of the electronic services. Nearly 30 per cent of the respondents are in the age groups of 21-30 and below 20.

Age

		Frequency	Per cent
Valid	Below 20	7	5.4
	21-30	30	23.1
	31-40	41	31.5
	41-50	37	28.5
	51 and Above	15	11.5
	Total	130	100.0

A majority of the people surveyed has studied at least matriculation (secondary school certificate) which is 31.5 per cent, while nearly 21 per cent of the respondents are illiterates. Over 30 per cent of the respondents have finished graduation or post graduation.

Education

		Frequency	Per cent
Valid	Upto SSC	41	31.5
	Intermediate	19	14.6
	Degree	33	25.4
	Post Graduation	7	5.4
	Other	3	2.3
	Illiterate	27	20.8
	Total	130	100.0

Over 28 per cent of the respondents said they are peasants while those doing farm work represent about 21 per cent of the sample size. Nearly 32 per cent of the respondents are pursuing an independent occupation while 4.6 per cent are into government service. Whereas 9.2 per cent of those surveyed said they have 'other' occupation while the remaining 5.4 per cent said they are non-agricultural labourers.

Occupation

		Frequency	*Per cent*
Valid	Agriculture	37	28.5
	Agriculture Labour	27	20.8
	Non-Agriculture Labour	7	5.4
	Government Service	6	4.6
	Independent Occupation	41	31.5
	Other	12	9.2
	Total	130	100.0

City utility services are a common knowledge in India and Vijayawada has high levels of awareness of them. Almost 95 per cent of the respondents have either heard or have used the VOICE services while a little over 5 per cent have not heard of them.

Awarenss

		Frequency	*Per cent*
Valid	Heard	14	10.8
	Not Heard	7	5.4
	Heard and User	109	83.8
	Total	130	100.0

On the transparency scale, VOICE scores less than e-Seva with only 77 per cent of the respondents replying positively. A significant number of the respondents – 23 per cent of the sample size – do not see or perceive transparency in the electronic delivery of services.

Transparency

		Frequency	*Per cent*
Valid	Yes	100	76.9
	No	30	23.1
	Total	130	100.0

On the accountability front too, VOICE fails to impress. Of those surveyed, 30 per cent said VOICE lacks accountability while the remaining 70 per cent respondents have a positive view on this count. This can be explained in terms of backup linkages and traditional ways of functioning of the corporation staff. Linkages have now been established with e-Seva and the programme still retains its identity.

Accountability

		Frequency	*Per cent*
Valid	Yes	91	70.0
	No	39	30.0
	Total	130	100.0

There seems to be quite a contrast in terms of responsiveness of the programme. As many as 90 per cent of the respondents believe there is a semblance of responsiveness in VOICE which they suggest has to be established at all levels in the corporation and the services it delivers.

Responsiveness

		Frequency	*Per cent*
Valid	Yes	117	90.0
	No	13	10.0
	Total	130	100.0

VOICE covers only a few of the services and delivers them nominally. However, there has been a phenomenal change when the programme was integrated with e-Seva in 2005. Prior to that availability of services was bleak. When we visited VOICE centres in 2006 the perception of the people on the availability of services was moderate. Nearly 77 per cent of the respondents said services were available, but those holding the opposite view form a significant number which is 23 per cent of the sample size.

Availability of Services

		Frequency	*Per cent*
Valid	Yes	100	76.9
	No	30	23.1
	Total	130	100.0

As is the case with the availability of online services in VOICE, their utility is also on a moderate scale. Only 68 per cent of the respondents had utilized these services while the remaining had not or yet to utilize them.

Utility of Services

		Frequency	*Per cent*
Valid	Yes	88	67.7
	No	42	32.3
	Total	130	100.0

Electronic services are more popular with urban masses and they have accepted them whole heartedly all over the country. Vijayawada denizens are quite conscious on the usefulness of the VOICE project. Nearly 88 per cent believe the services are very useful and should be expanded to cover all the utilities while only 12 per cent suggest there is nothing that can be made use of from them.

Use of the Programme

		Frequency	*Per cent*
Valid	Yes	114	87.7
	No	16	12.3
	Total	130	100.0

Time factor counts primarily for all the dwellers of the city, especially in availing civic services. Previously, they used to spend a day or a half for getting services. This was the opinion of more than 92 per cent of the respondents. There are even some who claim to have spent two days and they form 8 per cent of the sample size.

Time Taken for Services Before e-Governance Programme

		Frequency	*Per cent*
Valid	1/2 Day	73	56.2
	1 Day	47	36.2
	2 Days	10	7.7
	Total	130	100.0

With the introduction of VOICE, time spent on availing civic services has gone down to less than 10 minutes and the maximum time required for complex services is less than 30 minutes. Exactly 90 per cent of the respondents said they spent only 10 minutes at the VOICE counters.

Time Taken for Services Under e-Governance Programme

		Frequency	*Per cent*
Valid	Within 10 Min	117	90.0
	Within 30 Min	13	10.0
	Total	130	100.0

The Cost Factor

Lesser time and lower costs define the success rate of an electronic governance programme that delivers civic services online. With VOICE there has been a drastic fall in the costs required to procure civic services. Before that people used to spend Rs. 50 to 100. Nearly 77 per cent of the respondents subscribed to this view.

Money Spent Before e-Governance Programme

		Frequency	*Per cent*
Valid	Rs. 25	30	23.1
	Rs. 50	77	59.2
	Rs. 100	23	17.7
	Total	130	100.0

Money Spent After e-Governance Programme

		Frequency	*Per cent*
Valid	Rs. 15	111	85.4
	Rs. 25	19	14.6
	Total	130	100.0

Civic services are now cheap with VOICE gaining ground by the day. The minimum that people spend on utility services is Rs. 15 while the maximum limit is Rs. 25. Those who had spent less than Rs. 15 for 85 per cent of the sample group and the remaining 15 per cent put the cost at Rs. 25.

Satisfaction

		Frequency	*Per cent*
Valid	High	86	66.2
	Moderate	44	33.8
	Total	130	100.0

Since all the services have not been included under the VOICE programme the levels of satisfaction among users are bound to be moderate. Only 66 per cent of the respondents said they were satisfied with the electronic services while 34 per cent of them claimed they were satisfied, but on a moderate level.

REFERENCES

1. The then Chief Minister N. Chandra Babu Naidu inaugurating VOICE services.
2. Statue of Krishnaveni on the Prakasam Barrage.

SAUKARYAM, VISAKHAPATNAM

Saukaryam (meaning facility) was launched in Visakhapatnam Municipal Corporation. Under this project, a Metro Area Network (MAN) encompassing 120 Sq. Km has been created through broadband/leased circuits. A large number of banks for accepting municipal payments and various Municipal Offices have been connected to each other. A LAN encompassing all wings of the Municipal Corporation forms the backbone to the MAN. Being web enabled, it provides access to citizens through a utility driven website for multiple services. For citizens without access to the Internet or computers, fully computerized City Civic Centres on the network have been created, that deliver identical services.

The project covers the whole gamut of civic services ranging from the facility of online payment of dues to allowing lodging of grievances online or filing building plan applications and getting their status without running from pillar to post. There also is a facility for the hospitals to send Birth and Death information online helping citizens get their certificates instantal. As the Municipal Corporation enters into the daily lives of the citizens in many ways, all such multifarious areas have been covered. Now at the click of a button, citizens can see the garbage movement performance, water supply plan of their street and also the updated infrastructure works being executed in their city. It also provides the contractors online tender notices, entrepreneurs and philanthropists business opportunities and social possibilities the town entails. It has an online forum for the citizens to vent their grievances, air their opinions and stimulate necessary social change. In short, every service extended by City Corporation is being extended online under this project.

The prime motto of the project has been to improve the interface of the citizens with other government departments, as well as, to give them an integrated payment gateway. Simplifying the whole process, the project conceptualized an innovative approach. It opened a multi utility centre on the metro area network. Calling, 'Bill Junction', has been self explanatory to the citizens. The process creates an online window to the citizens to pay all their utility bills under one roof. This offers a multi pronged advantage of being the ultimate payment solution.

The conceptualization of project began in September 2000 and was dedicated to the citizens for implementation by January 2001. Like most of the IT projects, the Project has been evolving since then, adding additional services and features, day by day. Offering the citizens all the Civic Services, through a user friendly, transparent and accountable method, is the USP of this Project. The project was subsequently merged with e-Seva and the centres are now called Saukaryam e-Seva centres.

Services Provided

- On line payment of Municipal Dues through Networked Banks.
- Payment of Property Tax.
- Payment of Water Tax.
- D & O Trade Licenses.
- Advertisement Tax.
- Lease Rents.

Citizen Charter *(City Civic Centre)*

- Issue of Birth and Death certificates.
- Registration of Building Applications.
- Registration of Tap Applications.
- Registration of UGD service connections.
- Miscellaneous payments and registrations.
- Registration of Complaints and Grievances such as Garbage removal, Cleaning of Drains and Dustbins, Pipeline leakage's, Repairs to Street Lighting, Repairs to Roads and Fixing of House Tax).

Bill Junction *(e-Seva Centre)*

It is an integrated payment gateway for all Government bills. Right now the centre is collecting payment of Electricity bills in addition to other Municipal dues.

The conceptualization of project began in September 2000 and was dedicated to the citizens for implementation by January 2001. Like most of the IT projects, the Project has been evolving since then adding additional services and features day by day. Offering the citizens all the Civic Services through a user friendly, transparent and accountable method is the USP of this Project.

Project Outcome

The results have been stupendous. Ever since the project has been commissioned, the work has become the talk of the town. The citizens are surprised and enthused by the case with which their needs are getting attended to, without having to run from pillar to post as before. The complete networking and computerization today enables the corporation to get real time demand/collection statements that help in monitoring of cases with huge pending amounts, thereby improving the tax collection efficiency.

Due to the web-enabling of this network, citizens are able to get access to the information pertaining to their property assessment, and they are also able to see the calculations that have gone into it. The on-line payment module through net banking also allows the citizens to make the payment directly from the comfort of their homes. This has improved the collection efficiency and an additional Rs. 20 crore was collected during 2002-03, as a result of which the Corporation is able to extend more and better civic services.

Over 2000 people make use of this facility every day, either through the banking network, through the City Civic Centre or through the Internet. There are over 45,000 registered users for the Corporation website, while the civic centre receives over 200 citizens every day, reflecting its popularity across the range of communities.

The project has been declared as the pilot project for municipal governance and is being replicated in various municipalities and corporations across the state and other parts of the country. Visakhapatnam Municipal Corporation has also applied for its patenting and has entered into a MOU with a private company for the international marketing of this product. The project has already branched out into other areas of utility payments like telephone bills and registration and has tied up with electricity department for collection of bills on line.

Awards and Distinctions

1. NIUA Award For the Year 2001.
2. Short listed for Stockholm challenge Award 2001.
3. UNDP Award for the year 2002.
4. CSI Award for the year 2002.
5. CRISIL Award for the year 2003.

Scaling Up

The opening of e-Seva kendras has resulted in a significant increase in the Visakhapatnam Municipal Corporation's revenue which has gone up from Rs. 20 crores to Rs. 70 crores during last three years. More such centres would come up in rural areas. Three-lakh transactions are taking place every year after the introduction of these units, which bagged awards from the United Nations Development Programme and other organizations.

About Visakhapatnam

Visakhapatnam, better known as Vizag, is a port city on the East coast of India. The city is a harmonious blend of the magical past and the bustling present and is home to a peaceful community living in the midst of golden beaches, lush green fields, verdant valleys and splendid monuments from the past. This beautiful city is said to have derived its name from the deity 'Visakha' (the God of Valour). The history of the town can be traced back to Ashoka the Great (273-232 B.C.) when this was a small fishing village of the Kalinga Empire. Later on this port town successively passed from the Andhra Kings of Vengi to the Pallavas, Cholas and the Gangas. In the 15th century Visakhapatnam became a part of Vijayanagar Empire. The British took charge of this beautiful land and transformed this into a busy and flourishing port town. Today it has emerged as an important port on the east coast of India. The port of Vizag handles the maximum cargo in the country and promises to become one of Asia's major ports by 21st century. Today, the city is on the threshold of a major technological revolution through which the civic services rendered by its Municipal Corporation are being thrown open to the citizens using information and communications technology which could be the first of its kind in the country.

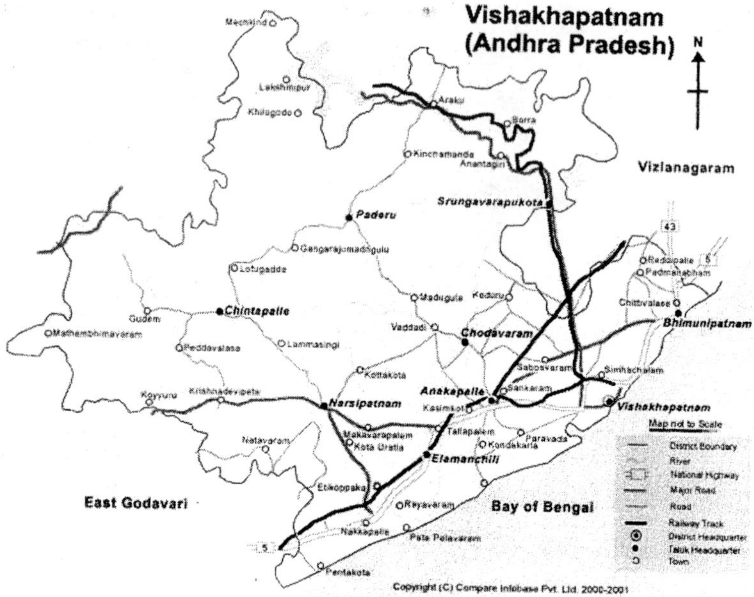

Location and Topography

Located on the East coast of India, in 17°42' North latitude and 82°02′ East range of hills. Based on topographical conditions, the city and its environs can be divided into four categories viz. Hilly region, Upland tracks, Rolling plains and Plains. The major hill ranges of the city are Kailasa and Yarada hill ranges. The Kailasa hill range stretches from Simhachalam to MVP Colony on the north flank of the city. The city which appears like a small basin is surrounded by the Yarada hill popularly known as Dolphin's nose (358m) on the side of the Kailasgiri hills on the north, with the Bay of Bengal forming the eastern wall. The coastal line runs from north east to south west over a distance of six kilometres. On the west there is an extensive tidal basin called Upputeru now under reclamation. Beyond Yarada there is a valley followed by another range of hills.

Climate

The climate of Visakhapatnam has no appreciable seasonal changes. Being close to the sea, the level of humidity is high. The fluctuations in temperature are fairly uniform in character, except during the dry months when the rise in temperature is higher than it is during the monsoon period. From February onwards, the temperature rises progressively till May, which is the hottest month. During the years 1931-60 the maximum average (mean) temperature was 34°C. This has been showing an upward trend with the minimum and maximum for the period of 1975-81 being reported as 38°C and 29°C, respectively. In recent years, it has not been uncommon for the day temperature to exceed 43°C during May. December, January represent the coldest period of the year.

The average annual rainfall for the city and its surroundings is of the order of 95 centimeters with the bulk of the rain coming from north-east monsoon. During the period between September and November, storms and depressions originating in the Bay of Bengal cross the east coast in the neighbourhood causing heavy rains and gales. As per Thornthwaite's classification, Visakhapatnam and its environs come under the semi—arid (D) category. All the elements of climate viz. temperature, pressure, wind, rainfall, relative humidity and other weather phenomena hardly exist and exhibit a well marked variation while January is the coolest month of the year with average temperatures of 30.0°C and 22.5°C respectively.

Economy

The city was originally a small fishing village. Mainly due to its natural harbour, it has developed into a major port city. It has experienced rapid industrialization with the onset of major industries viz., Oil Refinery, a private sector fertilizer factory, Hindustan Zinc Smelter and Visakhapatnam Steel Plant. The constructions of the outer harbour and Steel Plant have considerably changed the character of the city. On account of rapid industrialization and urbanization there has been tremendous amount of migration into the city. Today the services and information technology contribute significantly to the economy.

Information and Technology

Computer Department was started in 1988 with Xenix based server duly connecting three number of terminals. Since then, pertaining to the requirements, it has been expanding its horizons owing to the integrated development of multi-platform Environment. Computer Department now is being sufficed by Infrastructure capable enough

to handle needful requirements of the Municipal Corporation. It is located in the main block of the Corporation with an extent of 2000 sft. It is equipped with around 70 Desktop Systems which in turn connected to the servers of multiple platforms like NT, Unix, and Linux. Owing to its expansions, presently, it is maintaining around 3 kms Local Area Network and Established a Connectivity up to 40 kms (approx) Metro area Network. Services of Municipal Corporation mainly cater to the needs of the public like Online Birth and Death Registration, Online Tax Collection and many more. In addition to the above, huge data processing is being done.

Impact of e-Governance on Indian Society: A Case Study of Saukaryam, Visakhapatnam

We carried out the present study to gauge the impact of e-governance on society as part of which the e-services project of Saukaryam in Visakhapatnam, AP, was selected as a case study. Study was taken up at select centres in the city. The total sample size is 121 of which men are 80 and women 41, that is 66 and 24 per cent respectively.

Sex

		Frequency	*Per cent*
Valid	Male	80	66.1
	Female	41	33.9
	Total	121	100.0

The respondents fall in the age groups of below 20, 21-30, 31-40, 41-50 and 51 and above. Those above 31 years of age to the maximum limit are a majority among the users of the electronic services and they represent 66 per cent of the respondents. Nearly 44 per cent of the respondents are in the age groups of 21-30 and below 20.

Age

		Frequency	*Per cent*
Valid	Below 20	17	14.0
	21-30	36	29.8
	31-40	28	23.1
	41-50	25	20.7
	51 and Above	15	12.4
	Total	121	100.0

A majority of the people surveyed has studied at least matriculation (secondary school certificate) or intermediate which is 58 per cent, while nearly 35 per cent of the respondents are either graduates or hold post-graduation degrees. Only 6.6 per cent of the respondents are illiterates. This signifies the high level of literacy in this coastal city.

Over 31 per cent of the respondents said they are either peasants or do farm work. Nearly 35 per cent of the respondents are into government service while those pursuing an independent occupation account for 18 per cent of the sample size. Also, those claiming to be doing other works include 18 per cent of the sample size and only 5 per cent said they do non-agriculture work.

City utility services are a common knowledge in India and Vizag has high levels of awareness of them. Almost 95 per cent of the respondents have either heard or have used the Saukaryam services while a little over 5 per cent have not heard of them.

Education

		Frequency	*Per cent*
Valid	Upto SSC	34	28.1
	Intermediate	35	28.9
	Degree	36	29.8
	Post Graduation	6	5.0
	Other	2	1.7
	Illiterate	8	6.6
	Total	121	100.0

Occupation

		Frequency	*Per cent*
Valid	Agriculture	28	23.1
	Agriculture Labour	1	.8
	Non-Agriculture Labour	6	5.0
	Government Service	42	34.7
	Independent Occupation	22	18.2
	Other	22	18.2
	Total	121	100.0

Awareness

		Frequency	*Per cent*
Valid	Heard	10	8.3
	Not Heard	6	5.0
	Heared and User	105	86.8
	Total	121	100.0

On the transparency scale, Saukaryam is moderate with only 70 per cent of the respondents replying positively. A significant number of the respondents—30 per cent of the sample size—do not see or perceive transparency in the electronic delivery of services.

Transparency

		Frequency	*Per cent*
Valid	Yes	85	70.2
	No	36	29.8
	Total	121	100.0

On the accountability front too, Saukaryam has not shown enough mettle. Of those surveyed, 63 per cent said it lacks accountability while the remaining 37 per cent respondents have a positive view on this count. This can be explained in terms of backup linkages and traditional ways of functioning of the corporation staff. Linkages have now been established with e-Seva and the programme still retains its identity.

Accountability

		Frequency	*Per cent*
Valid	Yes	45	37.2
	No	76	62.8
	Total	121	100.0

There seems to be quite a contrast in terms of responsiveness of the programme. As many as 91 per cent of the respondents believe in the responsiveness of Saukaryam which they suggest has to be established at all levels in the corporation and the services it delivers.

Responsiveness

		Frequency	*Per cent*
Valid	Yes	110	90.9
	No	11	9.1
	Total	121	100.0

Saukaryam covers only a few of the services and delivers them online. However, there has been a phenomenal change when the programme was integrated with e-Seva in 2005. Prior to that availability of services was selective. Over 65 per cent of the respondents said services were available, but those holding the opposite view form a significant number which is 35 per cent of the sample size.

As is the case with the availability of online services in Saukaryam, their utility is also on a moderate scale. Only 60 per cent

Availability of Services

		Frequency	*Per cent*
Valid	Yes	79	65.3
	No	42	34.7
	Total	121	100.0

of the respondents had utilized these services while the remaining had not or yet to utilize them.

Utility of Services

		Frequency	*Per cent*
Valid	Yes	72	59.5
	No	49	40.5
	Total	121	100.0

Electronic services are more popular with urban masses and they have accepted them whole heartedly all over the country and Vizag with high levels of literacy is no exception. However, lack of adequate services is putting off many a prospective user. Nearly 65 per cent believe the services are very useful and should be expanded to cover all the utilities while nearly 35 per cent suggest there is nothing that can be made use of from them.

Use of the Programme

		Frequency	*Per cent*
Valid	Yes	79	65.3
	No	42	34.7
	Total	121	100.0

Time factor counts primarily for all the dwellers of the city, especially in availing civic services. Previously, they used to spend a day or a half for getting services. This was the opinion of more than 75 per cent of the respondents. There are even some who claim to have spent two days and they form 25 per cent of the sample size.

With the introduction of Saukaryam in 2000 by Sanjay Jaju, time spent on availing civic services has gone down to less than 10 minutes and the maximum time required for complex services is less than 30 minutes. Nearly 82 per cent of the respondents said they spent only 10 minutes at the VOICE counters while the remaining spent nearly 30 minutes at the counters.

The Cost Factor

Lesser time and lower costs define the success rate of an electronic governance programme that delivers civic services online. With Saukaryam there has been a drastic fall in the costs required to procure civic services. Before that people used to spend Rs. 50 to 100. Over 98 per cent of the respondents subscribed to this view.

Time Taken for Services Before e-Governance Programme

		Frequency	*Per cent*
Valid	1/2 Day	61	50.4
	1 Day	30	24.8
	2 Days	30	24.8
	Total	121	100.0

Time Taken for Services Under e-Governance Programme

		Frequency	*Per cent*
Valid	Within 10 Min	99	81.8
	Within 30 Min	22	18.2
	Total	121	100.0

Money Spent Before e-Governance Programme

		Frequency	*Per cent*
Valid	Rs. 25	2	1.7
	Rs. 50	68	56.2
	Rs. 100	51	42.1
	Total	121	100.0

Money Spent After e-Governance Programme

		Frequency	*Per cent*
Vaild	Rs. 15	102	84.3
	Rs. 25	19	15.7
	Total	121	100.0

Civic services are now cheap with Saukaryam e-Seva centres gaining ground by the day. The minimum that people spend on utility services is Rs. 15 while the maximum limit is Rs. 25. Those who had spent less than Rs. 15 for 85 per cent of the sample group and the remaining 15 per cent put the cost at Rs. 25.

Satisfaction

		Frequency	*Per cent*
Vaild	High	88	72.7
	Moderate	33	27.3
	Total	121	100.0

City portals have the ability to offer wide range services to people with different needs. This has been the experience in the West where city portals give comprehensive information on anything and provide services to the potential with external links. Saukaryam can still scale up its operations in this regard. As regards to the satisfaction level, the project scores moderately with over 72 per cent of the respondents claiming to be satisfied with the services. However, the remaining users are satisfied only moderately.

REFERENCE

1. Vabatarani Temple in Vizag.

BHOOMI, KARNATAKA
(Computerized Registration of Lands Project)

Background

The Centrally Sponsored Scheme on Computerization of Land Records (CLR) commenced in the financial year 1988-89 with 100 per cent funding from the Union Rural Development Ministry as a pilot project in eight districts viz; Rangareddy (Andhra Pradesh), Sonitpur (Assam), Singhbhum (Bihar), Gandhinagar (Gujarat), Morena (Madhya Pradesh), Wardha (Maharashtra), Mayurbhanj (Orissa) and Dungarpur (Rajasthan) to remove the loopholes inherent in the manual systems of maintenance and update of Land Records besides meeting the requirements of various groups of users. It was decided to computerize core data contained in land records, to assist planned development and make records accessible to people/ planners and administrators.[1]

In Karnataka, data entry work with regard to land records started in 1995, but up to 1999 there were only a few concrete benefits. In 1999-2000, modifications were made in the software and all the databases were updated when the Bhoomi project was launched in 2000. About 6.7 million farmers own 20 million land holdings in Karnataka. The crucial document which records various parameters and information pertaining to land-holding is the Record of Right Tenancy and Cultivation (RTC). Earlier, these records were maintained by 9,000 Village Accountants (VAs) who served farmers in about 27,000 villages of 177 taluks.

The Bhoomi project, implemented by the Department of Public Administration and Revenue (DPAR), makes available a computerized Record of Rights, Tenancy and Crops (RTC) to all landowners at a kiosk in the taluka office, on payment of Rs.15 per RTC. The department is promoting private franchise models in which the franchisees have to bear the cost of the infrastructure and the

Internet connection. They can charge more than what is normally charged at the taluka office.[2]

Description of the Project

This computerization of land registration project was spearheaded by the then State Additional Revenue Secretary Rajeev Chawla[3] and had already computerized 20 million records of land ownership of 6.7 million farmers.[4] Significantly, the project curbs corruption, as farmers had to bribe the village accountants to get their land records in the manual system. Now, all that a farmer has to do is pay Rs. 15 and get a print-out of his/her Record of Rights, Tenancy and Crops (RTC). Touch-screen kiosks at district offices help farmers view their records directly.

In this system, when a change of ownership takes place through sale or inheritance, farmers can apply for a 'mutation[5]' of the land record at the Bhoomi centre. Each application is given a number, which can be later used to check the status of the application. The computer generates notices which are handed over to the village accountants. The Revenue Inspector approves changes to the land record 30 days after the notices are served, provided that there are no objections. It takes a few days for the approval to reach the Bhoomi kiosk, where it is immediately scanned. The updated RTC is printed at the Bhoomi kiosk and handed over to the village accountant for his or her record. The new owner receives a copy on demand. Another significant aspect is that the Bhoomi kiosks create scanned copies of the original mutation orders and notices to avoid litigation troubles.[6]

Goals and Objectives

- To facilitate easy maintenance and regular update of land records.
- To make land records tamper proof.
- To provide farmers easy access to their land records.
- To create databases of land revenue, cropping pattern, land use, etc.
- To utilize the data for planning and formulating development programmes.
- To enable usage of this database by courts, banks, private organizations and Internet Service Providers (ISPs).

Planning

A pilot project for the computerization of land records in Karnataka started in 1989, initiated by the Government of India. The project for computerization of land records for all districts in the state was sanctioned in 1996. The aim was to create computer records from the manual data. However, since no provision was made to install computers at sub-district level, online updating of these records was not possible.

The Bhoomi project was launched in 2000 with the aim of computerizing the system for maintaining land records, thereby permitting online updating. In the first phase, the project was implemented as a pilot in five talukas in the Bangalore Rural district; and later rolled out to all the 177 talukas. The required software was designed and developed in-house by the National Information Centre.

The first on-line kiosk of India was started in Sakleshpur. The then Chief Minister of Karnataka S.M. Krishna inaugurated the first land records kiosk in his home town Maddur on 6th February 2001. The first computerised taluk, Bangalore (South), was inaugurated by M. Venkaiah Naidu, the then Union Minister for Rural Development on 13th July 2001.

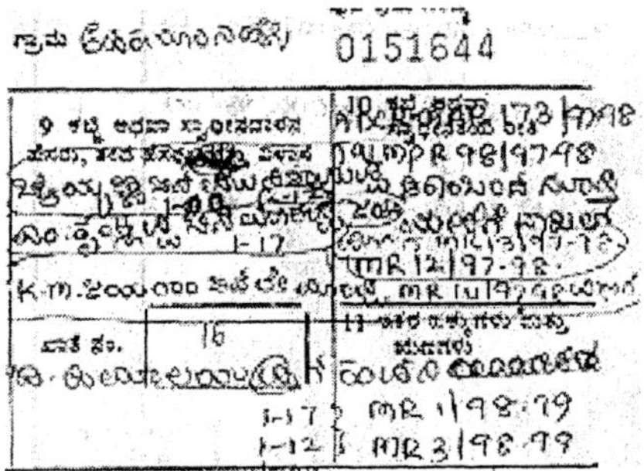

Services Provided

At the kiosks, there are two-computer screens, one of which performs the operation and the other which shows the transaction being performed to the clients. Just by providing the name of the owner or the plot number, one can collect copies of the land parcel. Farmers can file online requests at these kiosks for a change of ownership, sale or inheritance. These are important transactions for initiating the mandatory process known as mutation for effecting necessary changes in the RTC. Each request is assigned a number, and notices are then generated from Bhoomi, which are served by the Village Accountant, on interested parties. After waiting for a statutory period of 30 days from the date of serving the notice, the Revenue Inspector (RI) passes the mutation order in a register maintained for this purpose. The mutation order passed by the RI is processed in Bhoomi and a new RTC is generated, duly incorporating the details of the new owner. As a part of this process, the mutation order is scanned to take care of non-repudiation. While the mutation records are pending for orders of the RI, a farmer can trace the status of the application, using the number provided to him/her.

Mutation

Mutation is the process of updating textual information, of the changes in data, due to sale, inheritance, partition, donation, gift, mortgage, grant from the government, conversion of land, acquisition, court orders, will, etc. Nearly 90 per cent of the mutations are due to registration of the documents and remaining 10 per cent are reports received at the taluk Bhoomi centre directly from the public.

Phodi (Division of Land)

Acceptance of Mutation in Bhoomi is followed by Phodi in Survey section. Phodi is a series of activities, like giving notices to the interested parties, surveying the field, drawing a *mahajar* statement, mapping, recording measurement, information on adjacent lands, etc. The entire process of phodi would normally take 30 days.

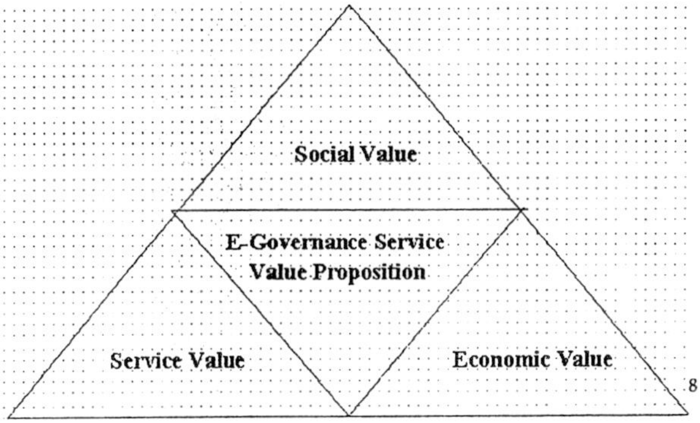

Existing Practice

Acceptance of mutation in case of any RTC, a multiple ownership RTC is created with the same survey number, and sent to survey section for phodi. After Phodi it comes back to Revenue Department. The corresponding multiple ownerships RTC are then split with separate survey numbers.

Types of ownerships maintained in RTCs in Bhoomi are as follows:

1. Single ownership
2. Multiple ownership
3. Pyki Ownership[9]

Status of Incorporation in RTCs

Type 1 RTCs are in tune with Akarbandhas. They are written after incorporation of the phodi data.

Type 2 and 3 RTCs are to be converted to Type 1 by incorporating the phodi data.

Phodi (division of land) will be taken up as and when a mutation case comes up in that RTC. Backlog can be completed in an incremental way.

Presently in Bhoomi, completed Phodi data is incorporated electronically through another mutation process, called 'Mutation Phodi'. New RTCs are generated with new survey numbers in Bhoomi. Thus, for each mutation transaction, there are two processes in Bhoomi; one is the regular mutation and the other is the Phodi mutation. There are plans to make every RTC in Bhoomi as single ownership, single survey number, single area and corresponding survey sketch.

Process Involved in Land Registration

The kiosk operator receives the mutation applications, only along with the pre-mutation survey sketch; enters the survey number and issues acknowledgement either in printed form to the persons in case of direct application, or electronically to the registration department in case of J slip.

The data would be pushed to Bhoomi backend for processing along with the physical records for verification and preparation of a checklist. The Data Entry Operator (DEO) enters the transaction as per the checklist. Shiresthedar approves the transaction and refers back to the DEO.

The DEO generates notice and forwards the record to the RI and the RI serves the notice through VAs and waits for 30 days. Based on the field report, RI has three options: (1) Give Provisional consent to Mutation (2) Rejection and (3) Refer to as a disputed case if objections are raised.

In case of RI provisionally consenting, it will be indicated to survey supervisor. RI now can not go back on his decision of consenting. The survey supervisor verifies the enclosed sketch; assigns new final subdivision numbers on the sketch itself and make the entries in the survey report sheet. He would allot new numbers to all new owners in the approved transaction and update the survey records like Akarbandh, tippan and atlas.

The survey supervisor indicates to Bhoomi that he has completed the phodi process and transmits the physical papers along with his report to Sheristhedar who sends it to the RI. The RI passes his final acceptance order in the mutation register and sends it to Sheristhedar. He verifies and sends it to DEO who later enters mutation details, subdivision numbers and scans the sketch.

New RTCs would be generated for each new subdivision numbers created in Bhoomi. Sheristhedar verifies and closes the transaction. The survey sketches would be made available to the public as prints of the scanned images. The sketch is also available for the surveyors whenever required for reference.

Target Group and Beneficiaries

All citizens of the state (residing in rural and urban areas) are the target groups and intended beneficiaries.

Institutional Arrangements

An additional secretary in the Revenue Department (Land Reforms) acts as the project manager, assisted by the Senior Technical Director, NIC. At the district level, the leadership role is given to the Deputy Commissioner. The administrative responsibilities are shared by the Assistant Commissioners, technical responsibilities by District Information Officers of the NIC, and implementation and monitoring tasks by the consultants appointed by the Bhoomi project. Revenue Sheristhedars (Deputy Tahsildars) have been made project leaders at taluka level, working under the direction of the Tahsildar.

At the grassroots level, there are revenue inspectors, village accountants and data entry operators. Except for the 28 consultants (one for each district and one for the state headquarters) appointed on an annual contract by the Bhoomi project, all tasks have been clearly defined with roles and responsibilities assigned to existing government staff. At the taluka level, one of the three Deputy Tahsildars is made responsible for Bhoomi. Five village accountants are trained and assigned the job of manning the Bhoomi counter and updating the records.

Technologies Used

All the 177 talukas are provided with one computer with 64 MB RAM (with two monitors), one printer, one scanner, one UPS, one battery for back-up and a generator. The computer at the counter is connected to a LAN and the server room has biometric equipment for fingerprints, two client machines for data updation and one printer. The front-end is written in Visual Basic v6 and the database in SQL server v7.0. The Operating System is Windows NT.

The software for the project was developed jointly by the Karnataka Revenue Department, the National Informatics Centre (NIC) and Compaq. It is proprietary software and incorporates Compaq's bio-logon metrics system, which authenticates users of the software using their fingerprint and makes it tamper-proof. Private data entry agencies tackled the work in an off-line mode at the taluks and the software was also made to accommodate variations in manual records across districts. A training module was also designed jointly by the department and NIC to train village accountants in handling data and transactions.

Primary Access Points

Bhoomi centres are operational in all 177 taluka headquarters of the state, providing a primary access point for all citizens. Each Bhoomi counter has two computer screens, one for the counter operator and another for the user. Most centres now have touch screen kiosks.

Benefits to Farmers

- Farmers can quickly get their land records from kiosks and are protected from harassment and extortion.
- They can lodge application for mutation (change in land title) to their land records at the mutation kiosks, get acknowledgement for the same and can monitor the progress using Touch Screen Kiosk (TSK). As against earlier time of 70-200 days, mutation now requires less than 30 days.

- Farmers can also get the official status report of their request for mutation.
- Access to farm credit has now become less cumbersome. Online connectivity to banks would ensure farm credit to farmers in less than 5 days as against 30 days in manual system.
- It would be easier for the farmers to pursue land related litigation in the court.

Evolution of Bhoomi

Phase 1 - End of March 2001

- Captured about 50 lakhs RTCs data of 50 sub-districts on digital media.
- Commencement of the project in 50 sub-districts.
- Trained revenue staff up to Village Accountant level on data entry operation - total number 8000.

Phase 2 - End of March 2002

- Captured the data on 15 million RTCs of remaining 127 sub-districts in digital form.
- The scheme began in remaining 126+1 sub-districts.
- One of the Kiosks is being used for additional cross-selling initiatives.
- Scheme decentralised to 5 Sub taluks (sub-districts) on experimental basis.

Phase 3 - April 2002 to March 2003

- Interlinking of sub-district level systems to district systems to put the data online.
- Use these data centres for disaster recovery.
- Manage the sub-district servers centrally from the district centres.
- Provide connectivity to Banks and Courts.
- Decentralise the scheme to about 100 sub-districts with private participation.
- Provide broad band to Bhoomi kiosks for various cross selling initiatives like provision of weather details and list of beneficiaries of government schemes etc.

Phase 4 - From March 2003 onwards

- Interlinking of district level data banks to the state level data warehouse.
- To provide EIS, GIS and other MIS data using multidimensional RTC hyper cubes.
- To carry online mutation facility up to village level.[10]

Awards Won

Silver to Bhoomi

C · A · P · A · M

Commonwealth Innovation Awards 2002

Won the Silver Award at the CAPAM Awards 2002
Finalist at the Stockholm Awards 2002
Finalist at the Tech Museum Awards 2002

Constraints and Challenges

Right from the inception, the Bhoomi project was faced with major hurdles. There were over 20 million land records of a dynamic nature, which required up date at least once a year. Like other major deficiencies in the land revenue system, the manual copies of land records too had a number of inaccuracies and inconsistencies. The question of data integrity was a major issue and the data structures were not uniform. Data were kept in multiple languages across the state. Data entry operations by multiple agencies had to be closely monitored since the objective was to build a robust process to facilitate data validation by the owners. There was stiff resistance to change from an exploitative system of land records which had operated for more than 300 years. It was necessary to change the mindset of over 10,000 revenue officials, VAs and RIs, and 1,500 officials from other departments.

The revenue officials involved in the project had no exposure to new information and communication technologies. There was an issue of lack of general acceptance of the deliverables of the project, particularly trust in the legal validity of the computer printouts amongst 6.7 million farmers. The project in the initial phase was supposed to be operated from the taluka level instead of village level, which required a change in the processes and procedures. Online updating of the system had to be built in to obliterate manual updating of records. The issue of manual records had to be discarded, which was a major procedural shift. The mutation system had to be robust and quick once it was decided that it would go online. The geographic expanse of the project (27,000 villages) was another major hurdle. There were power cuts ranging from six to10 hours in a day which also hindered the project. This compelled project managers to buy UPSs, batteries and generator sets in each taluka. Online mutation was incorporated at a later stage in the implementation of the computerized registration of lands project.

Project Outcomes

The generation time of the RTC has been reduced from 30 days to five to 15 minutes. Similarly, the mutation process cycle time has decreased from 90-180 days to 30-45 days. Crop record updating has increased to 90-100 per cent from 50-70 per cent. Nearly 65 per cent of the farmers are now able to use Bhoomi kiosks without any help and 75 per cent of the users transacted their business under the computerized system without seeking access to a revenue official. Besides this the computer-generated records had fewer errors than those provided manually. Significantly, corruption at the time of distribution of the copies of land records has come down drastically. Nearly a million farmers utilize the services of Bhoomi every year.

Scaling Up

The huge success of Bhoomi inspired other states to emulate the model and Haryana, Himachal Pradesh and a few other states put up a commendable performance. Karnataka now chairs a national committee for countrywide implementation of land records computerisation project. Bhoomi has been chosen as a mission mode project under NeGP by Government of India for nationwide roll-out. This will expedite the scaling-up of the project to other states while ensuring uniform implementation the country over.

The project has joined hands with the KAVERI system of Registration Department. The sale transactions are generated and sent on daily basis from Registration Department to Bhoomi system electronically through the State Data Centre (SDC) and Bhoomi collects and processes them as per the business processes. Bhoomi is also into survey activities. Every mutation of Bhoomi generates requests for survey. Bhoomi front-end also delivers the image of these maps to the public on demand.

The Department of Land Reforms under the Ministry of Rural Development is now planning to launch a Comprehensive Modernisation of Land Records (CMLR) system for farmers of India. The objective is to make all records of land in the country online by the end of 11th Five Year plan. As per the plan, aerial survey and digital mapping would computerize all land records and other immovable properties. These computerised records will be equipped with an automated system, which will keep records of all transactions that can be accessed online. The computerised records will be connected with a national Management Information System (MIS). This will generate a reliable database on land ownership, tenancy rights, crop details, land revenue, sources of irrigation and previous transactions. The proposed scheme will replace two existing central schemes of Computerisation of Land Records (CLR) and Strengthening of Revenue Administration (SRA).[11]

Current Status of the Project

- 200 lakh RTCs of 70 lakh farmers
- Self sustaining project: No financial support of State Government
- Old manual system fully disbanded
- Highly successful and acclaimed project
- National e-Governance award for the year 2003
- Commonwealth Innovation award for the year 2002
- UN public service Award -2006
- 1 million farmers get serviced every year
- National model for replication for all States
- Delivery of records in 5 minute
- First in First Out (FIFO) in mutation: No favouritism: Social equality
- Records available centrally at State Data Centre: all 200 lakh records centralized
- Taluks networked through a dedicated VSAT network
- 800 rural Tele Centres are being set up

Karnataka would be the only state in the country to have such an integrated system of land registration.

Survey on the Impact of e-Governance on Society: A Case Study of Bhoomi, Karnataka

We carried out the present study in 10 districts of Karnataka namely Bangalore Rural, Mysore, Madikeri, Mandya, Shimoga, Dakshin Kannada, Gulbarga, Raichur, Bidar and Bijapur. Responses were elicited from a total of 236 farmers who have used or users of Bhoomi. Of the total respondents 208 are male and only 28 are female – 88 and 12 per cent respectively. The respondents fall in the age groups of 21-30, 31-40, 41-50 and 51 and above.

Sex

	No. of Respondents	*Per cent*
Male	208	88.1
Female	28	11.9
Total	236	100.0

Age

	No. of Respondents	*Per cent*
21-30	18	7.6
31-40	76	32.2
41-50	103	43.6
51 and Above	39	16.5
Total	236	100.0

As far as the age composition is concerned, those falling in the age group of 41-50 form the majority with a representation of 43.6 per cent followed by those in the age group of 31-40 who constitute 32.2 per cent of the sample size. Nearly 17 per cent of the respondents are 51 and above while those under 30 are only 7.6 per cent.

That the respondents are mostly farmers or land owners from the rural areas is clear in this analytical description of the data. Over 40 per cent of the respondents have studied up to secondary school while 20 per cent hold a bachelor's degree. Nearly 15 per cent have studied up to Intermediate and only 6 per cent of the respondents have completed post-graduation. Over 19 per cent of the respondents are illiterates.[12] The figures correspond with the literacy statistics of Karnataka State.

Education

	No. of Respondents	*Per cent*
Upto SSC	95	40.3
Intermediate	35	14.8
Degree	47	19.9
Post Graduation	14	5.9
Illiterate	45	19.1
Total	236	100.0

Occupation

	No. of Respondents	*Per cent*
Agriculture	153	64.8
Government Service	28	11.9
Independent Occupation	37	15.7
Other	18	7.6
Total	236	100.0

Though Bhoomi project appears primarily designed for catering to the needs of farmers, people carrying on various occupations are also using its services. Nearly 65 per cent of the e-land registration services are farmers or dependent on agriculture while at least 16 per cent are carrying on an independent occupation.[13] Of the total users, 12 per cent are into government service while less than 8 per cent quoted other occupation. It is very significant to note that all 35 per cent of the users are non-farmers and have land holdings of varying stretches. It is clear from this data that Bhoomi has across the board clientage for its services, especially electronic registration of lands and issuance of computerized RTCs.

Awareness

	No. of Respondents	*Per cent*
Heard	27	11.4
Not Heard	7	3.0
Heard and User	202	85.6
Total	236	100.0

While it comes to generating awareness on e-governance in any government department, Bhoomi project has scored very high over every other e-programme of any department. This is very encouraging sign since the programme is aimed primarily at the rural masses and directly at those holding lands that normally are unaware or lack the abilities to understand an e-governance scheme. This is true when the literacy levels in rural areas of Karnataka are not more than 70 per cent for men and just about 60 per cent for women. Notwithstanding such bleak educational and awareness levels, Bhoomi has progressed really well over the years and got entrenched in the minds of the rural peoples. A whopping 97 per cent of the respondents reported that they are either using the services at Bhoomi kiosks or have heard about them. A mere 3 per cent claimed to have heard nothing on the programme. Sustained awareness campaigning by the state government and committed officials can be particularly attributed to this phenomenal success of the computerized registration of lands project.

Transparency

	No. of Respondents	*Per cent*
Yes	227	96.2
No	9	3.8
Total	236	100.0

Transparency and accountability are the key variables in estimating the success of an e-governance project. In these two critical areas, Bhoomi has attained huge success over the years. Over 96 per cent of the respondents agreed that there was transparency in the dealings at the Bhoomi centres which was not the case earlier. Every thing depended on what the village/taluk level officials had to say. The change seems to be better and a majority of the respondents feel they are happy with the phenomenal turn around in their dealings with the revenue department.

Accountability

	No. of Respondents	*Per cent*
Yes	218	92.4
No	18	7.6
Total	236	100.0

As far as accountability is concerned, Bhoomi is closely inching to the 97 per cent mark of transparency. However, the problem of accountability still persists on account of the institutional arrangements made for the finalization of a land transaction. The Village Accounts and the Revenue Inspector have the discretionary powers to withhold or delay the issuance of an RTC. Though over 92 per cent of the respondents said the dealings and services at the Bhoomi centres have a mark of accountability, nearly 8 per cent of the users still have doubts on the accountability factor involved in the transactions. This has to be plugged through institutional corrections which have nothing to do with the invincibility of an e-governance model.

Responsiveness

	No. of Respondents	*Per cent*
Yes	212	89.8
No	24	10.2
Total	236	100.0

Responsiveness to the needs and demands of the targeted population or users is another key variable that can sway public perception of an e-governance programme. It is by now accepted that transparency and accountability levels in Bhoomi project are high by any standards. However, that seems not to be the case when it comes to responsiveness. Over 10 per cent of the users said the project is not responsive to their needs or services. Here again, the problem could be with the institutional arrangements and personnel involved. Less than 90 per cent of the respondents feel the project is responsive. This critical area in terms of public perception has to be spruced up and scaled to attain the maximum levels of public trust.

Availability of Services

	No. of Respondents	*Per cent*
Yes	229	97.0
No	7	3.0
Total	236	100.0

The availability of services at Bhoomi centres in the taluks is quite high with 97 per cent of the respondents replying in the affirmative. Only 3 per cent of the users claimed services are not available. This is definitely not a depressing scenario. Even in the utility quotient nearly 94 per cent of the users had a positive opinion of the programme while over 6 per cent of the respondents claimed that the services at Bhoomi kiosks do not have a utility value. Utility is a relative term in the Bhoomi project as those who do not possess lands have a fairly negative view of its services.

Utility of Services

	No. of Respondents	*Per cent*
Yes	221	93.6
No	15	6.4
Total	236	100.0

Utility is a relative term in the Bhoomi project as those who do not possess lands have a fairly negative view of its services. That way all the services in an e-governance project cannot be made 100 per cent utilizable. Suggestions and demands from the people can be considered for adding new services and removing the ones that a majority of the users feel are irrelevant. Since the registration of lands demand immense pen and ground work, there seems to be no possibility of removing any services from the present bouquet.

Use of the Programme

	No. of Respondents	*Per cent*
Yes	223	94.5
No	13	5.5
Total	236	100.0

The usability of the Bhoomi programme is quite high for any e-governance programme. Over 94 per cent of the respondents say the programme is of much use to them while only less than 6 per cent claimed the opposite. Since land registration is a compulsory process and a visit to Bhoomi centre is inevitable, the usability of the programme is very high. The range of services obviously scales up the usability factor and Bhoomi has done a commendable work on this front.

Land registration is a cumbersome process in Indian public and revenue administration. This is particularly true in the rural areas where the personnel tasked with the revenue administration adopt a traditional approach in the registration of lands. In the

Time Taken for Services Before e-Governance Programme

	No. of Respondents	*Per cent*
1 Day	18	7.6
2 Days	76	32.2
3 Days	103	43.6
1 Week	39	16.5
Total	236	100.0

Time Taken for Services Under e-Governance Programme

	No. of Respondents	*Per cent*
Within 10 Min	178	75.4
Within 30 Min	58	24.6
Total	236	100.0

manual system, the timeframe taken for registration was more than a week and less than a month while the whole process of field survey, documentation, preparation of sketches and all took as many as six months (more than 180 days). Ever since the implementation of Bhoomi programme, this long period has come down to less that 35 days.

In the manual system, the time taken for actual registration was more than three days and less than a week. Nearly 60 per cent of the respondents agreed with this statement. Less than 40 per cent claimed the process took one to two days. In the Bhoomi system, this timeframe has come down drastically to less than 10 minutes and not more than 30 minutes for registrations requiring a cross verification. By all means, it is the time factor that has propelled the Bhoomi project to the pinnacle. This achievement is definitely a radical one and which has been recognized all over the country for replication.

Money Spend Before e-Governance Programme

	No. of Respondents	*Per cent*
Rs. 50	32	13.6
Rs. 100	130	55.1
Rs. 500	74	31.4
Total	236	100.0

Like in the time factor, Bhoomi has had a tremendous impact on people in terms of saving their costs in concluding a land transaction

Money Spend After e-Governance Programme

	No. of Respondents	Per cent
Rs. 15	201	85.2
Rs. 25	35	14.8
Total	236	100.0

with the revenue department. In the manual system, people used to incur expenditure from Rs. 100 to 500 apart from the registration fee. This was corroborated by more than 86 per cent of the respondents. The cost now has come down to as less as Rs. 15. More than 85 per cent of the users said they are now spending only Rs.15 for their work while at least 15 per cent of them put the cost at Rs. 25

Satisfaction

	No. of Respondents	Per cent
High	171	72.5
Moderate	54	22.9
Low	11	4.7
Total	130	100.0

Satisfaction in land registration is generally very low by Indian standards. However, the range of success that Bhoomi achieved in raising the satisfaction levels of people is outstanding for any e-governance project. There is no comparative data to deal with, but over 72 per cent of the respondents claimed their satisfaction with the Bhoomi project is quite high while nearly 23 per cent of the users said they are satisfied though on a moderate scale. Surely, this two levels cover over 95 per cent of the users and those who complained they have low levels of satisfaction with the services at Bhoomi are less than 5 per cent. This is an exceptional performance by any e-governance project with services involving a cumbersome process.

REFERENCES

1. www.planningcommission.gov.in (accessed 3rd December 2006).
2. www.bhoomi.kar.nic.in (accessed 3rd January 2007).
3. Rajiv Chawla is now serving as Managing Director of Karnataka State Food and Civil Supplies Corporation. He earlier worked in the capacity of secretary, e-governance, Government of Karnataka.
4. By the end of the fiscal year 2005-06.

5. Though online mutation module has been incorporated in the Bhoomi software, officials have to still carry out survey work as earlier.
6. www.bhoomi.kar.nic.in (accessed 2nd March 2007).
7.
8.
9.
10. Currently, this facility is available only at the taluk level.
11. *Indian Government plans to put land records online*, 3 January 2007, *Indian Express*.
12. The literacy rate of Karnataka State is nearly 70 per cent and while 80 per cent of the male are educated only 60 per cent of the women are literate.
13. Nearly 66 per cent of the population in Karnataka is dependent on agriculture as per the 2001 Census.

KARNATAKA VALUATION AND E-REGISTRATION (KAVERI)

Background

KAVERI is a comprehensive computerization project aimed at automating the entire registration process and speedy delivery of registered documents to the citizens of Karnataka. KAVERI has been operational since 2003. In 2007, 224 Sub-Registrar's Offices were delivering three key services: on line registration of property sale/ purchase deeds; issue of non-encumbrance certificate and issue of copies of a previously registered deed.

Planning

Initial efforts by the Department of Registration and Stamps in Karnataka towards computerization brought about only partial success. Despite computerization, the process of registration was time consuming; documents were not delivered on the same day; and integrated software could not be developed. Also, it required huge investment from the government. Besides, all 201 sub-registries could not be computerized at the same time.

Consequent to the delay, it was proposed to follow the Maharashtra model of e-Governance with the technical help of the Pune-based C-DAC in 2002 to automate the whole registration process on the principle of public-private participation on a Build-Operate-Transfer (BOT) basis for speedy delivery of registered documents. The computerization of the department was important because the Department of Stamps and Registration is the third highest revenue generating department for Karnataka, with a revenue target of Rs. 3415.20 crore in the fiscal year 2006-07 while the total expenditure was less than Rs. 40 crore. The department has staff strength of only around 1500 at 224 offices across the State. The first KAVERI centre was launched in the Rajajinagar SRO in Bangalore district in 2003.

Attributes of the Project

KAVERI is the first public-private partnership project to be implemented in Karnataka since 2003. The hassle-free procedure seeks to automate and streamline the workflow. The system provides comprehensive proof of authenticity of documents, afford publicity to transactions, prevent fraud, besides providing a facility for ascertaining whether a property has already been transacted, assuring security of deeds and titles in case the originals are lost or destroyed. The project would ultimately result in a transparent, accountable, responsible, improved, efficient and a user-friendly administration.

Institutional Arrangements

The project was started on a BOT (Build-Operate-Transfer) model, wherein a private partner was brought in to install, operate and maintain the hardware across all offices and recover his investments from service fees charged to the client in return of the services rendered. The contract period is for five years. The roles and functions of both the business partner and the department personnel are clearly laid out.

Pune-based C-DAC (Centre for Development of Advanced Computing) provided the software for the project, while CMS Computers Ltd. (AP Government's e-Seva service provider) and Electronics Corporation of India Ltd. (ECIL) are service providers for hardware, supporting software and maintenance. The state government spent Rs. 1.10 crore on the development of software, service providers invested around Rs. 40 crore on hardware, data entry and furniture for the system. The service providers are responsible for the execution and administration of the project, including manpower deployment, consumables planning, software installation and site preparation. They are allowed to charge Rs. 30 per page as 'scanning fee' from the public. They remit Rs. 5 to the Government and keep Rs. 25.

Registration Process

The KAVERI applications suite has been designed to take care of the entire registration process, inclusive of necessary report generation and property valuation. The 80-year-old, five-step procedure of registration was left undisturbed for the benefit of end users who have already adopted it. The general public was unaware of the

Organizational Chart of the Department

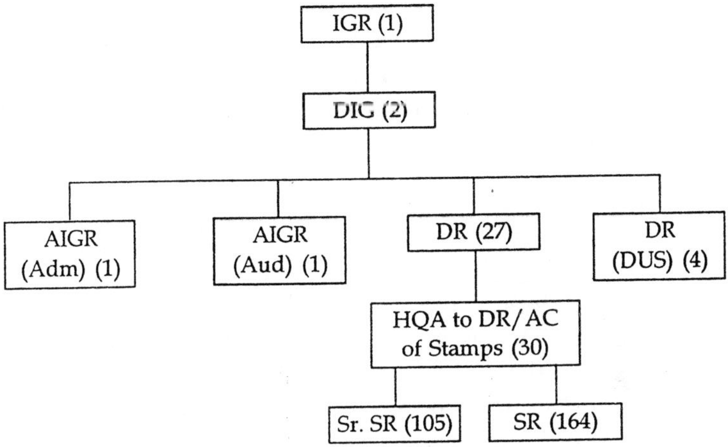

requirements to be fulfilled before going to the Sub-Registrar. Therefore each Sub-Registrar was provided a kiosk (with touch screen interface) also called Citizen Care Centre (CCC), which enables even a computer illiterate person to know the requirements for document registration like market value, stamp duty, registration fee, list of supporting documents, etc.

When a person wants to register documents he/she comes to the Sub-Registrar's Office, he gets an electronic token, which also assigns a timeframe for the applicant to present documents. The electronic token display system enhances the workflow of the system and the general public is able to attend at a prescribed time instead of waiting in queues at the Sub-Registrar Offices for hours together.

The Sub-Registrar then manually scrutinizes the submitted documents, decides on their type based on the schedule of the Karnataka Stamp Act and subjects them to PIS-II (Public Information System) scrutiny, which then computerizes it. The PIS-II checks the documents based on the information provided and generates a 'Check Slip'. The Check Slip mentions the end result of the documents, whether they would be registered through the system or whether they would be kept pending. Efforts will be made to return the documents to the party if they are not complete for registration through the system. The next step of receipt generation is a simple procedure with the help of a computer, since all fees have already been calculated, details of the presenter given and a number (either pending or normal serial) has been assigned to the document. The system generates a new receipt and all details about receipt are displayed. The operator then enters the details of payment and rechecks the fees calculated with the Sub-Registrar before finalizing the receipt. At this stage, the procedure of fee collection gets over and the operator sets stamp number 2 also called 'Fees Stamp' in consultation with the Sub-Registrar.

The admission and identification part is processed using Web camera and a finger print scanning device. When all the executors' photographs and thumb impressions are captured, the operator sets Stamp number 3 also called 'Admission stamp' in consultation with the Sub-Registrar. The identification part requires data entry of two witnesses present there. When the identification procedure is over operator puts Stamp number 4 called 'Identification Stamp' in consultation with the Sub-Registrar.

After the requirements of the document are completed, the Sub-Registrar asks the operator to register the document. The system rechecks all the necessary things before registering the documents and makes all data non-editable. Monthly, quarterly and annual reports are also prepared at the end of month or at specified time as and when required.

KAVERI software application suite can be classified on the following functional modules:

- Registration Module
- Valuation Module
- Reports Module
- Vendor Management System (VMS)
- Utilities Module
- Societies, Firms and Marriage Registration Module
- Scan-Archival Module
- Data Transmission Module
- Website

Advantages and Benefits

- Computerized 5-step document registration process.
- Auto valuation of property.
- Auto scrutiny of document.
- Immovable property valuation in urban and rural areas.
- Bar coded report generation (Daily, Monthly, Quarterly and

Yearly statements, Comparative statements etc.) at offices across the department hierarchy. Updated over telephone lines or website.

- Daily report generation for Sub-Registrar Office including Receipt, Indexes, Minute Book, Day Book, A Register, remittance etc.
- Gateway screen with online information display.
- Automatic fees and stamp duty calculations.
- Single data entry architecture.
- Automatic Database backup at local level.
- Advanced scanning system with features like black border, skew removal etc.
- Secure CD based Archival system.
- Exhaustive document search based on different parameters.
- Encumbrance Search certificate generation.
- Marriage registration.
- Firms and Societies registration.
- Data transmission and reception over dial-up telephone lines.
- MIS report generation at all levels in the hierarchy.
- Vendor Management software.
- Web enabled info base.
- Miscellaneous utilities to manage master info base like list of articles, jurisdiction etc.
- User friendly KAVERI installable software on CD.
- Bilingual interface (English and Kannada).
- Detailed User Manual in English.

Services Provided

At Sub-Registrar's Offices

1. Registration of all documents under the Registration Act, 1908.
2. Certified copies of the registered documents.
3. Encumbrance certificates of any property in the jurisdiction of the office.
4. Registration of marriages.
5. Certified copies from marriage register.

At District Registrar's Offices

1. Registration of Societies/Association under Karnataka Societies Registration Act 1960.
2. Registration of partnership firms under the Indian Partnership Act, 1932.

3. Certified copies from the Registers of Societies/firms.
4. Deposit/opening of wills under the Registration Act 1908.
5. Refund of stamps.
6. Adjudication of documents.

Technologies Used

Application Software

- Back end: MS SQL Server 2000 (Client + Server).
- Front End: Visual Basic 6.0.
- Language interface: ISM Office 2000 for Kannada language
- Install shield 6.0.
- Data reports/Crystal reports 8.5.
- Operating system: Windows 2000 (Server+Professional). All relevant service packs/upgrades.
- All relevant device drivers.

Website

- Back end: MS SQL Server 2000 (Server).
- Operating system: Windows 2000 Advanced Server.
- Domain name http://www.karigr.org.
- Website development using Microsoft Technologies.

Security Issues Handled

- Password protection for valid user (Provided by OS).
- Password protection for valid user (Provided by RDBMS).
- Envisaged Bio-metric logins (using Bio-metric devices).
- Password at application level.
- Password at database level (through the software).
- Triggers at table level.

Quality Standards Followed

- IEEE Standards.
- ISO 9001 :2000 Certified.
- CAG:IT Audit norms compliant.

Interoperability

- KAVERI is a completely object oriented software.
- ActiveX Exe, ActiveX DLL and OCX form a major part of the KAVERI Application Suite. Each component interacts and performs dependent as well as independent tasks.

Benefits for Citizens and Government

- The kiosks provide comprehensive information on the documents to be carried to the SR office and accept complete documents for presentation, thereby reducing the amount of paper work.
- Introduction of the electronic token system assigns a particular time to the applicant to present his documents, thus reducing unnecessary crowd gathering in the Sub-Registrar's office.
- The use of private participation in Government work has enhanced the productivity of the department. The private partners take care of the maintenance and operate the computers as per the guidance of the system, Sub-Registrar and various rules and regulations laid down by the Department. They also scan the document and verify the correctness of the same with the originals and burn the image data on to the CD.

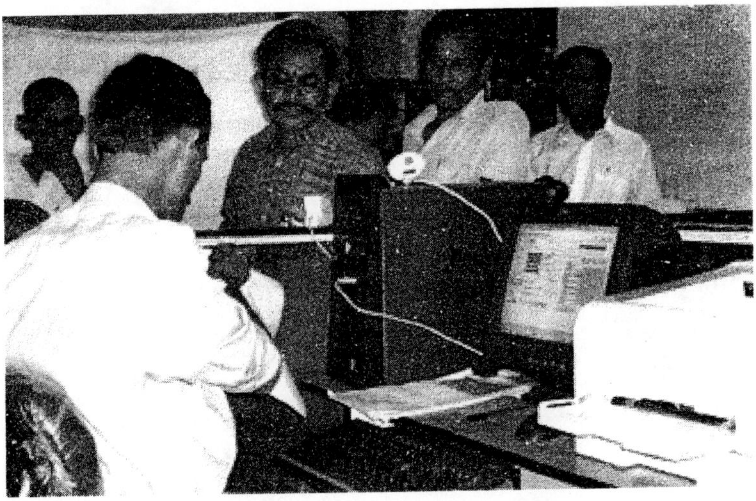

Targeted Beneficiaries

- Citizens residing in the State of Karnataka spanning an area of 191,791 sq km.
- The total population across the 27 districts of the state is 52,850,562 and comprises of 26,898,918 males and 25,951,644 females.

Linkages with Bhoomi

Bhoomi has joined hands with the KAVERI system of Registration Department. The sale transactions are generated and sent on daily basis from Registration Department to Bhoomi system electronically through the State Data Centre (SDC) and Bhoomi collects and processes them as per the business processes.

Project Outcomes

Efficient administration achieved by drastic reduction in the time taken in transaction processing, hassle-free procedure and reduced corruption. All transactions are predefined and hence all operations at the Sub-Registrar's Office are fully automated. In addition, the quality of the services has improved, as the staff is focusing more on creative work leaving the monotonous tasks of registration process to the computer. This has resulted in increased productivity at the departmental level, which in turn, has brought around a new synergy in the government at the highest level.

There has been an enhanced revenue collection for the state government with less expenditure on the KAVERI application suite maintenance and other investments. Being a PPP model, it is self-sustaining as the private partner has to install, operate, maintain the hardware and provide software support. In addition, the departmental staff has been trained by the C-DAC so as to make the transfer after the contract period easier. PPP model envisages zero spending for the Government, thereby making it scalable. An important aspect of is the imposition of user charges.

Award for KAVERI

KAVERI project was the winner of National E Governance Award in the year 2004. It was presented with the Silver Icon award.

Revenue, Expenditure and Registration in the Last Three Fiscal Years

Year	*Documents (in lakhs)*	*Income (in crores)*	*Expenditure (in crores)*
2004-05	11.99	1924.18	40.86
2005-06	10.15	2385.29	35.67
2006-07	14.13	3415.20	39.98

Scaling Up

27 new Sub-Registrars Offices created out of Bangalore North, Bangalore South, Kengeri, K.R. Puram, Yelahanka and Anekal Sub-Registrars Offices vide Government Notification under Reference started functioning from the 2nd of April 2007. As of now all the 224 Sub-Registrars Offices have been computerized and the total staff strength is over 1500.

Constraints and Challenges

In KAVERI, the transactions of property registration are a mandatory. Increase in tax revenue can not be attributed to computerization alone. A more transparent system of valuation and growth in property transactions can provide greater explanation for tax growth. However, in all cases, computerization seems to have allowed the agencies to cope with high growth in number of transactions. Then, there is a problem of transition when the government takes over the management of electronic registration from the private entrepreneurs after the expiry of contract period which is five years (2008). Corruption and delays still pose a big problem in registration of property documents though there is a marked improvement in the quality of services delivered online.

Capacity building for stamps and registration department staff is one major area of concern. Projects that serve rural clients are demanding on the cost front for any government. Bhoomi kiosks are functioning well, but increase in scope and varied nature of services can put undue burden right from the operator level up to the issuing authority. Accessibility to Internet is another major area of concern where a vast digital divide exists in predominantly agrarian states like Karnataka. All these issues have to be factored in before expansion of the linkages can be taken up to the panchayat level.

Survey on the Impact of e-Governance on Society: A Case Study of KAVERI, Karnataka

The study on the impact of KAVERI project was carried out in 10 districts of Karnataka namely Bangalore Rural, Mysore, Madikeri, Mandya, Shimoga, Dakshin Kannada, Gulbarga, Raichur, Bidar and Bijapur. Responses were elicited from a total of 239 are either users or have used e-registration services. Of the total respondents 207 are male and only 32 are female—87 and 13 per cent respectively. In Indian society, particularly in matters of property and economy, male dominate the scenario and this reflects in the sample size that we got.

Sex

	No. of Respondents	*Per cent*
Male	207	86.6
Female	32	13.4
Total	239	100.0

Age

	No. of Respondents	*Per cent*
Below 20	2	.8
21-30	18	7.5
31-40	89	37.2
41-50	64	26.8
51 and above	66	27.6
Total	239	100.0

The respondents fall in the age groups of below 20, 21-30, 31-40, 41-50 and 51 and above. However, the major users of electronic registration services are primarily in the age groups of 31-40, 41-50 and 51 and above. This has to keep in with the traditional role of a family head to perform all registration of property or lands on behalf of his entire family.

The KAVERI project encompasses the whole of Karnataka and is well entrenched even at the rural level with deep linkages to the already successful e-governance project, rather online registration of land process called Bhoomi. The survey sample has thrown up quite a large percentage of illiterates, mostly farmers and those pursuing traditional occupations in villages. Nearly 22 per cent of

Education

	No. of Respondents	Per cent
Upto SSC	108	45.2
Intermediate	16	6.7
Degree	36	15.1
Post Graduation	27	11.3
Illiterate	52	21.8
Total	239	100.0

the respondents are illiterate with no formal education. More than 50 per cent of the respondents—52 per cent to the precise—have either completed matriculation or Intermediate. Surprisingly this is on lower side of education levels in our study.[3] Those really with an authority of education form 26.4 per cent of the sample size.

Occupation

	No. of Respondents	Per cent
Agriculture	156	65.3
Government Service	30	12.6
Independent Occupation	38	15.9
Other	15	6.3
Total	239	100.0

The occupational status of the respondents is in tune with the 2001 Census details of Karnataka. Over 65 per cent of the respondents are in the agriculture sector while 16 per cent of them are pursuing an independent occupation.[4] Those in the government service form only 12.6 per cent of the sample size while over six per cent are into other occupations.

Awareness

	No. of Respondents	Per cent
Heard	29	12.1
Not Heard	7	2.9
Heard and User	203	84.9
Total	239	100.0

Though literacy levels and occupational status confirm the rural status of Karnataka, it is not surprising to note the high levels of awareness among the masses on the implementation of e-governance programmes particularly that cater to their basic needs. As in the case of Bhoomi, there is high level of awareness on KAVERI project in the state with 85 per cent of the respondents claiming to be aware or have used electronic registration services. Less than 3 per cent of the respondents have not heard while those in the know of the project are over 12 per cent.

Transparency

	No. of Respondents	*Per cent*
Yes	224	93.7
No	15	6.3
Total	239	100.0

The number of documents that are getting registered online is increasing by the year in Karnataka. In the fiscal year 2006-07, nearly 14.13 lakh documents were registered through the KAVERI programme while this figure was only 10.15 lakh the preceding year. This in itself explains the popularity of the online registration process and reflects the perception of the people on the transparency levels involved herein. Nearly 94 per cent of the respondents claimed or vouched for transparency in the programme while those holding the negative opinion form only 6.3 per cent of the sample size.

Accountability

	No. of Respondents	*Per cent*
Yes	207	86.6
No	32	13.4
Total	239	100.0

There has been a marked reduction in the levels of corruption in electronic registration of property and other title deeds after the implementation of the KAVERI project. However, as is the case with land registration, well-entrenched traditional ways of operation by the government staff and middlemen is yet to be eradicated comprehensively. In contrast to the Bhoomi programme, perception of accountability in KAVERI is on the lower side. Over 13 per cent of the respondents do not see or perceive accountability in the registration process while the remainder thinks positively of the project.

Responsiveness

	No. of Respondents	*Per cent*
Yes	204	85.4
No	35	14.6
Total	239	100.0

Complete automation of the registration process and increase in the numbers of staff in the registration and stamps department in Karnataka over a period of time has brought in a positive change in the outlook of the personnel.[5] Creative innovations on the part of the personnel have turned around the department which now leaves all the 5 steps of registration to the computer. The main outcome of this being increased responsiveness on their part. Over 85 per cent of those surveyed believe there is responsiveness in the programme. However, this is on the lower side when compared with Bhoomi. Nearly 15 per cent of the respondents replied in the negative on this aspect.

Availability of Services

	No. of Respondents	*Per cent*
Yes	198	82.8
No	41	17.2
Total	239	100.0

The process to link KAVERI with Bhoomi so that services can be taken to the level of sub-registry offices is yet to take a concrete shape. KAVERI services have spread only up to taluk level. The ground situation is that Bhoomi kiosks at the grassroots level have not been integrated with the KAVERI network and people have to visit the taluk office for availing the services. This is reflected in citizens' perception on the availability of electronic registration of property services. Over 17 per cent of the respondents claimed that services are not available. This is quite a significant number. Linkages at the grassroots level can help reduce this problem. On the positive side, over 82 per cent of the respondents say services are available and affordable.

Utility of Services

	No. of Respondents	*Per cent*
Yes	206	86.2
No	33	13.8
Total	239	100.0

Registration of property is a must at all levels and citizens utilize these services wherever they are. When such provision is made available to people at the grassroots level utility levels can be very high. Even in this adversity, over 86 per cent of the respondents are utilizing KAVERI services while less than 14 per cent have not or yet to utilize them.

Use of the Programme

	No. of Respondents	Per cent
Yes	212	88.7
No	27	11.3
Total	239	100.0

E-governance programmes have struck a chord with even those who have no use for them. This is the case with all the programmes that we covered as part of this study and KAVERI is no exception. Nearly 89 per cent of the respondents say the programme is very useful or can be of use to them in future. This can be scaled up further as we have seen in the case of Bhoomi which was supported by 95 per cent of the respondents.

Time Taken for Services Before e-Governance Programme

	No. of Respondents	Per cent
1 Day	13	5.4
2 Days	76	31.8
3 Days	110	46.0
1 Week	40	16.7
Total	239	100.0

Barring the preliminary documentation work, the registration process hardly takes any time in the case of KAVERI. This is not the case with Bhoomi where the process is tedious and time-consuming. Before KAVERI, that is prior to 2003, the minimum time for property registration was three days to one week. This was the opinion of nearly 63 per cent of the respondents. Those who said the timeframe ranged from 2 to 1 days form 37 per cent of the respondents.

There has been a drastic change in this aspect with the implementation of this programme. Now, the process of registration hardly takes 10 minutes and the maximum limit is less than 30 minutes. Nearly 68 per cent of the respondents claimed they are

Time Taken for Services Under e-Governance Programme

	No. of Respondents	*Per cent*
Within 10 Min	162	67.8
Within 30 Min	77	32.2
Total	239	100.0

getting their work done in less than 10 minutes while the remainder put the timeframe as less than 30 minutes.

Money Spend Before e-Governance Programme

	No. of Respondents	*Per cent*
Rs. 50	17	7.1
Rs. 100	135	56.5
Rs. 500	87	36.4
Total	239	100.0

On the cost front too, there is marked reduction. This involves travel and the documentation costs. In the case of KAVERI, user charges are levied to the range of Rs. 15 to Rs. 25. Over 75 per cent of these charges go to the private entrepreneurs while the government benefits hugely from the stamp and registration duties. Previously, expenditure on registration was anywhere between Rs. 50 and Rs. 100. This is confirmed by 93 per cent of the respondents.

Money Spend Under e-Governance Programme

	No. of Respondents	*Per cent*
Rs. 15	188	78.7
Rs. 25	51	21.3
Total	239	100.0

Electronic registration has brought down the costs for citizens. With KAVERI, people spend as less as Rs. 15 for registering their property documents. This is the opinion of nearly 79 per cent of the respondents while the remaining put the costs involved at Rs. 25. Truly, this is what people expect of electronic delivery of services which here means electronic registration.

Reduction in time and costs for citizens availing government services is the first outcome of e-governance projects. Normally, satisfaction levels on this count should be high for a programme like KAVERI. However, it fails to match with the high satisfaction levels

Satisfaction

	No. of Respondents	Per cent
High	82	34.3
Moderate	147	61.5
Low	10	4.2
Total	239	100.0

of Bhoomi which got a 72.5 per cent approval from the users. Those who professed high levels of satisfaction with KAVERI form only 34.3 per cent of the respondents. One positive signal from the citizens is that a majority of them – 61.5 per cent of the respondents – have moderate levels of satisfaction on electronic registration services. Further outreach and simplification of the institutional processes in KAVERI can place it on a par with Bhoomi. This can bring in a renewed synergy in the Bhoomi-KAVERI interoperability as well.

REFERENCES

1. Work at a Kaveri kiosk in Bangalore Rural District.
2. Capt. Amarinder Singh, the then Chief Minister of Punjab Presenting Gold Medal to D. Satya Murty, IAS, Inspector General of Registration and Stamps, Bangalore, at Chandigarh on 24th October, 2002.
3. The literacy rate of Karnataka state is nearly 70 per cent and while 80 per cent of the male are educated, only 60 per cent of the women are literate.
4. Nearly 66 per cent of the population in Karnataka are dependent on agriculture as per the 2001 Census.
5. The staff in the Stamps and Registration Department, Karnataka was around 1000 in 2003 when the Kaveri project was launched. It has increased to over 1500 by April 2007 and covers all the 224 Sub-Registrar Offices in the state.

BANGALORE ONE, BANGALORE, KARNATAKA

Background

The Government of Karnataka is keen to provide integrated services to the citizens deploying the tools of Information and Communication Technology (ICT) so as to enhance Speed, Convenience, Certainty and Accountability in providing such services through the concept of a 'One-Stop-Shop' facility. Accordingly, the state government decided to implement an e-Governance project called the Bangalore One or B1 Project on the lines of similar projects implemented elsewhere in India, especially e-Seva that was successful in Hyderabad and other major towns of Andhra Pradesh. The Bangalore One project has been successfully launched on 2 April, 2005 with 14 service centres providing 24 different services (18 government and 6 private) to citizens of Bangalore.

The state government got the Hyderabad-based National Institute of Smart Government (NISG) to implement the project with funds from the Ministry of Information Technology and the United National Development Programme (UNDP). There are now 16 centres in the city providing a wide range of services to the denizens residing within the limits of the Bangalore Mahanagara Palike (BMP).[1] The implementing agency of the project is the Department of Administrative Reforms, Government of Karnataka, but the project was spearheaded by the Bangalore Water Supply and Sewerage Board (BWSSB).

About Bangalore City

Located on the Deccan Plateau in the south-eastern part of Karnataka, Bangalore has an estimated metropolitan population of 6.8 million making it India's fifth-largest metropolitan area. It is spread in 225 sq. kms. Though historical references to the city predate AD 900, a written history of continuous settlement exists only from 1537. In that year, Kempe Gowda I, whom many regard as the architect of modern Bangalore, built a mud fort in the city and established it as a province of the Vijayanagara Empire. Bangalore was also ruled by the Sultanate of Bijapur, the Mughals and their feudatories, the Wodeyars, Hyder Ali and Tipu Sultan, Wodeyars and British East India.

During the British Raj, Bangalore developed as a centre for colonial rule in South India. The establishment of the Bangalore Cantonment brought in large numbers of migrant Tamil Nadu and Andhra Pradesh and North Indian workers for developing and maintaining the infrastructure of the cantonment. Bangalore remained part of British East India until Independence in August, 1942.[2]

After India gained independence in 1947, Bangalore evolved into a manufacturing hub for public sector heavy industries—particularly aerospace, telecommunications, machine tools, heavy equipment, space and defense. The establishment and success of software services firms in Bangalore after the liberalization of India's

economy has led to the growth of information technology industry. Bangalore is referred to as the *Silicon Valley of India.*[4]

Geographical Location

Bangalore is situated in the southeast of the South Indian state of Karnataka. It is located in the heart of the Mysore Plateau (a region of the larger Precambrian Deccan Plateau) at an average elevation of 920 m (3,018 feet). It is positioned at 12.97° N 77.56° E and covers an area of 696.17 km² (269 mi²). Bangalore District borders with Kolar District in the northeast, Tumkur District in the northwest, Mandya District in the southwest, Chamarajnagar District in the south and the neighbouring state of Tamil Nadu in the southeast. The Bangalore Urban district is divided into three taluks: Bangalore North, Bangalore South and Anekal. The Bangalore North taluk is a relatively more level plateau, while the Bangalore South taluk has an uneven landscape with intermingling hills and valleys.

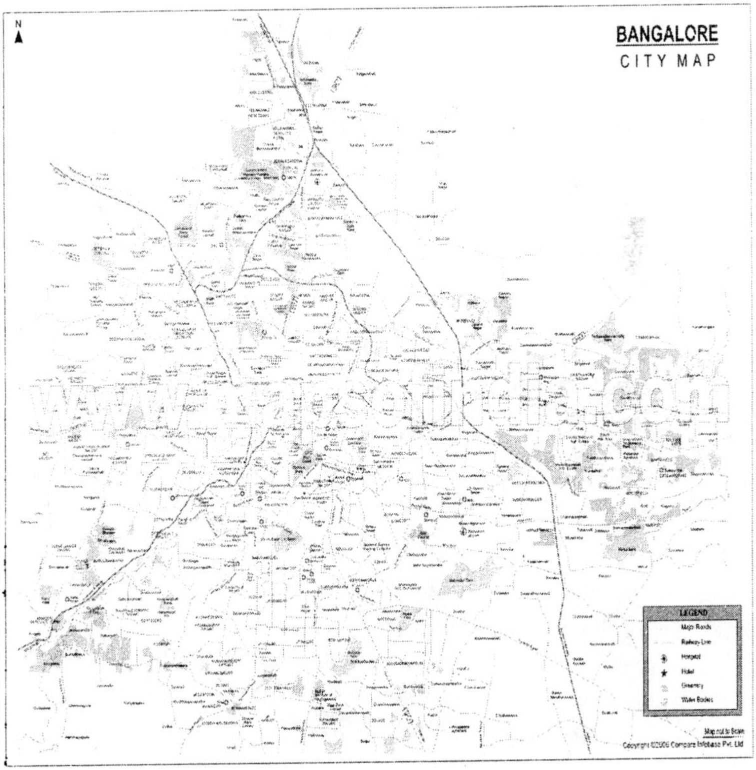

Bangalore has a handful of freshwater lakes and water tanks, the largest of which are Madivala tank, Hebbal Lake, Ulsoor Lake and Sankey Tank. Groundwater occurs in silt to sand layers of the alluvial sediments. Bangalore receives adequate rainfall from the Northeast Monsoon as well as the Southwest Monsoon.

Economy of Bangalore

Bangalore's Rs. 260 crore-economy (2002–03 Net District Income) makes it a major economic centre in India. Indeed, Bangalore is the fourth largest and the fastest growing market in the country. Its per capita income of Rs. 49,000 (US$ 1,160) is the highest for any Indian city. The city is the third-largest hub for high net worth individuals after Mumbai and Delhi. Bangalore is home to over 10,000 individual dollar millionaires and around 60,000 super-rich people who have a capital surplus of Rs 4.5 crore and Rs. 50 lakh respectively.

In the 1940s industrial visionaries such as Sir Mirza Ismail and Sir Mokshagundam Vishveswarayya played an important role in the development of Bangalore's strong manufacturing and industrial base. Bangalore is headquarters to several public manufacturing heavy industries such as Hindustan Aeronautics Limited (HAL), National Aerospace Laboratories (NAL), Bharat Heavy Electricals Limited (BHEL), Bharat Electronics Limited, Bharat Earth Movers Limited (BEML) and Hindustan Machine Tools (HMT). In June 1972 the Indian Space Research Organisation was established here under the Department of Space.

By the late 1990s, the city got the sobriquet 'Silicon Valley of India' because a large number of Information Technology companies were set up here which now contribute at least 38 per cent of India's $ 2.27 billion IT and software export market.[7] Bangalore's IT industry is divided into three major clusters – Software Technology Parks of India, Bangalore (STPI); International Technology Park Bangalore (ITPB) and Electronics City. Infosys and Wipro, India's largest software companies, have their campus in Electronics City. As a result of all this, Bangalore's place in the global IT map is prominent.[8]

The city has also emerged as the major biotechnology hub in India. Approximately 158 of the 320 biotech companies are based there, with total revenues of Rs. 1,400 crore. Further, fifty-five per cent of India's biotechnology companies are located in Karnataka. The Government of Karnataka is committed to establishing a biotechnology corridor for the development of the biotechnology industry in Karnataka.[9]

Significance of Bangalore One (BI)

The Bangalore One (B1) Project seeks to redefine public service through its focus on the common man. The vision of the B1 Project is to provide to the citizens of Karnataka, all G2C and G2B One-Stop services and information of departments and agencies of Central, State and Local Governments in an efficient, reliable, transparent and integrated manner on a sustained basis, with certainty, through easy access to a chain of computerized Integrated Citizen Service Centres (ICSCs) and through multiple delivery channels like

Electronic Kiosks, mobile phones and the Internet. The prime objective of the project is to be the One-Stop-Shop for all C2G interactions.

A complex initiative like an Integrated Service Project has to be necessarily implemented in a phased manner. And, the state government has decided to adopt phased approach in the expansion of the project. It is estimated that Bangalore would eventually need about 50 citizen service centres to provide about 100 G2B, G2C and B2C services in Bangalore City. The government has set up 16 service centres (14 in the first phase) in different parts of the city to provide 24 basic services of 11 government departments. The list of 16 service centres is provided in centres in Bangalore link of B1Contacts. The vision of B1 is to eventually bring all the G2C and G2B services within the purview of B1 project so as to obviate the need for citizens and business people to visit the Government offices except for specialized and complex services.

Objectives of B1 Project

1. To enhance the accountability, transparency and responsiveness to citizen's needs.
2. To provide cost-effective methods of service provision to the departments and agencies.
3. To provide efficient and real-time MIS and EIS to the departments.

4. To ensure speed and certainty of providing the services through enforcement of a Service Level Agreement with the selected Partner.
5. To enable the government departments and agencies to focus on their core functions and responsibilities by freeing them from the routine operations like collection of revenues and accounting, issuing of certificates etc., and thereby enhance the overall productivity of the administrative machinery.

Evaluation of the Project

B1 Project will be evaluated periodically through independent agencies to ascertain whether these objectives are being achieved, adopting an appropriate structured methodology. For instance, the E-Governance Assessment Framework (EAF) designed by the Department of Information Technology, Government of India. The purpose is to ensure that the project satisfies the basic tenets of an e-Governance project like people-orientation, scalability and cost-effectiveness in providing various services online.

Outcomes of the Project

The outcomes of the project can be prioritized as below:

1. Citizens should get governmental services on any time, at anywhere without the limitation of jurisdiction of a particular office or a particular department or an agency.
2. The quality of services has to match with that of services in the private sector.
3. Citizens' Charter as a blueprint for quality assurance.
4. Citizens should be able to see the government as a single window for all services.

The G2C Structure

Bangalore One (B1) provides the citizens of Bangalore with a one stop interface with the Government of Karnataka. Citizens' interaction with government departments will be under a single umbrella. Such a set up allows the citizens to avail numerous services of several government departments, through one window. A brief description of the participating departments has been given below:

- ***Bangalore Electricity Supply Company (BESCOM):*** BESCOM is responsible for power distribution in six districts of

Karnataka. BESCOM covers an area of 41,092 sq. kms. with a population of over 16.8 million.

- *Bangalore Mahanagara Palike (BMP):* The municipal corporation's major task is related to civic development within the Greater Bangalore Metropolitan Area. This translates into an area of 224.66 sq. km with a population of 6.8 million. The notable tasks of the BMP are the orderly development of the city (including zoning and building regulations), health, hygiene, licensing, trade, and education through its network of schools and junior colleges. These tasks are now being carried through the B1 centres.
- *Bangalore Police Service:* BPS is endowed with the responsibility to maintain law and order, traffic management, and implementation of social legislation are its functions. That translates into ensuring communal harmony, bringing culprits to book, and order on the roads and parking lots. Its vision is that of a people-friendly police.
- *Bharat Sanchar Nigam Limited (BSNL):* When it comes to connecting the four corners of the nation, and much beyond, one reliable name is that of the BSNL. It is now working round the clock to take India to the world through provision of world class telecom services for the people of India. In order to facilitate the citizens of Bangalore with the usage of different services provided by BSNL, the department has integrated its certain citizen-specific services with Bangalore One.
- *Regional Transport Office (RTO):* The Transport Department is one of the largest revenue earning Departments in the State of Karnataka dealing with various Transport related matters like Driving Licenses, Registration of Motor Vehicles, Grant and Renewal of Permits and other regulatory and enforcement functions. In order to facilitate the citizens with the usage of different services provided by the RTO, the department has integrated its certain citizen-specific services with Bangalore One.
- *Regional Passport Office (RPO):* Regional Passport Authority is the Passport Issuing Authority. Currently it has a Server based network for collection of the application forms at their respective offices. The department has integrated its certain citizen-specific services with Bangalore One.

- *CellOne:* Customers of CellOne can now avail their bill payment through any of the Bangalore One centres. In addition to this, they can access the B1 web portal to make their CellOne bill payments online.
- *Department of Labour:* This department is endowed with the responsibility to get all the shops and commercial establishments, which come under the jurisdiction of the state government laws. It also looks after the renewal, amendments and surrender of various registrations. Currently, registration of shops and commercial establishments can be done through B1 centres.

New Services on Offer

Flight Booking

Customers can book the Domestic Flight Tickets, throughout all the Bangalore One centres, provided they are available. There is a facility for booking 4 seats per ticket.

Train Booking

Customers can book train tickets at all the B1 centre online. A maximum of six berths can be booked. Citizen will be provided an Electronic Reservation slip along with the Bangalore One Receipt, at the end of the transaction.[12]

Passport Services

All applications received in B1 Centres are invariably forwarded to the Passport Office within two working days after submission. The accepting Centre will generate the unique file reference number for each application using their software, enter the personal details of the applicant into the system, and scan the photograph and signatures. The data and images will be transferred to the Passport Office electronically, so that they can be directly read into the system at the Passport Office. The papers relating to police verification will also be sent directly to the concerned police authorities, by these centres. The applications will thereafter be physically sent to RPO Bangalore for further processing, as per precise time-lines agreed between the two sides.

Roll Out of the Project

The B1 project was launched on 2nd April 2005 with the inauguration of 14 centres in Bangalore. With the opening of these centres, the citizens will not have to stand in long queues to pay monthly or other bills at conventional or manual counters. They will be able to complete transactions in 10-15 minutes at the e-Kiosks in air-conditioned facility. Payments for other services such as stamps and registration, passport applications, birth and death certificates, license renewal and traffic fines will also be available at the e-Kiosks, with each centre having 15 counters. Now there are 16 centres in the city.[14]

Facilities at the B1 Centres

To make the e-Kiosks customer-friendly, the centres have been installed with a TV set, coffee/ tea vending machines, Internet facility, an Automated Teller Machine (ATM) and a well-stacked collection of newspapers, magazines and books. There are 15 counters at each centre to provide services. There is a seating facility for 50 visitors. All modes of payments—barring debit card—are accepted at any counter which officers any kind of service. There is an electronic queue management system. Housekeeping is done professionally and there is an adequate security at the centres.

Technical Structure

Services at the B1 centres are being run on a Microsoft.NET platform, have been put together by a consortium including CMS Computers and Ram Informatics. The same partners executed a similar project, *e-Seva* in Andhra Pradesh, and bagged orders for such e-governance initiatives in Maharashtra and Uttar Pradesh.

Technology

- 3-tier architecture.
- Oracle 9iAS Application server on Sun Solaris.
- Servers of different departments are connected to the B1 Data Centre, which is in turn connected to different ICSCs.
- The connectivity is point-to-point leased line, with ISDN as backup.

System Developed/Implemented by: CMS Computers Ltd. and Ram Informatics Ltd.

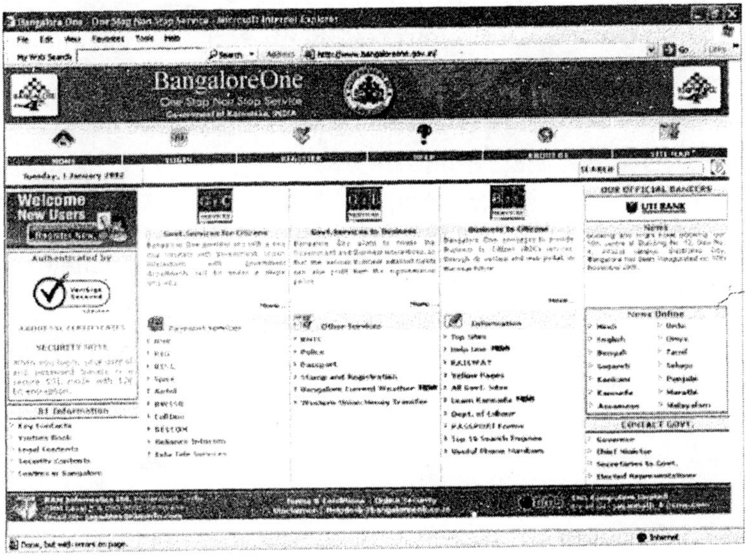

Transactions at B1 Centres

The total number of transactions per month at all the B1 centres is approximately 40 lakh while the total monthly collection is approximately Rs. 32 crores.

Future Plans

In the next phase, the number of Bangalore One service centres would be scaled up to 50. The scope of the services provided would also be expanded to about 200 services which would include G2B and B2C services. Bangalore One is envisaged to move to smaller cities, towns and finally cover all the rural areas in the state.

The implementation of Integrated Citizen Services requires extensive work by the government. The state government plans to set up 1,000 tele-centres on the lines of Bangalore One all across the state and predominantly in the rural areas. This was disclosed by Vipin Singh, Director, Bangalore One.

Survey on the Impact of e-Governance on Society: A Case Study of Bangalore One (B1)

We carried out the present study to gauge the impact of e-governance on society as part of which the e-services project of Bangalore One (B1) was selected as a case study. The service centres we covered in our study include Air Port Road, JP Nagar, Jayanagar, Kalasipalayam, Malleshwaram, Shanti Nagar, Vijayanagar, Yeshwantpur and Infosys Campus.

Age and Sex of the Respondents

Responses were elicited from a total of 242 users—166 male and 76 female—falling in the age groups of under 20, 21-30, 31-40, 41-50 and 51 and above. Male respondents account for 68.6 per cent of the sample size while the female respondents form the remaining 31.4 per cent.[16]

Sex

	No. of Respondents	*Per cent*
Male	166	68.6
Female	76	31.4
Total	242	100.0

Age

	No. of Respondents	*Per cent*
Below 20	15	6.2
21-30	92	38.0
31-40	49	20.2
41-50	37	15.3
51 and above	49	20.2
Total	242	100.0

Education

A majority of the people surveyed have finished their under graduate studies (bachelors degree) whose percentage is 46.7, which 20.2 per cent of the respondents have studied at least up to SSC. Over 13 per cent of the B1 users have done technical courses (here referred to as other) while 10 per cent studied up to Higher Secondary School (Plus 2). Those who have finished post graduation form 6.6 per cent of the sample size. Interestingly, only 3.3 per cent of the respondents said they are illiterate.[17]

Education

	No. of Respondents	Per cent
Upto SSC	49	20.2
Intermediate	24	9.9
Degree	113	46.7
Post Graduation	16	6.6
Other	32	13.2
Illiterate	8	3.3
Total	242	100.0

Occupation

The city's workforce structure is predominantly non-agrarian, with less than 6 per cent of Bangalore's workforce being engaged in agriculture-related activities.[18] This was found to be true in our study too and the percentage of respondents involved in agriculture (both as farmers and farm labour is roughly over 2 per cent. The majority is those with an independent occupation—they form 53 per cent of the total respondents. At least 20 per cent of the users we covered are in government service while the same per cent of the respondent are undertaking 'other' occupation. Those involved in non-agriculture labour are roughly over 6 per cent.

Awareness on B1 project

Over 88 per cent of the respondents covered under the study have heard and are users of the services provided at the B1 centres. This has to keep with the literacy rate of this fast evolving commercial hub of south India. Over 8 per cent of the respondents are aware of the project, but are not using it for various reasons. And those who

Occupation

	No. of Respondents	Per cent
Agriculture	4	1.7
Agriculture Labour	1	.4
Non-Agriculture Labour	15	6.2
Government Service	48	19.8
Independent Occupation	128	52.9
Other	46	19.0
Total	242	100.0

Awareness

	No. of Respondents	Per cent
Heard	20	8.3
Not Heard	8	3.3
Heard and User	214	88.4
Total	242	100.0

have not heard anything about the e-services constitute only 3.3 per cent of the total sample size. It has to be noted here that Bangalore is the first and foremost IT and ITES centre in the country and it is natural for a majority of the people (in the present case nearly 97 per cent said they are aware of B1 programme) to have up to date information on the e-governance models in the city as well as the state.

Transparency in Transaction

Transparency in dealings or transactions between the government and the citizens through an e-governance model has been considered as a critical variable in all the studies done on an international scale. Unfortunately, B1 has not been able to live up to the standards of the city denizens who are the most educated and have a broader understanding of information and communication technologies and their application in areas of administration, including service delivery. Nearly one-fourth—24 per cent of the total respondents—do not have a positive view when it comes to transparency in dealings at the B1 centres. However, those who claimed that there is transparency in the running of the centres are not a substantial majority; they form only 76 per cent of the total respondents.

This kind of negative perception is very high for any e-service delivery programme in the country. Mostly it has to do with the public relations component of the B1 project and the officials responsible for propagating e-governance both at the city level and also at the state level. There is need for a rethink on the crucial aspect of an e-governance programme and a concerted campaign launched to dispel the wrong notions among the users.

Transparency

	No. of Respondents	*Per cent*
Yes	184	76.0
No	58	24.0
Total	242	100.0

Accountability

On the accountability factor, the respondents do not have as much a negative perception as is the case with transparency. Over 86 per cent of the respondents claimed that there is accountability in the functioning of the e-service centres while over 13 per cent replied in the negative. We have already noted that unless the levels of transparency and accountability are scaled up there would be a bleak future for any e-governance programme like the B1. The participating departments have to adapt themselves to the ever increasing expectations of the e-service users in terms of these two factors both on an individual and collective plane.

Accountability

	No. of Respondents	*Per cent*
Yes	209	86.4
No	33	13.6
Total	242	100.0

Responsiveness

Responsiveness of an e-governance project definitely elevates it in stature as well as popularity. Any number of studies on e-governance has concentrated on this key feature in eliciting the response of the users. The expectations of e-users are rising by the month and this reflected in major studies. Responsiveness here is to consumers' demand for more services, expansion of jurisdiction of e-service delivery centres, world class quality in the delivery of services and complaints and suggestions thereto. This attribute has to be very strong evoking a positive response to the scale of 95 per cent and above.

Bangalore One seems to be still evolving on the responsiveness front, with only 81 per cent of the total respondents reflecting positive signs. Almost one-fifth (19%) of the respondents have a negative perception towards the programme. Officials concerned with running this e-governance project have to take into account complaints and suggestions of the consumers by setting up separate cells.

Responsiveness

	No. of Respondents	*Per cent*
Yes	196	81.0
No	46	19.0
Total	242	100.0

Availability of Services

Bangalore One started with 24 services from 11 participating departments and is planning to include more and more services in its expansion phase. Services are being made available in a 24 × 7 model that includes Sundays (from 9 am to 3 pm). The project has not been scaled up when it comes to provision of services that are fundamental in nature. There is a deep dissatisfaction among the users of B1 on the availability of services at the centres. Over 32 per cent of the respondents were unhappy with the range of services that are being provided through B1. This is a significant minority and can't be wished by policy makers who are determined to scale up e-governance all over the country.

Availability of Services

	No. of Respondents	*Per cent*
Yes	164	67.8
No	78	32.2
Total	242	100.0

Only when the bouquet of services is wide and attractive can any service provider elicit maximum response and returns from the customers. Back up measures and front office management of customers on the question of availability of services has to be strengthened with due emphasis on adding services demanded by majority of the people.

Utility of Services

From the analysis of the above table it is clear that the availability of services is not up to e-governance standards and needs an urgent rectification. However, customers are availing the services of Bangalore One to the maximum extent. Nearly 90 per cent of the respondents claimed that they are utilizing the services on offer at B1 centres. However, more than 10 per cent said the present services do not have utility value. The utility factor needs to be scaled up to more than 95 per cent so as to make the services viable and amenable to the people.

Utility of Services

	No. of Respondents	*Per cent*
Yes	216	89.3
No	26	10.7
Total	242	100.0

Use of the Programme

That an e-governance model or an e-service delivery project has high quotient on the usability front needs no repetition. Fortunately, this has been the case with most of the e-governance programmes in the country including Bangalore One though it lacks inherent strength on certain key issues. Almost 97 per cent of the respondents said the programme is very useful while less than 3 per cent had doubts on its usability.

Use of the Programme

	No. of Respondents	*Per cent*
Yes	235	97.1
No	7	2.9
Total	242	100.0

The Time Factor

The time required to finish off or conclude a governmental transaction is the direct indicator of the success that e-governance models have achieved all over the world. In the previous traditional model of governance or administration redtapism and bureaucratic stubbornness on even matters of easy conclusions took a toll on the time of people doing business with the government. This traditional or fundamentalist approach of the departments and the officials manning them has undergone a radical change after the implementation of e-governance in the early years of this decade. Previously it would take not less than one day to conclude a transaction with the government. Over 53 per cent of the respondents agreed with this statement. At least 17 per cent of the respondents in the present study claimed that it used to take them even two days for a work to be done.

Time Taken for Services Before e-Governance Programme

	No. of Respondents	*Per cent*
1/2 Day	73	30.2
1 Day	129	53.3
2 Days	40	16.5
Total	242	100.0

Time Taken for Services Under e-Governance Programme

	No. of Respondents	*Per cent*
Within 10 Min	184	76.0
Within 30 Min	58	24.0
Total	242	100.0

Things have changed for the better under e-government modules. At least 76 per cent of the respondents claimed that they finish off their work at the B1 centres in less than 10 minutes while 24 per cent said it takes less than 30 minutes for them to conclude a transaction or a host of transactions. Since those claiming to be spending at least half hour at B1 centres constitute roughly one-fourths of the users, it is advisable to further bring down this time-frame so that customer satisfaction levels soar further.

Reduction in Costs

As is the case with time, citizens are particular on the money factor too. Expenditure on concluding government transactions is one thing that the law-abiding citizens hate very much, especially in this age of liberalization and globalization which has spawned a new awakening among the educated masses on where the moneys from the taxpayers go. The governments are

Money Spend Before e-Governance Programme

	No. of Respondents	*Per cent*
Rs. 25	32	13.2
Rs. 50	136	56.2
Rs. 100	74	30.6
Total	242	100.0

Money Spend Under e-Governance Programme

	No. of Respondents	*Per cent*
Rs. 15	206	85.1
Rs. 25	36	14.9
Total	242	100.0

increasingly trying to project transparency in budget formulation as well as allocation of funds.

Prior to the implementation of e-governance, over 56 per cent of the respondents were paying at least Rs. 50 while over 30 per cent claimed to incur Rs. 100 to conclude a governmental transaction. Only 13.2 per cent said the cost was less than Rs. 25.

With the advent of e-governance models, there has definitely been a huge dip in the expenditure of the utility bill-paying citizens. Under the Bangalore One project, the cost incurred by an individual for a governmental transaction has come down to a nominal Rs.15. Over 85 per cent of the respondents supported this view while nearly 15 per cent of the users pegged the cost at Rs. 25. Complex transactions require a lot of time to be done with and the expenditure incurred in the process in only a fraction of what the people used to spend earlier in a traditional governance module.

Overall Satisfaction

On the public satisfaction front, Bangalore One is yet to match other e-service delivery projects like e-Seva. Those really satisfied with the functioning of the B1 programme form only 69 per cent of the total respondents. This is relatively less as we see this scale in e-Seva project. Over 22 per cent of the users are satisfied though on a moderate scale. Less than 9 per cent of the respondents said their satisfaction levels are relatively low, but wanted drastic improvement in the services being provided through B1 centres.

Satisfaction

	No. of Respondents	*Per cent*
Highly Satisfied	167	69.0
Moderately Satisfied	54	22.3
Lowly Satisfied	21	8.7
Total	242	100.0

Though Bangalore One has brought in fundamental changes in the way the public service delivery systems function, it has not been able to live up to the high expectations of an enlightened citizenry. Though the usability and utility quotient of B1 programme was never in doubt, lack of adequate levels of transparency, responsiveness coupled with non-availability of services that are of fundamental value are the critical variables that need to scaled up as to make the e-service delivery project a comprehensive and wholesome one.

REFERENCES

1. Visit www.bmponline.org
2. Hasan, Fazlul, 1970, *Bangalore Through the Centuries*, Historical Publications.
3. Karnataka Vidhana Soudha is a historical landmark in the city of Bangalore. *Source:* www.flickr.com (accessed 2nd March 2007).
4. Sundara Rao, BN, 1985, *A History of Bangalore*, CSSR Publications.
5. Map of Bangalore City, Source: www.mapsofindia.com (accessed 2nd March 2007).
6. Pix of Infosys campus in Bangalore *Source*: www.econ.ucdavis.edu (accessed 2nd March 2007).
7. India's Foreign Trade: 2006-07 (April-March), A Ministry of Commerce, GoI Report.
8. Taeube, F., 2004, Culture, Innovation and Economic Development: The Case of South Indian ICT Cluster, www.intech.unu.edu (accessed 22nd February 2007).
9. www.genengnews.com (accessed 12th June 2007).
10. Satyavathi, (left) Director, Bangalore One and Jagannath, (2nd left) Regional Manager, CMS Computer exchange MoUs on December 20, 2004. J. Sathyanarayana, CEO, National Institute of Smart Government (right) is also seen. Source: *Business Line.*
11. A Bangalore One centre on the Airport Road.
12. For information on services, customers can log on to www.bangaloreone.gov.in.
13. Union Minister of State for External Affairs E. Ahmed inaugurating

regional passport office services at the Malleshwaram B1 centre in Bangalore on the 5th of June, 2006.

14. The sixteen B1 centres are located in the following areas: Air Port Road, Banashankari, HBR Layout, JP Nagar, Jayanagar, Kalasipalayam, Malleshwaram, Nagarabhavi, RT Nagar, Rajaji Nagar, Shanti Nagar, Tannery Road, Vijayanagar, Yeshwantpur, Shrirampuram, Infosys Campus.
15. A view of Bangalore One website (www.bangaloreone.gov.in).
16. The population of metropolitan Bangalore has been estimated at 6.8 million in the year 2002-03. Women make up 47.5 per cent of the total population in the city.
17. As per the 2002-03 studies, the literacy rate of Bangalore city is over 87 per cent. This is high for any Indian metropolitan city after Mumbai.
18. Census of India 2001.

AKSHAYA, MALAPPURAM, KERALA

India has been on the path of rapid development ever since it opened up its economy to the world in the early 1990s. Along with liberalization came new technologies which transformed the way public institutions functioned.[1] Many ICT for Development (ICT4D) programmes were launched in the country. The southern state of Kerala that has high literacy rate and better PQLI (Physical Quality of Life Indicators) standards[2] embraced the new pattern of development much later (in 2000) than the rest of the country, but has witnessed unprecedented success.

The Task Force on IT implementation in the government recommended that the state adopt a strategy of administrative reforms-based computerization simultaneously with highly visible and immediately implementable citizen interface projects.[3]

One such success project—as many have hailed it—is the grassroots people-oriented project launched in October 2002 called Akshaya, under the supervision of the State IT Mission. It was conceived originally to bridge the digital divide in Kerala and to act as a catalyst for socio-economic development. The project has established 630 multi-purpose community technology centres, each with 5-10 computers, in Malappuram District in North Kerala—a Muslim majority district. The Akshaya programme is now ready for a state-wide rollout, aiming at 6,000 centres, which would cover the whole state.[4]

About Malappuram

Malappuram is one of the 14 districts in the state of Kerala. Situated between the Nilgiris hills on the east and the Arabian Sea on the west, the district of Malappuram—literally the land atop the hills—is remarkable for its unique natural beauty. The district was formed in June 1969 amalgamating the distant and backward areas of the erstwhile Kozhikode, Perintalmanna and Ponnani taluks of Palakkad. In the north, it is bounded by Kozhikode and Wayanad districts and in the south, by Palakkad and Thrissur districts. The district has a geographical area of 3550 square kilometres which is 9.13 per cent of the total area of the state. With regard to area, Malappuram district ranks 3rd in the state. The total population of the district is 30.96 lakh (Male: 1,759,479 Female: 1,870,161).[5] While the density of population is 1022, the sex ratio is at 1063 females per 1000 males. Literacy rate is over 90 per cent (male 92% and female 86%) which is more or less the same for rural and urban areas. Muslims form the majority community in the district followed by Hindus and Christians. As per the latest data, here is a community-wise breakup: 24,84,576 (Muslim), 10,57,418 (Hindu) and 1, 75,495 (Christian).[6]

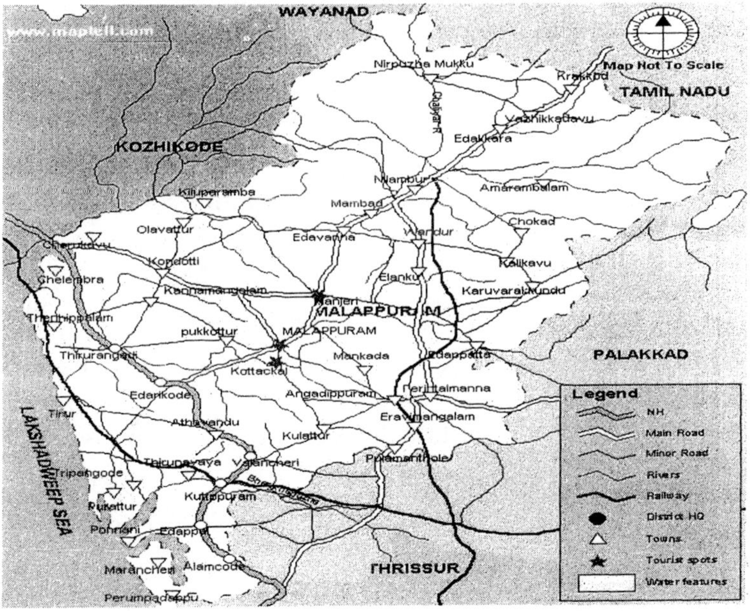

Area: 3350 sq km Population: 3.6 M Pop. Density: 1022 M/F Ratio: 1063
Literacy: 90.9% Decadal Growth: 9.42%
Household size: 5.3% Urban Pop: 9.7%

The district accounts for the largest number of emigrants (more than a fifth of the nearly 1.5 million Keralites) and receives about 17 per cent of the total external remittances to the state.[7] However, domestic commodity production is low and, in 2002-03, Malappuram's per capita income of Rs. 16,766 was the lowest among all districts in the state. The primary sector contributes 17.86 per cent of the district income, the secondary sector 19.90 per cent, and the tertiary sector, 62.24 per cent. 2.36 lakh educated unemployed are registered with various employment exchanges in the district.

Headquarters of the District Administration is at Malappuram with Collectorate and main offices in the Civil Station, established in the erstwhile headquarters of the Territorial Army. The district has two Revenue Divisions with headquarters at Perintalmanna and Tirur and 6 taluks, namely Eranad, Nilambur, Perintalmanna, Ponnani, Tirur and Tirurangadi.[8] The district has a coast line of 70 kms and the total forest cover is 1, 03,417 hectares, i.e., 28.47 per cent of the total geographical area. Four important rivers of Kerala flow through this district. They are: Chaliyar (Beypore) Kadalundipuzha, Bharathapuzha and Tirurpuzha.[9]

Background

The Akshaya project in the rural Malappuram District of Kerala is the first district-wide e-literacy project in India, and one of the largest known Internet Protocol (IP) based wireless networks. Through a test network of over 600 village telecentres, known as e-Centres, Akshaya has conducted one of the world's largest e-literacy drives, reaching to 600,000 households and representing more than 3.6 million people in less than a year from its launch in November 2002. The project has created a unique brand of state-funded computer access centres, and simultaneously led to a massive wireless infrastructure, providing a wide range of services and making way to many future opportunities.[10]

Planning

Entrepreneurs were selected by February 2003 and given training. Over the next few months, a number of Akshaya centres, sporting their blue logo, sprang up across Malappuram, one of the backward districts in terms of social and economic development in Kerala. Eventually, 634 Akshaya centres would be set up, it was planned. As per the project report of the Kerala IT Mission, each centre would entail an investment of Rs. 3.83 lakh for its 10 computers and other paraphernalia, plus working capital.

The government ensured the Akshaya project priority funding from banks and term loans to cover half the project cost were arranged. The project went on steam in May 2003, and by February 2004, over 5.80 lakh people in Malappuram knew how to log on to a computer, open a file, save it, surf the Internet and send e-mail. By then, the world took note of Malappuram.[11]

Approach to the Study

There have been many studies by reputable research organizations and academic institutions on the phenomenal success of the Akshaya programme. Many came out with interesting facts and figures entwined with the success story. However, the emphasis of this study has been not only on the positive aspects of the programme but also the overall impact it had on the perceptions and ethnic and cultural values of the dominant Muslim community of Malappuram, hitherto considered backward in all spheres of life compared to others in the rest of Kerala. The basic premise has been on the impact of the ICTs on society which implies the relative satisfaction of users or customers on the functioning of ICT tools in governance—plainly e-governance—in terms of transparency, accountability and responsiveness.[12]

Key Indicators of Good Governance

The process of economic liberalization brought in new concepts in public administration the world over. Previously, hard indicators such as resources and outputs were the norm to monitor performance. What is now called good governance was one of the key concepts that came to be accepted as *the* norm in sound financial management as well as in the smooth functioning of the economic system. Key factors like accountability and transparency were given added emphasis coupled with introduction of soft indicators like citizen and user satisfaction targets.

There is now an increasing demand for information on performance in relation to governance as a whole—which includes quality of life indicators. There have been ever growing concerns at the level of trust that the governments enjoy and the negative impact it has on government and on cohesion of society. It has now been established clearly that more trust and more satisfaction invariably result in good governance. It is by now clear that citizens' trust in government and user satisfaction are key indicators of good governance.[13]

In our study, key indicators like public awareness on the e-governance programmes, availability of services, their utility and usability, reduction in time and costs in the payment of utility bills have been factored in. These key indicators in totality reflect the realistic impact the Akshaya programme had on society which is a distinct composition of communities in Malappuram district.[14]

Technology: Impact on Society

It has been an accepted fact that technology is most effectively deployed in pursuit of some premeditated developmental plans rather than as an outcome itself. However, in many cases, technology is decided upon and then a development opportunity is sought to which it can be applied.[15] Very often, this leads to the deployment of inappropriate technologies, when simpler alternatives would have been more appropriate.

In fact, high technologies (ICTs) tend to deliver maximum output when they appropriated by the organization and the community to provide assistance with problem that they themselves have identified and sought solutions for, and project promoter should adopt measures, including education and awareness rising, to encourage this form of technology adoption to take place. This would inevitably result in success and this has been true in the case of the Akshaya programme that started off as a pilot project in Kerala.

Delivery of Services

Another major outcome has been the remarkable improvement in the delivery of services. Here again, the stress was on long-term sustainability of the e-services. Normally, community development projects that use ICTs will grow in effectiveness as the number and quality of information services that they provide grow. This has surely been the case with Akshaya. It is now offering a wide range of services including e-payment, e-krishi, e-governance, content development, computer-aided learning for students, exam online, business tie up, capacity building programmes to citizens, course programmes, mapping of natural resources, mainly water, GPS, connectivity and others.

Project Outcomes

The project has established the fact that the PPP model can be effectively mobilized to launch community programmes, helping to bridge the digital divide. A major part of the investment was borne by private entrepreneurs in establishing the centres. Local bodies too contributed towards the e-literacy programme. The state government spent about Rs. 3 crore for promotion and content development. The e-literacy programme targeted about 5.9 lakh people and nearly 35,000 were certified. The community, on the whole, accepted Akshaya kendras as centres for communication and e-literacy. The long-term sustainability of the project can be determined once the kendras are effectively networked with the provision of sufficient bandwidth.

Bureaucratic Acceptance and Adaptability

Besides the entrepreneurs and the centre staff, the Akshaya project has 20 permanent staff members (the total staff in the Akshaya centres is about 1890 – with an average of 3 persons per centre). A total of 105 Social Animators trained and positioned for the campaign period. Besides this, 25 persons are working permanently with the Internet Service Providers (ISPs). Nearly 40 companies/corporates operate through the Akshaya network and have positioned at least 50 persons on an average for coordination. All the policemen and personnel from the Kerala State Electricity Board and the Rural Development Department were trained in the programme. Also, over 100 teachers were trained in communication skills by the British Council. However, major part of the work at the Akshaya centres is carried out by the entrepreneurs who have been trained specially for the purpose.

Indian bureaucracy that is relatively new to the concept of good governance – or e-governance – has been struggling hard to come to terms with new ways of performance appraisal. Here the accent is on accountability and transparency that would directly translate into 'soft' indicators like satisfaction targets in the budget and citizens' satisfaction on the services provided. The key concept of transparency when put into action would mean that citizens' are hungry for more information and more openness on policy formulation and implementation. That would also mean increased participation of the stakeholders.

What has been unique in the case of Akshaya programme -- a pilot project – is that the entire district administration went out of its way to make it a huge success story. Traditional approaches hitherto dominant at the district level were set aside and the 20 permanent staff -- on deputation from various state government departments – put in their best efforts. The Town and Country Planning Department was tasked with identifying geographical locations. It chose 801 locations for community technology centres that were located on main/link roads with telephone connections and power supply. The centres were set up using private-public partnership (PPP) model and these were put under the supervision of ward implementation committees of panchayats and municipalities. The District Coordinator of Akshaya has a District Programme Officer (campaign) and an Assistant Mission Coordinator (implementation). There are 13 block level coordinators who have been appointed on contract and 100 panchayat coordinators who execute and monitor the project.

Despite such a favourable policy and administrative scenario, there are certain key issues that are yet to be addressed at the ground level. Resistance to introduction of new technologies has been witnessed profoundly at the panchayat level among staff belonging to key departments of the state government like revenue and agriculture. The lackluster performance of the e-krishi programme bears testimony to this fact. Officials and staff at the agriculture department strongly oppose this concept with the notion that entrepreneurs may misuse their position and make profits from online sale of farm produce. Revenue officials and staff too have similar concerns. They fear losing their traditional grip over the administrative process mainly related to clearance and movement of files. The traditional bureaucratic mindset is yet to attune itself to the ever changing facets of governance—in other words e-governance.

Community: Response and Participation

The major outcome of the introduction of new technology in the relatively less developed Malappuram District in Kerala has been the paradigm shift in the cultural and social ethos of various communities, notably the Muslim community. The Akshaya programme in its early phase of e-literacy brought profound changes in the attitude of the rural folk, in that it gave a good opportunity to the fairer sex to catch with the latest communication technologies. Previously, Malappuram district had high teledensity which was more than the national average. It lacked the infrastructure for providing Internet connectivity. Things moved at such a fast pace that not only the basic infrastructure was put in place but broad bandwidth was also made available to all the community technology centres (CTCs).

The literacy level in Malappuram is nearly 95 per cent, but it lags behind the other districts of Kerala in terms of key social indicators. Despite this, the people of the district showed remarkable temperament in waking up to the new technological challenge. The role of Kudumbashree members — about 4500 women — was crucial in mobilizing people for the e-literacy campaign.

It was clear at the outset that there was little or no enthusiasm for new technology among various communities and most of the people preferred enhanced allocation for education and health rather than investing in ICTs. The Muslim community which is traditionally conservative raised serious concerns, notably the abuse of computers and the Internet. Similarly, there was a staunch resistance from commercial, cooperative and rural banks to provide loans to entrepreneurs without collateral assurance. The state government took the initiative and provided budgetary support for the e-literacy campaign when the local bodies expressed their inability to set aside funds for the same.

Survey on the Impact of e-governance on Society — A Case Study of Malappuram, Kerala

The study we undertook covered 26 blocks in Malappuram district and the sample was selected randomly. The total number of respondents is 235-131 men (55.7% of the sample size) and 104 women (44.3%).

Sex

		No. of Respondents	Per cent
Male		131	55.7
Female		104	44.3
Total		235	100.0

The sample size covered all the age groups with emphasis on regular users of the ICT tools in governance—in the age groups between 21 and 50.

Age

		No. of Respondents	Per cent
Below 20		25	10.6
21-30		48	20.4
31-40		69	29.4
41-50		75	31.9
51 and Above		18	7.7
Total		235	100.0

Nearly 85 per cent of the respondents are literate and others fall under the category of illiterates are regular users.

Education

		No. of Respondents	Per cent
Upto SSC		67	28.5
Intermediate		49	20.9
Degree		65	27.7
Post Graduation		15	6.4
Other		4	1.7
Illiterate		35	14.9
Total		235	100.0

Interestingly, 49 per cent of the respondents are carrying on their occupation independently while only 22.1 per cent of them are in the agriculture sector.

Coming to awareness levels, nearly 99 per cent of them have either heard or regular users of e-services.

We shall now explain the response of the regular users in key terms or indicators that determine good governance, viz. transparency,

Occupation

	No. of Respondents	*Per cent*
Agriculture	52	22.1
Agriculture Labour	6	2.6
Non-Agriculture Labour	9	3.8
Government Service	13	5.5
Independent Occupation	115	48.9
Other	40	17.0
Total	235	100.0

Awareness

	No. of Respondents	*Per cent*
Heard	81	34.5
Not Heard	3	1.3
Heard and User	151	64.3
Total	235	100.0

accountability, responsiveness and reduction in time and costs in availing services from various departments of the government. These key determinants were chosen in accordance with the international standards in the study of governance models, notably after the introduction of ICT tools in the processes of administration and governance and their overall impact on society.

Previous studies have already established the huge success that the Akshaya project achieved in its pilot stage in Malappuram district. This study is an extension, but an important one in that it focused on the impact that new technologies make on culturally conservative communities. The major point here is that Malappuram is a relatively backward district in Kerala in terms of key social indicators, populated mainly by the Muslim community which by all means is the least developed section of Indian population only next to scheduled tribes.

Akshaya's success was mainly due to its positive impact on conservative groups hitherto not exposed to new information and communication technologies. The acceptance of the project was so comprehensive that within a few years of its introduction people from various sections began demanding more and more services from the e-kiosks—Akshaya centres or Community Technology

Centres (CTCs). Their enthusiastic response only reflects their growing levels of trust in e-governance models and trust comes from mainly from transparency, accountability and responsiveness in those models. The other key factor that determines the inevitability of good governance is the reduction of costs for users or customers in securing various services from both the public and private sectors.

Transparency

	No. of Respondents	*Per cent*
Yes	204	86.8
No	31	13.2
Total	235	100.0

In terms of transparency, Akshaya project scores very high over every other e-governance programme in the country. Nearly 87 per cent of the respondents—204 out of 235—vouched for transparency of the project while only 13 per cent of them are apprehensive. Their apprehension can be attributed mainly to strong and traditional ties with the administrative personnel at the block and panchayat level. While there should be no doubt on the levels of transparency in the project, it is to be noted that there are still people who demand physical proof for the work done and the transactions made.

The other major factor that determines the levels of trust among the customers or users of the ICT tools in governance is 'accountability'. The term is understood in different ways in various societies. Indian society lays major emphasis on trust and this comes mainly from accountability. Akshaya has set up high standards of accountability in its functioning at all levels. Over 87 per cent of the respondents—205 out of 235—said they believed in the accountability of the project while only 12.8 per cent of them still have some apprehensions as in the case of transparency of the project.

Accountability

	No. of Respondents	*Per cent*
Yes	205	87.2
No	30	12.8
Total	235	100.0

The PPP model adopted for the implementation of the project and the midway closure of some Akshaya centres for lack of viability seems to be the reason for this reluctance among people to believe in its accountability. Here we should understand their 98 per cent of the users pay their utility bills without caring for transparency or accountability. The overall accountability factor, well that needs to be established firmly not only by the administration but also the entrepreneurs.

Trust levels definitely improve with responsiveness on the part of the administrative model or process. E-governance is linked to three basic indicators—accountability, transparency and responsiveness. The last factor can be explained in terms of the ability of the e-governance programme to respond to the queries of the customers or users and provide instantaneous solutions. Akshaya has done a good job in this important sector with 79 per cent of the respondents confirming its responsive nature.

Responsiveness

	No. of Respondents	*Per cent*
Yes	185	78.7
No	50	21.3
Total	235	100.0

However, nearly one-fifth (21.3 %) people surveyed did not come out in favour. This is where the change managers should step in and they may include active citizens and officials determined to change the ways in which the administration functions.

Though Akshaya centres were established to cover each and every family in all the panchayats and municipalities of Malappuram district, it can be said that this goal is still distant one on account of geographical constraints. The district is unique in its geographical features with Arabian Sea on one side and the undulating Nilgiri hills on the other. Besides there are many natural streams and forests that make physical connectivity an arduous task. Each centre was to cover at least 5000 members of 1000 families and provide basic services. Lack of enthusiasm seen initially among the officials and entrepreneurs can be blamed for the incomprehensive penetration of services. Nearly 78 per cent of the respondents said services are being made available to them through Akshaya centres.

However, 22 per cent of the people surveyed said they are yet to avail the services and that they are very much eager to have services

Availability of Services

	No. of Respondents	Per cent
Yes	183	77.9
No	52	22.1
Total	235	100.0

delivered to them through community technology centres located in the vicinity of their residential area.

When the penetration of services is not up to the envisaged levels, naturally that is bound have its impact on the utility of services as well. Of the total 235 people surveyed 172 (73.2%) said they were utilizing the various services at the centres.

Utility of Services

	No. of Respondents	Per cent
Yes	172	73.2
No	63	26.8
Total	235	100.0

However, a substantial number of respondents (26.8%) replied in the negative. This has mainly to do with the connectivity levels of the centres and lack of awareness among the people on the various services on offer at the centres. This huge discrepancy in availability and utility of the services has to be plugged with a set time frame so as to make the project fully viable and replicable in other parts of the country.

Akshaya project since its e-literacy phase has involved a major proportion of the population which is evident in the use of the programme indicator. Nearly 229 of the 235 respondents—97.4 per cent of the total respondents—said they had used or using the programme in one way or the other.

Use of the Programme

	No. of Respondents	Per cent
Yes	229	97.4
No	6	2.6
Total	235	100.0

Only a miniscule per cent of the respondents (2.6%) said they had not used nor were using the programme. The success of the projects lies in its usability to a majority of the population targeted. The e-literacy drive covered almost 98 per cent of the targeted population and was instrumental in enhancing the capability of the people to use the latest information and communication technologies for various purposes. This aspect has to surely reflect in the utility of services as well. Unfortunately, this is not the case as we analyzed it in the previous indictor.

Reduction in time and costs is the most evidential form of any e-governance programme or project. Cuts in the amounts of time and money spent for availing various services from both the public and private sector determines the range of success of an e-governance model. Akshaya has been largely successful in reducing the timeframe required to conclude any transaction of the citizens with the government.

Time Taken for Services Before e-Governance Programme

	No. of Respondents	*Per cent*
1 Day	1	.4
2 Days	115	48.9
3 Days	119	50.6
Total	235	100.0

Previously, it took at least two to three days to finish the business with the government agencies. This was confirmed by almost all the respondents we surveyed (see the tables and charts below). After the introduction of services—e-services or online services—at the Akshaya centres, the time a user or a consumer spends to conclude a transaction or multiple transaction has come drastically to less than half hour (30 minutes). Normally, payment of utility bills and the related transactions take not more than 10 minutes. They are mostly done in a span of couple of minutes or within 10 minutes. More than 64 per cent of the respondents say it takes less than 10 minutes to pay utility bills at the Akshaya centres while 35 per cent of them say they finish their work within 30 minutes.

Time Taken for Services Under e-Governance Programme

	No. of Respondents	*Per cent*
Within 10 Min	151	64.3
Within 30 Min	84	35.7
Total	235	100.0

The Akshaya centres can improve their levels of delivery to the maximum if they adopt the model followed by Friends centres in all the district headquarters of Kerala. However, logistical problems remain as they were at the beginning of the programme. Only 10 computers are being maintained at present at the centres and these are mostly used for browsing and e-mailing, payment of examination fee and other educational purposes. The entrepreneur in most cases uses one or two terminals for governmental transactions.

There is also a dearth of capability among the staff privately employed at the centres to conclude such business. They are confined only to keeping the records and collection of money for using the terminal. In its outward presence, any Akshaya centre resembles to that of an Internet café. The Akshaya project authorities should try to give them a new and functional look of a utility centre.

Reduction in costs is another area where the project seems to have made a remarkable progress. This is evident in the responses of the people surveyed. More than 92 per cent of the respondents said they used to incur an expenditure of Rs. 50 to Rs. 100 for any transaction with the governmental agencies before the e-governance programme came into vogue. Nearly 5 per cent of them said it even cost them Rs. 500 for major transaction.

Money Spend Before e-Governance Programme

	No. of Respondents	*Per cent*
Rs. 25	6	2.6
Rs. 50	145	61.7
Rs. 100	72	30.6
Rs. 500	12	5.1
Total	235	100.0

This situation has changed substantially after the introduction of various services at the Akshaya centres. Nearly 45 per cent of the respondents said it is now costing them less than Rs. 15 to pay utility and other bills online at the centres while 34 per cent of them said the cost has come down to Rs. 25. Only 21.3 per cent of the respondents claim that they are spending Rs. 50 for availing e-services.

However, the cost can still be brought down to a minimum of Rs. 10 as is the case with the Friends Centres. The departments

Money Spend Under e-Governance Programme

	No. of Respondents	*Per cent*
Rs. 15	105	44.7
Rs. 25	80	34.0
Rs. 50	50	21.3
Total	235	100.0

involved with the e-project can adjust the costs so that the Akshaya entrepreneur does not lose on his income.

The perception of the people towards any e-governance programme or project hinges hugely on the level of trust it generates and on the overall level of satisfaction it inculcates among the users or customers in the delivery of services. People's faith in Akshaya programme has so far been comprehensive by and large and that needs to be expected in terms of satisfaction. Of the 235 users surveyed 156 (66.4%) say they are satisfied with the programme to a large extent while 52 of them (22.1%) say they are satisfied, but only moderately.

Satisfaction

	No. of Respondents	*Per cent*
Highly Satisfied	156	66.4
Moderately Satisfied	52	22.1
Lowly Satisfied	27	11.5
Total	235	100.0

There are at least 11.5 per cent of the respondents (27) who expressed lower levels of satisfaction with the e-governance project and the related services. Since one-thirds of the population is satisfied only on a moderate or lower level, a course correction process has to be initiated to streamline the services. The participating departments can evaluate their services individually and come out with a more comprehensive programme for service delivery to the users or customers.

REFERENCES

1. Heeks, R. "Building E-Governance for Development", i-Government Working Paper Series, Paper No. 11, 2001b, Institute of Development Policy and Management, University of Manchester. Available in http://www.man.ac.uk/idpm/idpm_dp.htm#ig
2. Physical Quality of Life Indicators like infant mortality (13%), female

literacy (87.86%), and life expectancy at birth for males (70.2) and females (76.6), are well above all-India levels. The Human Development Index for Kerala was 0.638 in 2001, as against the national figure of 0.472. Source: *Census of India* 2001, and *SRS Annual Reports*, Directorate of Economics and Statistics, Government of Kerala.

3. Department of Information Technology, Government of Kerala, *Task Force Report* (Department of Information Technology, Government of Kerala, 1999).
4. www.keralaitmission.org (accessed March 15th 2006).
5. Registrar General and Census Commissioner, India, National Census, 2001.
6. Govind, Biju, "Increase in Muslim Population in the State," *The Hindu*, September 23, 2004.
7. K.C. Zachariah; E.T. Mathew and S.I. Rajan, *Impact of Migration on Kerala's Economy and Society* (Working Paper No. 297, Centre for Development Studies, Thiruvananthapuram, 1999).
8. www.kerala.gov.in (accessed 12th March 2006).
9. www.mlp.kerala.gov.in/gen.htm (accessed 12th March 2006).
10. Joyojeet Pal, Sergiu Nedevschi, Rabin K. Patra, Eric A. Brewer, 2006, *A Multi-Disciplinary Approach to Shared Access Village Computing Initiatives: The Case of Akshaya.*
11. *Information and Communication Technologies for Development: A Comparative Analysis of Impacts and Costs from India*, 2004. A report for a project funded by Department of IT and Infosys Technologies.
12. See Methodology part.
13. Bouckaert, Geert & Van de Walle, Steven, 2003, Comparing measures of citizen trust and user satisfaction as indicators of good governance: difficulties in linking trust and satisfaction indicators, *International Review of Adminstrative Sciences.*
14. See introduction to the Akshaya Programme.
15. Harris, Roger and Arora, Rajesh, 2006, *Empowering the Poor: Information and Communications Technology for Governance and Poverty Reduction — A Study of Rural Development Projects in India*, UNDP-APDIP, Elsevier, 2006.

FAST, RELIABLE, INSTANT AND EFFECTIVE NETWORK FOR DISBURSEMENT OF SERVICES (FRIENDS), KERALA

Background

FRIENDS—Fast, Reliable, Instant and Efficient Network for Disbursement of Services—an integrated citizen-centric e-governance project, was started in 2000 in Thiruvananthapuram, the capital city of the state of Kerala. The chief motivating and implementing agency of this project is the Kerala State Department of Information Technology and the urban civic bodies played a major role in making the concept of e-services an instant success besides earning a wider popular support for it.

The FRIENDS centre or Janasevana Kendram (Janasevana means serving the people, Kendram means centre) is a one-stop integrated service delivery point. The aim of the project is to provide a single-window payment mechanism for government-to-citizen interaction. It envisages facilitating the collection of various payments pertaining to payees within specified area limits like corporation municipality etc. at a single centre. Every FRIENDS centre has multiple counters—normally between 10 and 20—and the payees can remit any payment at any counter. The customer/ client/ consumer will be given an acknowledgement note/receipt for the amount remitted at the FRIENDS centres.[1]

Planning

The FRIENDS project has been implemented by the Information Technology Department, Government of Kerala through the Information Technology Mission in collaboration with various departments like the Kerala State Electricity Board, Kerala Water Authority, BSNL, Revenue Department, Civil Supplies Department, Motor Vehicles Department, Universities and the Local Bodies of the State. Centre for Development of Imaging Technology (C-DIT),

Government of Kerala is the Total Solutions Provider (TSP) for the FRIENDS project. It started off as a pilot project in the capital city of Thiruvananthapuram in June 2000. Subsequent statewide rollout started in June 2001.[2] FRIENDS or "Fast, Reliable, Instant and Efficient Network for Disbursement of Services" was started in 2000 in Thiruvananthapuram by the Kerala State Department of Information Technology with the help of local bodies. On an average, 700 to 1000 people visit each centre every day.[3] Ever since the launch of the Friends project, the collection received through Friends centres has crossed Rs. 250 crore.

The unique features of the FRIENDS centres are the following:

- FRIENDS Janasevanakendram is a one-stop Service Centre where remittances can be done quickly and various other services received.
- The Centre works from 9 am to 7 pm (in two shifts) on all days including Sundays. The Centre will be closed on other public holidays including Second Saturdays.
- A computer controlled queue and token management system eliminates the queue and avoids long waiting time.
- Emphasis is given to provide a comfortable ambience to the public.
- There would also be help desks, which would provide information on the remittances.
- There would be a facility to record suggestions/complaints, which will be seriously reviewed on a regular basis and corrective actions taken.

FRIENDS centres are intended to function as per the principle of "Collect and Remit" and "Receive and Forward" methods and offer the following services:

1. Water Bills
2. Telephone Bills
3. Electricity charges
4. Payments to Civil Supplies Department
5. Payments to Revenue Department
6. Payments to Local Body
7. Payments to Motor Vehicles Department
8. Payments to Universities

Participating Departments[4]

Following are the state government departments that have widespread participation in the programme, mainly in terms of collection of revenue and disbursement of services:

- Kerala State Electricity Board (KSEB)
- Kerala Water Authority (KWA)
- Local Bodies
- Civil Supplies
- Revenue
- Motor Vehicles
- Universities
- Bharat Sanchar Nigam Limited (BSNL)[5]

FRIENDS Technical Structure

Every counter at FRIENDS has one Celeron 650 computer (10 GB hard disk, 64 MB RAM), one 80-column dot-matrix printer, one fake currency detector and one Queue Management System. The client terminal at the counter uses only Internet Explorer to browse software from the server and to send data to the server. Computers at the counter act as dumb terminals. They are linked into a LAN with the server. The server is a Pentium III (956 MHz, 26 MB RAM, 30 GB HD with RAD configuration). There is a backup server of almost the same configuration. There are three hard disks in the server, each of 9 GB, in RAD configuration for rebuilding the data if one of the hard disks crashes. The server uses Visual Basic at front end and SQL Server 7.0 for data bases. The software for the centres was developed with ASP, Windows 2000 and SQL RDBMS. One important feature is a provision for adding more modules and a queue management system. Client/server architecture, consisting of a network of one powerful server (Windows 2000 Server/MS SQL Server 7.0 - Pentium III 850 MHz or above) and 10 to 20 normal PCs (Windows 98/Me—Celeron 600 MHz or above), is used in each centre.[6]

Mode of Payment

Each Friends centre has 10 counters (only Thiruvananthapuram centre has 20 counters) to collect remittances from the general public. No user charges are charged from citizens. No service charge is collected from government departments for the services provided (only BSNL pays Rs. 6 per transaction service charge to the Government). All the payments are received in cash. There are no payments by Cheque or bank drafts, but credit cards are accepted.

Implementing Agency

The Kerala State IT Mission is the autonomous nodal IT implementation agency for the Department of IT, Government of Kerala which provides managerial support to the Department's various initiatives. Kerala State IT Mission is a team of professionals from the industry and the Government and is headed by the Director with the Secretary-IT as the Chairperson.

Technical Support

The entire technical support of FRIENDS is provided by the Centre for Development of Imaging Technology (C-DIT). The C-DIT is a Total Solution Provider in information technology for the Government of Kerala. It also functions as the southern regional video software production facility of the National Council for Science and Technology Communication (NCSTC), New Delhi. The Web Services, GIS, Video Communication, Animation, Educational Informatics and Optical Image Processing are some exclusive teams that offer a range of products and services in the fields of information communication technologies.

Institutional Arrangements

Each FRIENDS centre is managed by one Project Manager (PM) appointed by the Government from any of the participating departments (at Thiruvananthapuram there are two PMs). There are two System Administrators for each FRIENDS centre for two shifts. These are trained personnel brought on deputation from the Centre for Development of Imaging Technology (CDIT). There are 20 operators posted for 10 counters (53 in Thiruvananthapuram). They are designated as CSOs and are posted to FRIENDS on deputation from the participating departments. There are no accountants, clerks or peons in FRIENDS centres. The Project Manager reports directly to the Director, Kerala IT Mission, Thiruvananthapuram.[7]

Expansion

Following are the services that have been incorporated in Friends project since its inception:

- Collections relating to LIC
- Air India reservation re-confirmation system
- Introduction of Touch Screen facilities for dissemination of information to the public in all the 14 centres.[8]

Stakeholders

The major stakeholders include the State Government, the citizens, the employees of FRIENDS, participating public agencies/ departments and Kudumbasree units (self-help groups of women from below the poverty line who have undertaken some of the auxiliary data entry and related work for the centres). Government was able to provide better services to the citizens and also demonstrate the benefits of ICT tools in governance. Citizens now get better services at lower direct and indirect costs. Employees were deployed from participating departments with a common designation of Service Officer.

Costs and Benefits

The FRIENDS centre in Thiruvananthapuram required some INR 40 lakh worth of capital investment (including software). It was the pilot centre, and has 20 counters. The other centres in district headquarters, with an average of 10 counters, had an initial investment of Rs. 20 lakh each. The average monthly recurrent expenditure incurred by each centre comes to Rs. 60,000 to 70,000, which includes hardware maintenance charges and payments on account of rent, electricity, etc. These costs are borne centrally by the Department of IT. The salaries of service officers are an additional recurrent cost, covered by those government departments that collect payments at the centres. However, the Bharat Sanchar Nigam Limited (BSNL) does not provide staff at the centres. Instead, it provides a transaction payment of Rs. 5 BSNL-related transaction, giving an average monthly income for each centre of Rs. 150,000.

Photographs

Transactions at the Friends centre in Ernakulam, Kottayam and Thiruvananthapuram[9]

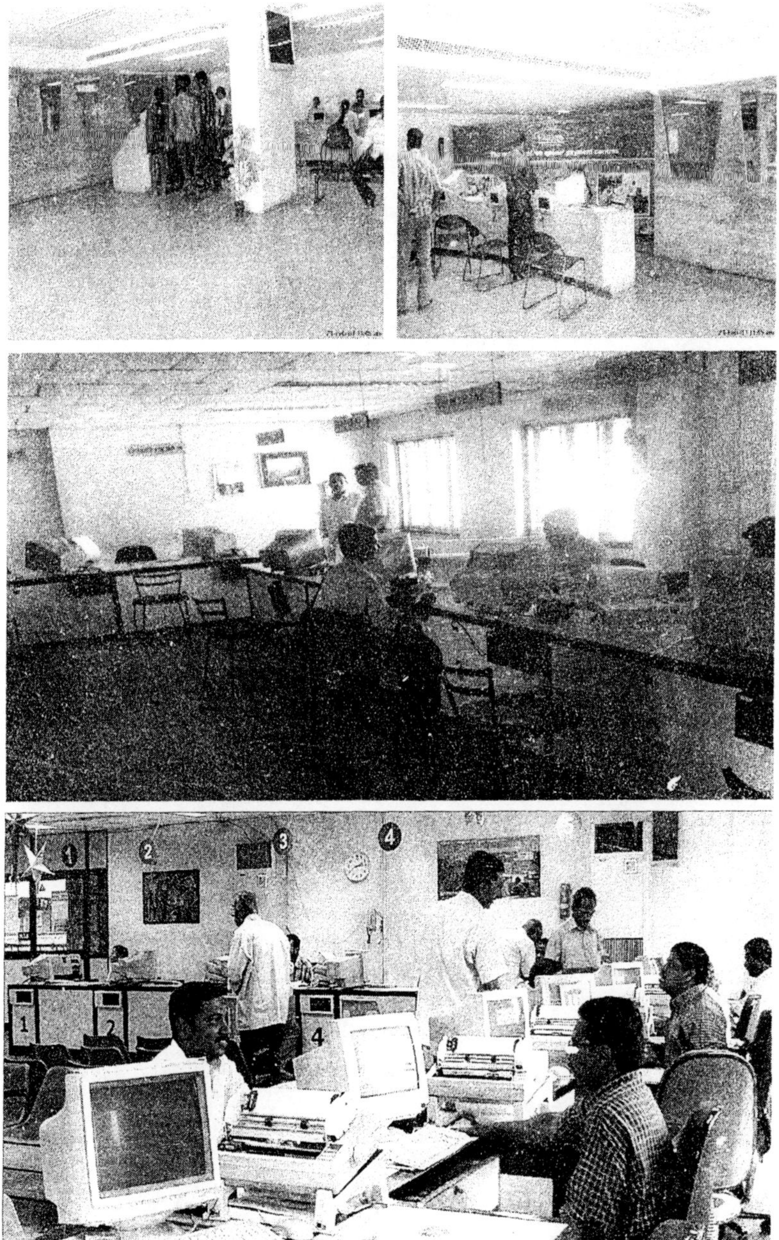

A normal scene at the Friends centre in Thiruvananthapuram. [10]

DET NORSKE VERITAS

MANAGEMENT SYSTEM CERTIFICATE

Certificate No: 03545-2006-AQ-BOM-UKAS

This is to certify that

FRIENDS JANASEVANA KENDRAM
(A PROJECT OF KERALA STATE IT MISSION)

at

Saphalyam Complex, Palayam, Thiruvananthapuram - 695 033, Kerala, INDIA

has been found to conform to the Quality Management System Standard:

ISO 9001:2000

This Certificate is valid for the following product or service ranges:

SERVICE OF COLLECTION OF RENT, RATES, DUTIES AND TAXES ON BEHALF OF GOVERNMENT DEPARTMENTS, PUBLIC SECTOR ORGANIZATIONS, ACCOUNTING AND TRANSFER OF COLLECTION TO CONCERNED ORGANIZATIONS

Initial Certification date:
2006-03-09

Place and date:
Chennai, 2006-03-09

This Certificate is valid until:
2009-03-09

for the Accredited Unit:
DNV CERTIFICATION B.V., THE NETHERLANDS

013

The audit has been performed under the supervision of:

Jetey Thomas
Lead Auditor

D.K.S. Moorthy
Management Representative

Lack of fulfilment of conditions as set out in the Appendix may render this Certificate invalid.

DNV CERTIFICATION B.V., [illegible], [illegible] Rotterdam, The Netherlands TEL INT: +31 10 [illegible], FAX: +31 [illegible]

11

Key Factors

Front-end First Approach

Back-end computerisation in government departments in countries like India faces major hurdles in the form of resources and procedural hassles. Many a project with back-end operations end up as stand alone projects due to socio-politico and economic factors. Consequently, citizens are forced to run from one agency to another to complete their transactions. FRIENDS had two critical factors that favoured it enormously. The first is the delivery of services without waiting for the completion of back-end computerisation. The second is the integration of service delivery through a single window despite severe opposition from various departments and employee organizations.

Participatory Model

Whereas the criticality of administrative reforms is not an issue to discuss here, it is important to focus on a reform strategy for delivering quick and high-visibility gains to all sections of society. FRIENDS has been successful in this aspect in that it evoked instant and tremendous response from the users. The very nature or design of the project is enough to ensure credibility for the use of information and communication technology tools in government.

Approach to the Study

There are quite a number of studies and surveys on the impact of the Friends project on society. They made interesting observations on delivery of services, public trust and satisfaction and the like.

However, the basic approach of our study has been on the overall impact Friends had on various sections of society and in various ways. The key issue that was given emphasis is the impact of the ICTs in governance which is the relative satisfaction of users or customers in terms of transparency, accountability, responsiveness and reduction in cost and time.[12]

On Delivery of Services

That an e-governance model improves delivery of services is a well established fact. Many a study has pointed out to this phenomenon. In our study, we looked at the nature of services provided and the response of the users on the various dimensions of those services, their levels of satisfaction and further expectations. Employing ICTs in any service delivery programme will only add more services to it in a progressive fashion. FRIENDS on a broader plane reflects this trend. It added the following services ever since its inception in 2000: collection of LIC premium, Air India reservation re-confirmation and installation of touch screens for dissemination of information.

Project Outcomes

There has been a tremendous development on the service delivery front with the setting up of FRIENDS centres in all the major cities and towns (district headquarters) of Kerala. The number of transactions is going up by the month. For instance, in the year from April 2002 to March 2003, nearly 232,000 transactions were carried out at Malappuram centre. There was a huge increase in the number of transactions with BSNL deciding to collect rentals through the centres. Though the number of services has increased over the years, users want more services to be included as well as extending the jurisdiction of the centres. Now utility bills are being collected only within the purview of the city or district headquarters. People want more centres in the major towns of all districts with a wider jurisdiction.

Survey on the Impact of e-Governance on Society: A Case Study of FRIENDS Project

We carried out the present study at FRIENDS centres in the districts of Kozhikode, Wayanad, Malappuram, Palakkad, Ernakulam, Kottayam and Thiruvananthapuram. Responses were elicited from a total of 232 users—159 male and 73 female falling in the age groups of under 20, 21-30, 31-40, 41-50 and 51 and above.

Sex

	No. of Respondents	*Per cent*
Male	159	68.5
Female	73	31.5
Total	232	100.0

A majority of the people surveyed are graduates—40 per cent—while only 3.4 per cent of the respondents (eight out of 232) are illiterates. This has to do with the high literacy rate in the state of Kerala.[13]

Age

	No. of Respondents	*Per cent*
Below 20	15	6.5
21-30	99	42.7
31-40	39	16.8
41-50	35	15.1
51 and above	44	19.0
Total	232	100.0

Education

	No. of Respondents	*Per cent*
Upto SSC	47	20.3
Intermediate	36	15.5
Degree	94	40.5
Post Graduation	15	6.5
Other	32	13.8
Illiterate	8	3.4
Total	232	100.0

Occupation

	No. of Respondents	*Per cent*
Agriculture	4	1.7
Agriculture Labour	1	.4
Non-Agriculture Labour	15	6.5
Government Service	44	19.0
Independent Occupation	123	53.0
Other	45	19.4
Total	232	100.0

Since all the Friends centres are either in major cities or district headquarters which are major towns, you can see a drastic change in the nature of the respondents' occupation. While a majority of the respondents is pursuing an independent occupation—53 per cent—only 2.1 per cent (5 of 232 that include 4 agriculturists and 1 farm labour) are in the farm sector. Those in the government service tally up to 19 per cent which again is the same for those pursuing other occupations.

Awareness

	No. of Respondents	Per cent
Heard	20	8.6
Not Heard	8	3.4
Heard and User	204	87.9
Total	232	100.0

As in the case of literacy and occupation, you can perceive a definite urban trend in the case of awareness on the e-services delivery project. Nearly 88 per cent of the respondents have heard about FRIENDS and are regular users of the services provided at the centres. Among the non-users—who form 12 per cent of the respondents—8.6 per cent are in the know of the services being provided by FRIENDS while only 3.4 per cent have not heard anything on the e-governance programme.

Transparency

	No. of Respondents	Per cent
Yes	178	76.7
No	54	23.3
Total	232	100.0

Unlike Akshaya programme, FRIENDS has not come out well on the transparency front. A whopping 23.3 per cent of those surveyed have responded negatively towards the project. Though 76.7 per cent of the respondents said there was transparency in the transactions done at the centres, it is clear that a sizeable section does not think so. This has to do with the basic concept of e-governance that lays strong emphasis on public-private partnership. In the case of FRIENDS, it is purely a state venture where officials (special officials including) are deputed from participating departments. As it is, there is a widespread negative feeling among people when it comes to levels of transparency in government departments and this is reflected in the present study.

Accountability

	No. of Respondents	Per cent
Yes	194	83.6
No	38	16.4
Total	232	100.0

Transparency and accountability compliment each other to the maximum extent. Nearly 16.4 per cent of the respondents said there is little or no accountability in the functioning of the e-service centres. This is a significant minority. However, majority of the respondents —83.6 per cent—sounded positively when the issue of accountability was raised. This is mainly due to widespread awareness among the people on the processes involved in the functioning of FRIENDS centres.

Responsiveness

	No. of Respondents	*Per cent*
Yes	169	72.8
No	63	27.2
Total	232	100.0

Bureaucratic underpinnings in the functioning of FRIENDS centres reflect themselves very strongly. The perception of nearly 27.2 per cent of the respondents is that officials manning the counters are utterly unresponsive. This critical factor can mar the further spread of the programme if ever attempted. Change in the nature of institutions to the positive side is essential for any e-governance model to be successful and replicable.

Availability of Services

	No. of Respondents	*Per cent*
Yes	142	61.2
No	90	38.8
Total	232	100.0

Utility of Services

	No. of Respondents	*Per cent*
Yes	191	82.3
No	41	17.7
Total	232	100.0

Use of the Programme

	No. of Respondents	*Per cent*
Yes	209	90.1
No	23	9.9
Total	232	100.0

While the usefulness of the project is very high—90 per cent of the respondents confirmed this—and the utility is also high at 82.3 per cent, it is necessary that all the major services be included under the project. This is clear as nearly 39 per cent of the respondents reported lack of availability of services at the centres. Simultaneously, the jurisdictional limits of the centres have to be expanded, a view expressed by most of the respondents.

Time Taken for Services Before e-Governance Programme

	No. of Respondents	*Per cent*
1/2 Day	72	31.0
1 Day	122	52.6
2 Days	38	16.4
Total	232	100.0

The scale of success of an e-governance project hinges largely upon the key factor of reduction in time and costs for the users in availing civic services. Prior to the introduction of FRIENDS programme it took almost a day for 52.6 per cent of the respondents to complete a governmental transaction while 31 per cent said the time-frame was half a day. To view this factor in its utmost severity, a look at the responses is necessary. Nearly 16.4 per cent of the respondents claimed that it took them two complete days to conclude a transaction at various government departments.

Time Taken for Services Under e-Governance Programme

	No. of Respondents	*Per cent*
Within 10 Min	174	75.0
Within 30 Min	58	25.0
Total	232	100.0

Things have changed for the better after the introduction of the e-services project. Nearly 75 per cent of those surveyed said they are now finishing their business at the centre within 10 minutes whereas it takes less than half hour for the remainder to get their work done. This is the most encouraging sign for the prospects of new e-governance models and projects not only in the well-educated state of Kerala but also in the entire country.

Comparatively there has been a huge reduction in costs for availing services after the establishment of e-service centres. The concept of single window service provision has been accepted largely

Money Spend Before e-Governance Programme

	No. of Respondents	*Per cent*
Rs. 25	41	17.7
Rs. 50	127	54.7
Rs. 100	64	27.6
Total	232	100.0

Money Spend Under e-Governance Programme

	No. of Respondents	*Per cent*
Rs. 15	190	81.9
Rs. 25	42	18.1
Total	232	100.0

by the citizenry since it saves a great deal of time, mostly to visit various departments that are located at different places. The average amount of money spent on travel and availing of services was Rs. 50 for nearly 54.7 per cent of the respondents earlier, which has now come down to only Rs. 15. A majority of the users—81.9 per cent—have confirmed this downslide in their expenditure after the introduction of e-services. More than 18.1 per cent claimed that they are spending up to Rs. 25 under the e-governance model. This cost can be further reduced or harmonized at Rs. 15, a view expressed by majority of the users.

Satisfaction

	No. of Respondents	*Per cent*
High	88	37.9
Moderate	86	37.1
Low	58	25.0
Total	232	100.0

The level of satisfaction among most of the users is positive only when it comes to few aspects like reduction in time and costs and the usefulness and utility of the e-services project. Only 75 per cent of respondents are satisfied either highly or moderately while the remaining 25 per cent have lower levels of satisfaction in availing services at FRIENDS centres. This is quite a disturbing scenario since the universal benchmark in this aspect has been plugged at more than 90 per cent.[14] Efforts have to be made to improve the overall satisfaction levels among the users by addressing the issues raised by them. A complete overhaul cannot be envisaged at this juncture, but a long-term correction course would surely help to boost the image and acceptance of e-services project like FRIENDS.

REFERENCES

1. www.friendscentre.net (accessed 13th January 2006).
2. www.keralaitmission.org (accessed 14th 2006).
3. This was the rough estimate given by the manager of the centre at Thiruvananthapuram in February 2007.
4. www.friendscentre.net (accessed 13th January 2006).
5. It is expected that more departments will join the project as it unfolds in the coming years.
6. Shirin, Madon; Kiran G.R., *Information Technology for Citizen-Government Interface, A Study of Friends Project in Kerala,* 2004.
7. Kerala IT Mission is the sole implementing agency of the Friends Project.
8. These services are yet to roll out at some of the centres in the state and a definite time-frame has not been set.
9. Photographs taken by the investigator on various field visits to Kerala.
10. Photograph downloaded from www.friendscentre.net (accessed 2nd November 2006).
11. ISO 9001:2000 certificate awarded to Friends centre, Thiruvananthapuram, at Chennai on 09.03.2006 (*Source:* www.friendscentre.net)
12. See Methodology part.
13. The literary rate of Kerala is 90.9 per cent as per the 2001 Census.
14. Most surveys at the international level have confirmed this standardization.

E-COLLECTORATE (DC* SUITE), PALAKKAD, KERALA

Background

Restructuring of administration began in right earnest in Kerala in the early 1990s with the State Government setting up an advisory committee with top and the whole process was termed "Modernizing Government Plan." The MGP was conceived as a comprehensive reform package for overhauling Government towards enhancing transparency, efficiency and effectiveness in delivery of services to citizens at all levels of administration. In implementing the scheme, the Kerala Government made a radical departure from the conventional, emphasis on results and outcome as against the usual emphasis on activity-based management.

Service Delivery Project (SDP) is one of the fast track projects under MGP to improve the quality of services delivered by Government to the people of Kerala, particularly the poor. DC* Suite is part of the Mission Mode Projects conceived by the National e-Governance Plan. National Informatics Centre is the implementing agency of this programme, which was inaugurated on the 24th of October 2004 by the then Chief Minister Oomen Chandy. The e-district project was conceptualized by the National e-Governance Plan (2006). It is currently spread over 30 districts across 17 Indian states. 20 pilot projects have been successfully implemented.[1]

Description

DC* Suite covers 22 functional areas of Collectorate, and includes electronic file management system, revenue recovery management, public grievance monitoring system, etc. Information is made available to public through touch screen kiosks, interactive voice response systems etc. The project highlights the concept of paperless office maintaining an effective networking of G2G, G2C, and G2E communication between and among the various governmental departments, public and the employees respectively. The architecture framework of the suite is divided into 'back office modules', 'middleware internet services' and e-Services (front end services)'. A communication network mode named 'Tappal' is adopted that gives lateral value addition to the entire system.[2] However, only three districts in the entire country had been recognized as model e-districts and they include Tiruvarur, Palakkad and West Godavari.

Genesis of the Project—The Tiruvarur Initiative

Tiruvarur, a riparian district in the Cauvery delta, was carved out of Thanjavur and Nagapattinam districts on 1 January 1997. Agriculture is the backbone of the economy in this district which has a population of about 1.1 million, and a very high level of poverty and associated backwardness. But this has not come in the way of e-Governance initiatives. The transformation from manual governance to e-Governance began in February 1999. The district did not receive any funds from the state budget for this initiative. A non-profit organization, District Welfare Committee was floated to mobilize funds worth Rs. 2.5 crore. The Members of State legislature (MLAs) and Members of Parliament (MPs) contributed nearly half the sum mentioned above from their Local Area Development funds. Four software development centres were set up in the District Collector's Office itself employing around 30 software professionals. The district also had ushered in a Wi-Fi revolution by setting up the first wireless LAN (on 802.11b standard) connecting all the 20 offices in 14 different locations.

The major beneficiaries were agriculturists, land owners, students, widows, agricultural labourers above 65 years of age, schools, local body population, rural population, and people benefiting from social welfare schemes.

To educate the citizens on online services, a special campaign was organized in the year 2000. The promise was that the services would be provided within a maximum of 2 hours, including enquiry time, if any, and that no paper would be used in the whole exercise. In 2000, Tiruvarur conducted its first online annual audit of village accounts. In February 2001, an online data warehouse containing all local land records, as well as information for the public on the old age pension scheme, cultivation and harvest details, and other data were developed. Krishnagiri district in Tamil Nadu is also taking steps to become the first comprehensive e-district in the country.[3]

Scope of the Project

DC* Suite is one of the joint initiatives from NIC and NICSI for application integration and providing web enabled services to empower employees and public. The concept of e-District is a subset of the broader area of e-Governance. It is the application of technology in e-Governance from the district level downwards since 90 per cent of services are delivered at the local/district level. Starting with the Tiruvarur (Tamil Nadu) initiative in June 1999, there have been a number of e-District programmes that have been implemented in different states of the country like Gyandoot in Dhar District of MP, Fatehabad District in Haryana, Community Information Centres (CIC) project in the north-eastern states, etc. The village of Bellandur on the outskirts of Bangalore is credited with being the first gram panchayat to introduce e-Governance.[4]

The reasons for implementing the project as part of the NeGP (2003) include:

- Districts are the primary delivery channel for Government Administration and electronic delivery of large number of services at the district level would greatly improve the quality of life of the citizens.
- Significant improvement in delivery of Government services by integrating other e-Governance initiatives by different departments (Land records, Property Registration, Agriculture, Passport, Police, etc.) could also occur.
- Establishing a Multi-Disciplinary centre for information accessibility for capacity building of the district administrative processes would also be created.
- Formulation of strategies for creating a Central data repository at the district level for all associate activities for improving district administrative processes by ensuring data and information are collected, stored, retrieved, used and exchanged in an efficient manner at all levels from 'top to bottom.'
- Support and integration of the e-Governance initiatives by Government of India such as Common Service Centres (CSCs) and Statewide Area Networks (SWAN).

Objectives of the e-district Project Include

- Implementation of an efficient electronic workflow system for District Administration
- Backend computerization of the core services provided through the district administration
- To redesign the processes for the core services to deliver them through the common service centres
- Infusion of transparency and accountability in operations
- Fast processing of public cases/appeals/grievances. Dissemination of information as per public requirements.

As part of the project, 22 key services provided through the District Administration have been taken up. These include:

- Public Grievance Redressal/Right to information
- Computerization of the ration cards
- Issuance of Birth/Death Certificates
- Issuance of Domicile certificate/ Caste Certification
- Electronic Payment collection for Bills/Government Dues
- Computerization of the Rural Employment Guarantee Scheme
- Computerization of Old Age pension
- Computerization of Arms license Issuance process
- Recovery Certificates
- Government Entitlements
- e-Filing
- Infrastructure Management
- Employees Database
- Computerization of Revenue Court Cases

The list of departments that have been included for designing and implementing the e-district model include:

- Registration Department
- Land Records Department
- Health Programmes
- Police
- Transport
- Agriculture

Technologies Used

The software is developed using Open Software Technologies LAMP. The applications, which are of public interest, will be given access through INTERNET, IVRS and Touch Screens based Kiosks using

standard software and web interfaces. DC* Suite is developed in Linux-Apache-MySQL-PHP (LAMP).

The project has made a good beginning in the e-Governance era reaching the grassroot level. The data centre established in the Collectorate has to offer many more services to the citizens through Internet, counters, SMS, IVRS, touch screens etc. It is only question of time for the next phases of the project to get completed, reaching the villages and panchayats through the wired and wireless modes, which is going to make revolution in the country.

e-Services layer is the front-end layer of DC* Suite which interacts with citizens and offer services to the citizens. There are several methods proposed in DC* Suite. The services are offered over touch screen kiosks, interactive voice response system, Internet and front-end counters. The first level proposal connects all taluks to the Collectorate and all other government departments through dial-up facility.

Middle layer is the Internet services layer, which offers lot of collaboration services and tools. E-mail, messaging, chat video conferencing, bullet in boards are a few worth mentioning.

Back office layer is the key functional area comprising of all 21 functional modules with which the government staff will work and carry out the backend operations.

IT infrastructure layer comprising of the data centre, terminal for each staff, academy hall, computer hall, VC hall etc.

Risk Management

Power Failure

Additional UPS is given and server with redundant power supply is used.

Hardware Failure

Standby server is provided with automatic scheduling of transaction log to the backup server

Database Crash/System Crash

Standby server is provided with automatic scheduling of transaction log to the backup server. Backup is taken to external media in a well defined backup plan.

Primary Access Points

Kiosks have been set up at the District Collectorate besides some select taluk headquarters (Ottapalam and Ponnani).

Constraints and Challenges

Though full scale automation has been achieved at the District Collectorate, a comprehensive integrated network that connects the DC* Suite with other offices at the headquarters has not been put in place. For instance, if a citizen files a complaint regarding law and

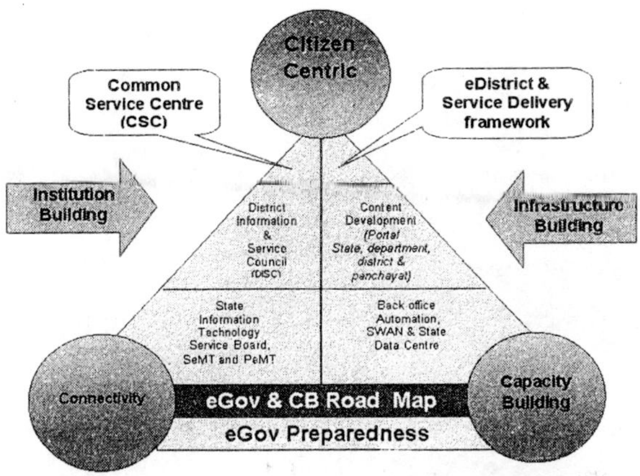

order issues, his case is sent to the District Superintendent of Police Office manually. This often results in undue delay in informing the complainant on the status of his file. Also, a full scale network that integrates all the talukas up to the panchayat level is yet to be developed. Such a network is in the realm of possibility in Malappuram District where Akshaya centres are omnipotent in every panchayat and in every village. The full potential of an automated Collectorate at Palakkad has not been achieved as the district lacks an entrenched network—up to the panchayat level. And, that is also the reason for the lower levels of satisfaction among the users of the services.

Scaling Up

Presently, the project is under implementation in Kasargod, Malappuram, Ernakulam, Thrissur, Kozhikode and Kottayam and will gradually be extended to all the districts in the state. DC* Suite Version 5.0, Collaborative open source software was released by K. S. Srinivasan IAS, District Collector, Palakkad on the 4th of October 2007. A customized version of DC* Suite, named MESSAGE, is now implemented in government secretariat.

In the month of September 2007, the Union Government under the National e-Governance Programme has granted Rs. 5 crore each to the districts of Kannur and Pathanamthitta for implementing the e-district project. There is still scope for improving the automation process further considering the lessons learnt from the Palakkad experience.

Project Outcomes

There has been a considerable reduction in time and costs for availing services at the Collectorate. The biggest beneficiaries are the farmers who now have tremendous access to information and services regarding agriculture and agricultural practices. Social and economic development schemes and the related information and literature are in the public domain as never before. The National Rural Employment Guarantee scheme is the best illustration for this.

About Palakkad District

Palakkad is one of the fourteen districts of Kerala. Its geographical position, historical background, rural natural, educational status,

tourist attractions and above all, the developmental activities that are carried out, are wide and varied. This district, situated almost in the centre of State, has no coastal line. The district opens the State to the rest of the country through the Palakkad gap. Bharathappuzha, the longest river in Kerala, originates from the highlands and flows through the entire district.

The district is one of the main granaries of Kerala and its economy is primarily agricultural. Agriculture engages more than 65 per cent of the workers and 88.9 per cent of the district's population is rural in nature. The proximity and easy approach to Tamil Nadu have caused the admixture of Malayalam and Tamil culture, here. Palakkad is part of the erstwhile Malabar district of Madras Presidency. There are five taluks, 163 villages, four Municipal towns and ninety Panchayats in the district. The district is divided into 13 Community Development Blocks for the effective implementation of various development activities.

Location

Palakkad district is situated in the South West Coast of India, bounded on the North by Malappuram in the East by Coimbatore of Tamilnadu, in the South by Thrissur and in the West by Thrissur and Malappuram districts. It lies between 10'21 and 11'14 North latitude and 76'02 and 76'54 East longitude. The total geographical area of the district is 4480 sq.km representing 11.53 per cent of the State's geographical area. The forest land per cent covers 136257 hectares. The Western Ghats has an average altitude of 5000 ft. except for two peaks of more than 6000 ft. The important peaks above an altitude of 4000 ft. are Anginda (7628 ft.), Karimala (6556 ft.), Nellikotta or Padagiri (5200 ft.) and Karimala Gopuram (4721 ft.)

Population

According to the 2001 census the population of the district is 26,17,072. The density of the population is 584 per sq. km. Decadal growth rate for the period 1991-2001 is 9.86 per cent in comparison with the State figures of + 9.42 per cent. The sex ratio of the district is 1068 females for 1000 males. The district has achieved over 85 per cent literacy in 2004.[11]

Administration

The present Palakkad district, as an administrative unit, was formed on the 1st of January 1957, comprising of Palakkad, Perinthalmanna, Ponnani, Ottappalam, Alathur and Chittur. When the Malappuram district was formed on the 16th of June 1969, Ponnani taluk excluding Thrithala firka and the villages of Vadakkekad, Punnayur and Punnayurkulam and Perinthalmanna taluk consisting of Mankada *firka* and Perinthalmanna *firka* excluding Karkidamkunnu and Chethalloor were transferred to Malappuram district. At present, the district consists of two revenue divisions, five taluks and 163 villages. The revenue divisions are Palakkad and Ottappalam. Palakkad, Alathur and Chittur taluks form the Palakkad revenue division and Ottappalam and Mannarghat taluks form the Ottappalam revenue division. There are 13 development blocks and 90 panchayats in the district. The total area of the district is 4480 Sq. km.

Basic Statistics

1.	Taluks	5
2.	C.D Block	13
3.	Municipalities	4
4.	Corporations	—
5.	Panchayats	90
6.	Revenue Villages	163
7.	Parliamentary Constituencies	2
8.	Assembly Constituencies	11
9.	District Panchayats	1
10.	District Panchayats Constituencies	26
11.	Block Panchayats	13
12.	Block Panchayats Constituencies	141
13.	Gram Panchayats	90
14.	Municipal Councils	4
15.	Total Population	2617072 (male 1265794 and female 1351278)[12]
16.	Literacy	85%

Survey on the Impact of e-Governance on Society: A Case Study of e-Collectorate, Palakkad, Kerala

Sex

		Frequency	*Per cent*
Valid	Male	175	73.2
	Female	64	26.8
	Total	239	100.0

We carried out the study on the impact of automated services at the district Collectorate, referred to as DC* Suite in the Palakkad district of Kerala. Responses were elicited from a total of 239 persons both from the rural and urban areas of the district and who are the users of e-Collectorate[13] services. Of the total respondents, 175 are male and 64 are female—73 and 27 per cent respectively.

Age

		Frequency	*Per cent*
Valid	Below 20	24	10.0
	21-30	66	27.6
	31-40	62	25.9
	41-50	60	25.1
	51 and above	27	11.3
	Total	239	100.0

The respondents fall in the age groups of below 20, 21-30, 31-40, 41-50 and 51 and above. However, those falling in the age groups of 21-30, 31-40 and 41-50 form the majority of users of the e-Collectorate services—above 78 per cent of the total respondents.

Education

		Frequency	*Per cent*
Valid	Upto SSC	67	28.0
	Intermediate	75	31.4
	Degree	64	26.8
	Post Graduation	12	5.0
	Illiterate	21	8.8
	Total	239	100.0

Though Kerala as a state boasts of literacy levels as high as 95 per cent (the districts with highest literacy rate in 2001 – Kottayam (95.82 per cent), Pathanamthitta (94.84 per cent) and Alappuzha (93.43 per cent) Palakkad is one of the districts with lowest levels of literacy which is 85 per cent [14] However, there has been a phenomenal growth in the following three years and the 2004 estimates suggest that the literacy rate in Palakkad is more or less 90 per cent. This is evident from our classification of the respondents at the e-Collectorate. Only 9 per cent of the users said they are illiterate while nearly 60 per cent of them have completed either Secondary School Certificate course or Plus Two. As many as 76 of the total 239 respondents claimed they are either graduates or post-graduates. This group represents 31 per cent of the sample size.

Occupation

		Frequency	*Per cent*
Valid	Agriculture	63	26.4
	Agriculture Labour	28	11.7
	Non-Agriculture Labour	13	5.4
	Government Service	38	15.9
	Independent Occupation	65	27.2
	Other	32	13.4
	Total	239	100.0

As we mentioned in the introductory part to Palakkad, the district is predominantly dependent on agriculture. As such, 38 per cent of the total respondents are directly related to that field. Those pursuing an independent are also significant in number and represent over 27 per cent of the sample size. Nearly 16 per cent of the people we surveyed are into government service and only 5 per cent said they are into non-agriculture services. Those pursuing other occupation form 13 per cent of the sample size.

Awareness

		Frequency	*Per cent*
Valid	Heard	30	12.6
	Not Heard	18	7.5
	Heard and User	191	79.9
	Total	239	100.0

As reflected in the literacy levels, the people of Palakkad district are quite consciousness about various developmental activities, including delivery of citizen services online. It is little wonder then that only 7.5 per cent of the respondents replied in the negative when questioned on the availability of electronic services at the district Collectorate. Of the remaining 92.5 per cent of respondents who have heard about e-Collectorate, nearly 80 per cent claimed they either availed or are availing electronic services. This suggests a majority of the people in the district are availing automated services at the Collectorate which in turn points out to the popularity of electronic governance services among the masses with high levels of literacy and general awareness.

Transparency

		Frequency	*Per cent*
Valid	Yes	190	79.5
	No	49	20.5
	Total	239	100.0

Normally, electronic delivery of citizen services is synonymous with transparency in administration. However, it is surprising to note that a little over 20 per cent of the respondents do not see any transparency in the automated services at the Palakkad Collectorate. This is quite a high level of mistrust for any e-governance programme. One comforting factor is that a little less than 80 per cent of the respondents believe in the transparency of DC* Suite services. There are a lot of reasons for this, but the major one is the traditional distrust of the masses from the rural areas on the modus operandi of district level officials at the Collectorate. A campaign to create more awareness among prospective users will help a great deal in removing any such misconceptions on transparency in the delivery of electronic services.

Accountability

		Frequency	*Per cent*
Valid	Yes	216	90.4
	No	23	9.6
	Total	239	100.0

There seems to be quite a contrast in peoples' perception on the levels of accountability in the DC* Suite programme. Of the 239 surveyed, over 90 per cent (216) believe there is either accountability or the programme appears accountable. Less than 10 per cent of the respondents believe there is little or no accountability in the e-district project services. While automated services appear to be accountable the same cannot be said the back-end processes involved in them.

Responsiveness

		Frequency	*Per cent*
Valid	Yes	219	91.6
	No	20	8.4
	Total	239	100.0

Responsiveness is one positive aspect of e-governance and is considered to be the driving force for many an e-governance project. When questioned on the levels of responsiveness in the e-Collectorate programme, over 91 per cent of the respondents replied in the affirmative and a little over 8 per cent of them feel there is no responsiveness in the delivery of automated services.

Availability of Services

		Frequency	*Per cent*
Valid	Yes	216	90.4
	No	23	9.6
	Total	239	100.0

A majority of the population in Palakkad district is rural and sustains on agriculture. DC* Suite services are those than can be availed only at the Collectorate or at the taluka level that has a similar suite, for instance, Ottapalam. Over 90 per cent of the respondents claimed services are available at the Collectorate while less than 10 per cent said there are no services that can be availed. This in fact is the result of selective automation of services.

As is the case with the availability of e-district services, there seems to be considerable hitches in the utilization of services. Not all services are included in the DC* Suite and this reflects clearly in the perception of the respondents. Their utility of services stands at 87.4 per cent while over 12 per cent claim to have not utilized or utilizing services at the district Collectorate. Unless the automated

Utility of Services

		Frequency	*Per cent*
Valid	Yes	209	87.4
	No	30	12.6
	Total	239	100.0

services are all encompassing and made available at the taluk and panchayat level, their utility may not go up. Currently, only a few taluks (Ottapalam and Ponnani) have taluk suites.

Use of the Programme

		Frequency	*Per cent*
Valid	Yes	233	97.5
	No	6	2.5
	Total	239	100.0

As mentioned earlier, Palakkad district has high levels of literacy and people here are aware on e-governance programmes. Over 97 per cent of the respondents believe DC* Suite is very useful and probably will expand further down to the Local Self Government (LSG) level. A negligible per cent of the respondents—2.5 per cent—has a negative opinion on the programme which they believe is of no use to them.

Time Taken for Services Berfore E-Governance Programme

		Frequency	*Per cent*
Valid	1 Week	27	11.3
	1 Month	127	53.1
	3-6 Months	85	35.6
	Total	239	100.0

That cases or files pending at the district level offices move at a snail pace is still an accepted reality, especially by those hailing from rural areas for reasons of accessibility and influencing power. There has been a considerable improvement in this situation after the implementation of e-governance programmes. Previously, the people of Palakkad used to wait for 3 to 6 months to get their files cleared at the collector's office. This was confirmed by over 35 per cent of the respondents. This may well be due to the complex nature of their cases. A majority of the respondents—53 per cent of the sample size—claimed they had to wait for at least a month to get their work done. A little more than 11 per cent of the respondents said it used to take a week for them to get their files cleared.

Time Taken for Services Under E-Governance Programme

		Frequency	*Per cent*
Valid	Within 1 Week	14	5.9
	Within 2 Week	58	24.3
	Within 1 Month	116	48.5
	Within 3 Months	51	21.3
	Total	239	100.0

With the introduction of DC* Suite services, the timeframe for clearance of files has reduced gradually to almost a half of what it used to be earlier. The range of six months has got down to three months with the average still being a month/fortnight. Over 21 per cent of the respondents said the average time they spend on this venture is less than three months. Almost half of the respondents—48.5 per cent to the precise—said the timeframe is less than a month. Those getting their work done within a fortnight represent more than 24 per cent of the respondents. Only less than six per cent of the respondents claimed it takes less than a week for getting their work done.

Money Spent Before E-Governance Programme

		Frequency	*Per cent*
Valid	Rs. 50 to Rs. 100	39	16.3
	Rs. 101 to Rs. 200	121	50.6
	Rs. 200 and Above	79	33.1
	Total	239	100.0

Expenditure for getting work done at the District Collector's Office was always on the high side, specifically in a district like Palakkad which is predominantly rural. Even after the implementation of automated services, there is only a marginal decrease in the costs for the citizens. Previously, people in the district used to incur an expenditure ranging from Rs. 100 to 200 and also above it. Over 33 per cent of the respondents claimed to have spent more than Rs. 200 for work at the Collectorate and over 50 per cent pegged the costs between Rs. 100 to 200.

Money Spent After E-Governance Programme

		Frequency	*Per cent*
Valid	Rs. 50	42	17.6
	Rs. 51 to Rs. 100	133	55.6
	Rs. 100 to Rs. 200	64	26.8
	Total	239	100.0

After the inauguration of DC* Suite services, the costs have down to less than Rs. 200 and more than Rs. 50. Nearly 27 per cent of the respondents say they are spending anywhere between Rs. 100 to 200 for their work while over 55 per cent claim to be spending between Rs. 51 to 100. This range (Rs. 51 to 100) appears to be the normal one in Palakkad. Those spending less than Rs. 50 represent more than 17 per cent of the respondents. Costs for availing automated services can be brought down to as low as Rs.25 if all the taluks have a DC* Suite modules. The expenditure can further be reduced to Rs. 10 if the services are extended to the grassroots level.

Satisfaction

		Frequency	*Per cent*
Valid	High	43	18.0
	Moderate	77	32.2
	Low	119	49.8
	Total	239	100.0

Time and costs have a lot of bearing on the peoples' perception of an e-governance project. Though services are automated they still have to put in lot of efforts to reach either the Collectorate or the taluk suite. The timeframe and the costs involved in availing services at the District Collector's Office more or less remain the same. This should not be the case with any mechanism that delivers citizens' services online. Further, the DC* Suite has to incorporate all the basic services, especially those catering to the rural masses. On the satisfaction front, the e-district programme suffers poorly only on account of the problems listed above. Almost half of the respondents (49.8%) said there is nothing to feel satisfied about DC* Suite services while the remainder has a moderate/high levels of satisfaction. Those feeling totally satisfied with the automated services represent 18 per cent of the respondents while 32 per cent are moderately satisfied.

REFERENCES

1. Modernizing Government Programme (MGP) Document, Government of Kerala, 2005-06.
2. www.palakkad.nic.in (accessed 12th January 2007).
3. Move afoot to make Krishnagiri first e-district in the country, 11th Nov 2006, *The Hindu*.
4. E-district: The Emerging Future, *ICTD Project Newsletter*, January 2007.
5. A sectional view of the fully automated district collectorate in Palakkad.
6. A public kiosk at the Palakkad Collectorate.
7. Graphical illustration of integrated network delivering citizen services at the district level.
8. Ottapalam taluk suite.
9. Palakkad district map.
10. A view of the Palakkad Fort.
11. Palakkad is backward in terms of literacy rate in Kerala state where the average literacy ranges between 95 to 91 per cent.
12. As per the 2001 Census figures.
13. The term e-Collectorate is synonymous with DC* Suite and e-district and there should be no confusion on their usage.
14. As per the 2001 Census.

4

Conclusion

The dynamics of public administration in India have altered drastically with the introduction of e-governance as a guiding concept in the late 1980s. Citizens, the world over, have been demanding smaller, effective and responsive governments, obviously inspired by the unprecedented and rapid success of finance capital in the global market. Consequently, policy makers began the search for smaller and efficient governments. On an evolutionary plane, reengineering of service systems, performance management, transparency in government operations, down sizing or right sizing the government workforce, emphasis on delivery of reliable and quick public services and ultimately citizen satisfaction came to be considered as benchmarks by most of the administrators. Quick decision-making, data-based planning, effective implementation through quantitative techniques seemed to have clinched the issue. This reformative pattern was no different in the Indian context, where the governments at the federal and state levels were in search of new techniques and technologies.

Information technology is very useful in reinvigorating the government/administrative systems by enhancing their capacity and efficiency. The potential and scope for application of IT in governing processes and transactions are enormous. E-government can transform traditional administrative systems through employment of information and communication technologies. A governance system that is committed to working with civil society, and by extension, private industry in a transparent and accountable way to reduce poverty, redress imbalances in access to resources, foster security and uphold social, economic, cultural, civil and political rights is the ultimate objective of e-governance theory. In practice, much depends on the collaboration patterns that the governments seek to establish.

E-Governance practices in India emerged and evolved mainly from native intuition, but under prescription for lesser and transparent government by international financial institutions, mainly the World Bank and the International Monetary Fund. However, the range of success of e-governance initiatives has not been uniform. The bottom-up demand for delivery of electronic services was bleak initially, but the change in public perception was for the better with the governments roping in private industry and service-oriented organizations gradually.

PPP Model

The Public-Private Partnership (PPP) model as is construed normally in a world that is fast witnessing globalization of all businesses and administrative trends, especially in the realm of e-governance, involves features such lesser government investment in electronic delivery of public services, collaboration in conceptualizing, designing and implementing the e-governance projects besides increased participation of stakeholders—both private and public—to saturate the levels and the reach of such projects. India is no exception to the general rule dictating PPP mode in e-governance.

The unprecedented success of e-governance in India can be rightly established with path-breaking e-governance models in the states of Andhra Pradesh, Karnataka and Kerala. These projects not only caused a jump in revenue collections of the two state governments, but also timely payment by the citizens. Time and costs for availing public services have come down drastically bringing in a positive change in peoples' perception of e-governance theory and practice. This holds equally true for both the rural and urban populace. The result of all these radical changes in public administration systems is the enhanced satisfaction level of the citizenry on delivery of public services and simplification of governmental procedures.

The development of network-based distributed systems that serve numerous and diverse constituents and improve the overall efficiency and functioning of government is a priority. In this regard, private players such as IT vendors perform a crucial role. However, in the case of India, the governments both at the central and state levels, are allowing participation only at the front-end and are handling all the back-end work. In programmes like e-Seva and Bhoomi, any private party can set up a kiosk, but the government provides all the support to run it. At the state level, governments are required to generate and develop content in local languages and this aspect brings in greater transparency in the delivery of public services.

Not only the private IT vendors, but also the community stakeholders need to play a greater role in generating and maintaining the content. The other feature in the PPP model is capacity building—both for public personnel and private operators. Connectivity up to the grassroots levels is imperative to ensure the success of any e-governance programme. The PPP design for e-governance involves adoption of different models like BOO (Build-Operate-Own), BOT (Build-Operate-Transfer) and BOOT (Build-Operate-Own-Transfer) for leveraging the technical, financial, and managerial capabilities of the private sector to implement a large number of e-Governance projects in a relatively short time framework and create the necessary impact.

Infrastructure for e-Governance

Setting up of Information Technology architecture, drafting competent cyber laws for protecting data integrity, enhancing the performance of back-end systems are the other key features of the public-private partnership (PPP) model in e-governance. Generation of software applications for e-projects from open source not only gives greater flexibility to the governments at the state level, but also generates lot of employment opportunities for local communities. This also helps in enhancing the technical competency of kiosk operators as well government staff at the grassroots level.

There's another major factor that sustains e-governance in developing societies like India, and it is that of Central funding for all pilots as well as constant support for research in e-governance. This was one of the major recommendations of the National Academy of Sciences (USA) when it presented a report to the federal government on "Technology, Research, Innovation and E-Government" in 2001. The Indian Government has every stake to offload in this critical factor that sustains e-governance in the long run. The government, in consonance with its double role of being a IT user and a long term investor in IT research – also research in e-governance – can gain a sound knowledge on the opportunities provided by IT advances and influence the development of IT than can help meet its own requirements. Such a synergy can be established through investment in the technology supply chain and through integration of all research modules.

For various ministries and departments, both at the central and state level, benefits from research can go well beyond the research results themselves. While there can be no replacement for institutional IT talent, collaborations with research agencies can be of great use to tap additional technical expertise, particularly high caliber research talent that is not easily available to the government.

Human resources in the administrative systems in India, at best, have been static over the years in terms of skill management and capacity building. This is one of the major handicaps in the developing and developed world as well. Technical competency among the public personnel is critical to the success of technology integration in administration, in other words, e-governance. While there have been several studies on this core issue in Western Europe and North America which offer tremendous insights to the respective government to overhaul the personnel management system, no such efforts have ever been attempted in India. The National Knowledge Commission has offered valuable suggestions with regard to IT infrastructure:

> *"It is important to provide nationwide secure broadband infrastructure and associated hardware, software and hosting facilities with easy access at all levels. This infrastructure should be based on user-pays principle and Public-Private partnership in investments and mutual accountability and efficiency. This infrastructure creation should be led by the Central Government to enforce a high level of security, uniformity and standards at every interface, regardless of state language, culture, legacy and financial health."*

With regard to standardization of e-governance practices, the NKC has this to say:

> *"At present various State Governments are doing their own thing to selectively computerize their processes and provide e-governance. Many of these programmes are vendor driven and not scalable. It is critical to develop and enforce citizen/business entitlement standards*

uniformly over all states and Central Ministries and functions, spanning from voting, taxes, certificates, financial products, law-enforcement and welfare for individuals, properties of land, institutions, businesses etc. These standards should not be hardware-centric and vendor dependent but should enable easy participation by any State, Panchayat Institution, business, NGO or citizen, whenever they decide. These standards, templates and data formats must be designed carefully by teams of experts drawn from government, IT companies, academia, R & D institutions and users/stakeholders who understand latest trends, technology, software, user interfaces and interoperability requirements."

E-Governance in India

Infusion of technology in administration is not a new phenomenon in India. The whole of 20th century witnessed great scientific and engineering marvels in the country. Our research history is over 100 years old. Significant achievements have been made in the areas of nuclear and space science, electronics and defense. India has the third largest scientific and technical manpower in the world; 162 universities award 4,000 doctorates and 35,000 postgraduate degrees and the Council of Scientific and Industrial Research runs 40 research laboratories that have made some significant achievements. In the field of Missile Launch Technology, India is among the top five nations of the world.

India has done a pioneering work in the field of information and communication technologies over the last two decades. The period from 1985 virtually saw India witnessing a communication revolution. However, the actual surge in the field of Information Technology (IT) began with the opening of the Indian economy to outside world in the early 1990s. As per the 2006-07 annual report of the Union Ministry of Commerce on India's foreign trade, software exports from India has crossed the $ 2 billion mark ($2.27 billion). Thanks to its foresight in steadily building up infrastructure in Science and Technology (S&T), India now has a far stronger technological base than most developing societies.

Telecommunication and Internet Penetration

Mobile telephony and Internet penetration has seen an upward swing in India after 1997. However, it is yet to reach the saturate levels on a par with other developing countries, especially China which has Internet penetration of over 12 per cent. As per the latest statistics from the International Telecommunication Union (ITU), India with a population of 1.12 billion has only 60 million internet users and little over 2.5 million broadband connections. Internet penetration is only 5.3 per cent when compared with the world average of 19 per cent. However, in terms of telephony penetration, India fares better with 21.20 per cent tele density. By the end of September 2007, there were 248.66 million subscribers (landline and mobile) across the country, according to Telecom Regulatory Authority of India report.

Though these figures do not paint a rosy picture as far as the country's readiness for e-governance is concerned, there has been a tremendous achievement on the ground, particularly in the field of public services.

Research on e-Governance

Further research in e-governance can be taken all over the country with emphasis on exploring new avenues for its application. Community organizations, cooperative bodies, industrial units, women's self-help groups, the National Rural Employment Guarantee Scheme, the Right to Information modules, all public-private collaborations in the fields of rural development, health, education, housing, sanitation, vaccination and slum development besides agriculture, animal husbandry, horticulture, sericulture, agro-based industries, food processing units, marketing can all be brought under the purview of e-governance systems in the pursuit of national development goals.

Once an integrated information and communications network is put in place with room for grassroots connectivity and interoperability the nation can really be on the path of inclusive development. Here again, there is a need to develop creative and innovative leadership and an efficient government workforce that is capable and willing to adapt electronic systems for governance. For this to happen, the Central Government should fund all the e-government programmes fully besides long term support for research in application of new technologies in governance. This was the pattern followed earnestly by the United States of America and other industrially advanced nations in achieving commendable goals in the field of e-governance.

Major Challenges and Constraints Facing e-Governance in India

Though much literature is available on the relative success of e-governance programmes in the country there has been little attempt at evaluating the critical challenges and constraints facing the concept of e-governance. The foremost challenge is the lack of literacy—by extension e-literacy. By any standards, literacy is not uniform in the rural and urban areas. Women's literacy is again a negative dimension. In this bleak scenario, expecting e-literacy levels that can sustain e-governance initiatives is almost impossible. Malappuram, the first e-literate district, is only one exception, and which is difficult to replicate not only at the state level (Kerala) but also on a national scale.

Considering the fact that a major chunk of the education sector is still owned by the government, budgeting and funding for IT education become a major concern. Cost also becomes a prohibitive factor when it comes to primary and secondary education segment because of the budgetary constraints. Even within the private sector, cost still acts as a dampener. Another fundamental challenge is the lack of appropriate authorities in charge of IT within the educational institutes to design and plan IT in terms of a strategic and integrated roadmap from a long-term perspective.

Lack of technical competency among the government employees is another hindering factor. Though definite statistics do not exist, the latest available figures point out that we have about 116,000 people in India engaged in scientific research and development (R&D) activity. This is in total contrast to the United States of America which has 1.3 million people in R&D, despite its total population of 290 million being less than a third of our one billion.

We have nearly 9 million science graduates, 2 million postgraduates and a lakh of PhDs. In addition, two million fresh students enroll for science degrees annually (though not all graduate), along with another 7 lakh in engineering. Thus there is no shortage, in terms of sheer numbers, of our technical manpower. The only thing lacking is the funding of R&D activity. A standard reason trotted out for this is shortage of funds. Another factor has been the absence of substantial demand for indigenous technology from the marketplace—an essential requirement for a healthy growth of S&T. Where new technology was deemed necessary, it was generally bought from abroad. Even as recently as 2004-05, the private sector contributed only 14 per cent of India's R&D expenditure, as compared to 63 per cent in the U.S. As it is, employment opportunities for the technically skilled are abysmally low and are confined to only public sector units like the BHEL, NTPC, ISRO, ECIL, etc. It is a fact that people with engineering and computer sciences background (those from IITs) are entering the Indian Administrative Service. However, they are at the top decision making level and are confined to developing e-governance modules. Their implementation at the ground level is still left to the technically disadvantaged personnel.

There is no denying the fact that there is a greater demand for technical skills in the private sector, especially after the opening up of economy in the early 1990s. Even in this sector we have a problem. Employers find most of our graduates not only inadequately trained, but un-trainable. For instance, our IT-BPO sector is expected to hire over a million more employees by 2010 but, according to an industry analyst, only 8-10 per cent of our 495,000 engineers graduating annually are qualified to work in this burgeoning industry. As a result, the IT giants in India hire several thousand graduates from abroad, even as 2 million science graduates remain registered at our employment exchanges.

Public service delivery in the key social and employment sectors is one that needs a radical overhaul. Traditionalism still pervades the administration in these critical sectors, including delivery of basic services to the masses. Nothing best illustrates this point than a terse comment by the Union Finance Minister P. Chidambaram at the India Economic Summit (2nd December 2007). He said: "We have very ambitious social sector programmes—in areas of employment, health, education and the outlays on them have been increased. But we still depend on tried and tested, but failed systems of delivery. There has been very little progress in public-private partnerships and devising alternative institutions to deliver goods and services to the masses rather than rely on the rigid bureaucracy that we have. I have no problem providing resources to states as long as outcomes are delivered. But are we getting bang for the buck?"

Commenting on technology in governance, Planning Commission Deputy Chairman Dr. Montek Singh Ahluwalia said: "You know technology change disrupts a system, and it's extremely difficult to know what the best way to take a system forward is."

Traditionalism is synonymous with clientage and corruption in administration. Feudal relations prevail at all levels of governance and corruption is rampant. These negative traits hinder any attempt at technological innovation in governance. Rigid bureaucracy at the top as well as technology resistance at the field level is the major stumbling block on the road to e-governance. Technology sensitization coupled with capacity building in a systematic and phased manner can be a solution, but these are still out of the realm of possibility considering the lack of basic skills among the public staff.

The efforts bringing the processes of governance in public domain is picking up gradually, but surely. This is in tune with the basic principles of e-governance termed as transparency, accountability and responsibility. Electronic services are more or less transparent, but what requires to be done further is in field of information outflow, expressed recently in the form of Right to Information (RTI). Comprehensive data is still a distant dream with no constant update of the information. In other words, a systemic data management is yet to be put in place. Problems on the supply side continue to plague the RTI Act as the officials are hostile and unhelpful towards applicants.

MAJOR FINDINGS OF THE STUDY

There is an increasing bottom-up demand for more electronic delivery of services in urban areas, particularly cities and towns. The success of e-Seva, FRIENDS and BangaloreOne illustrates this point.

There is a growing bottom-up demand for electronic delivery of public services in urban areas of the country. Though different models of electronic services are in operation, there is still a wide demand for inclusion of more and more services. On this front, e-Seva scores high over other programmes with nearly 64 services and can be truly considered as "one-stop" shop for citizens. It is planning to include more services in the future besides spreading to every municipality and mandal headquarters in Andhra Pradesh. City portals of Vijayawada and Visakhapatnam – VOICE and Saukaryam respectively – have merged with e-Seva for administrative and public convenience.

However, FRIENDS that started as early as 2001, has failed to replicate the success of e-Seva. It has not scaled up to the expected levels and remains confined to the jurisdiction of the state capital and the district headquarters. The service centres too are a few, barring Thiruvananthapuram which has nearly 20 centres. Also, the number of services is less compared to e-Seva and BangaloreOne, though the number of citizens availing services at FRIENDS centres is growing up very fast.

BangaloreOne, which is claimed to be technically superior to e-Seva, has not grown out of the capital city of Karnataka. The number of service centres is too less with only 16 centres operating in select areas of the city in contrast to e-Seva which has a service centre in almost every locality in the twin cities of Hyderabad and Secunderabad. The number of services is growing steadily, but there has been no effort to popularize them among the prospective users.

E-services can be implemented successfully even in the rural areas with innovative and productive modules. Projects like Akshaya, Bhoomi, CARD and KAVERI are shining examples in this context.

Though rural India is backward in terms of literacy and use of technology, it has shown a tremendous adaptability to technology in governance. The prime attributes the rural populace found indispensable in administration online are the time and cost factors. Technology has been leveraged in such a way that even illiterates can operate an electronic kiosk and know the status of their petition/work at the click of a button. Availing public services at a faster pace and with less costs was hitherto not in the realm of possibility for the rural masses.

Illiteracy has been the prime cause for the socio-economic backwardness of the rural peoples, but things are improving slowly and steadily over the last two decades. Telecommunications have improved in the last few years and according to the latest TRAI report, there are 57 million phones (land and mobile) in rural India. This number is expected to go up drastically in the next few years. Infrastructure for e-governance has been designed and developed in an innovative way to take technology to the door steps of the people. This situation can best be illustrated with the success of Akshaya, the first e-literacy drive in the country. At least one person from each family in Malappuram where Akshaya was implemented as a pilot received training in handling the desktop as well communicating through the Internet. That the Akshaya centres have evolved in full-blown community information centres that provide citizen services online speaks volumes of the success of the programme.

However, the ability of the entrepreneurs to sustain the centres for longer periods has not been uniform of the 630 centres that went into operation in the second phase of the project, only 350 are active now. The reasons for this lack of sustainability of the franchisee are varied, but the prime factor is the lack of innovativeness on the part of entrepreneurs to integrate services that are of great need to the local people. However, Akshaya, if replicated successfully, on a national scale can make India a true knowledge society.

Land is synonymous with property in rural areas and valid documents to support ownership of land are compulsory under revenue laws. The computerization of land records was taken up as a national project in 2000. However, only a few states have been successful in reaching the target (computerization of land records was supposed to be completed on a national scale by 2007). Karnataka is one of those states and has done a pioneering work. The state launched the Bhoomi project as part of the national plan in 2002 and a pilot was started early in 2001 to test its viability. Initially, the programme faced difficulty in piling up the databases, but picked up in a couple of years. Karnataka became a model for the entire country in electronic documentation of land records by early 2004.

The traditional model of land documentation took a lot of paper work and an extended timeframe that was not less than six months. In the present model, there is little or no paper work and the time for documentation has come down to less than a month. Issue of land documents hardly takes 10 minutes. Queries on pending files can be had online at the Bhoomi kiosk and a farmer can operate it on his own without bothering to see the revenue officials. Virtually every farmer and land owner has utilized or is utilizing the services at Bhoomi kiosks across the state. Though bureaucratic hassles have been eliminated in this model, the level of corruption is yet to come down. As of now, private personnel are managing the Bhoomi kiosks. That kiosk operators will work for longer period cannot be guaranteed. Hence, efforts should be made to improve the technical competency of the revenue staff to handle the kiosk operators. Only a few other states have taken up Bhoomi as a model for computerization of land records in the country. The Central Government has to frame guidelines in this regard and order all other states to adhere to them promptly in a set timeframe.

Registration of property was never so prompt before the implementation of CARD (Computer-Aided Administration of Revenue Department) in the state of Andhra Pradesh and KAVERI (Karnataka Valuation and e-Registration. In 2007, 224 Sub-Registrar's Offices in Karnataka were delivering three key services: on line registration of property sale/purchase deeds; issue of non-encumbrance certificate and issue of copies of a previously registered deed through the KAVERI programme. The first KAVERI centre was launched in the Rajajinagar SRO in Bangalore district in 2003. The timeframe to issue a sale deed has come down to less than 10 minutes in this electronic registration model. The registration department of

Karnataka has earned revenue to the tune of Rs. 3415.20 crore in the 2006-07 fiscal year, while the total expenditure was less than Rs. 40 crore.

CARD was introduced as a pilot at two Sub-Registrar Offices (SROs) as early as 1997 by the Department of Registration in Andhra Pradesh. The project was started on 4 November 1998. Presently, the project covers all the 287 SROs in 23 districts of the state. The CARD project registers 1.18 million documents and serves 5 million citizens in a year. Since the inception of the project, 4 million documents have been registered. The gross revenue earned by the department is more than Rs. 3,500 crores. The department is confident of achieving its target of Rs. 4,500 crore for the year 2007-08.

However, the success of KAVERI has been outstanding compared to CARD. It has also established effective linkages with Bhoomi at the taluka level and to some extent with BangaloreOne is Bangalore Rural district. Such interoperability can be achieved in Andhra Pradesh by integrating CARD, e-Seva and the proposed project for digitization of land records. Kerala too has enabling conditions to integrate electronic documentation with Akshaya and FRIENDS.

Total networking of district administration is in the realm of possibility. Effective coordination among various departments is crucial to set up an integrated network right from the village panchayat to the district level. E-Collectorate of Palakkad can be a model for the entire country.

DC* Suite (District Collectorate Suite) was inaugurated on the 24th of October 2004 in Palakkad by the then Chief Minister Oomen Chandy. The e-district project was conceptualized by the National e-Governance Plan (2006). It is currently spread over 30 districts across 17 Indian states. 20 pilot projects have been implemented successfully. DC* Suite covers 22 functional areas of Collectorate and includes electronic file management system, revenue recovery management, public grievance monitoring system, etc. Information is made available to public through touch screen kiosks, interactive voice response systems etc. However, the concept of e-district was put into practice in Tiruvarur district of Tamil Nadu as early as 1999 and in the year 2000 it conducted its first online annual audit of village accounts. In February 2001, an online data warehouse was developed. The district did not receive any funds and technological support from the State Government.

Coming to the Palakkad experience, though full scale automation has been achieved at the District Collectorate, a comprehensive integrated network that connects the DC* Suite with other offices at the headquarters has not been put in place. For instance, if a citizen files a complaint regarding law and order issues, his case is sent to the District Superintendent of Police Office manually. This often results in undue delay in informing the complainant on the status of his file. Also, a full scale network that integrates all the talukas up to the panchayat level is yet to be developed. Such a network is in the realm of possibility in Malappuram district where more than one Akshaya centre is functioning in every panchayat.

- Replication of successful technology modules on a national scale can save precious public money and pave way for funding of e-governance projects in unexplored avenues.
- Continuous and broad central funding for research in new technologies and long-term support for ongoing e-government projects can open up new opportunities for application of information and communication technologies in hitherto unexplored administrative areas.

E-governance in India is happening on account of certain key ministries/departments taking the initiative and launching e-governance schemes. A National e-Governance Plan (NeGP) was formulated, but in effect the ministries/departments have been plodding through on their own, managing projects, pursuing financial approvals and the like.

The Central Government has a major scheme for e-governance with a budget of Rs. 23,000 crore. This is apart from the state-level initiatives some of which are funded entirely from the state exchequer and some in partnership with the private players. Much of the investment—both by the Centre and the States—goes into setting up IT infrastructure and capacity building. For the 2006-07 fiscal alone, the Centre spent Rs. 300 crore as the Additional Central Assistance (ACA) for capacity building under NeGP.

Investment on infrastructure largely includes setting up the IT architecture, laying optical fibre cables, software packages for e-service modules, broadband Internet, maintenance costs along with training for the private operators and officials concerned. Funding of e-governance is imperative, but it needs to be done strategically and creatively. For instance, replication of successful electronic service delivery modules like e-Seva can be done on a national scale and the funds thus saved from investing in new software packages for similar modules can be routed to unexplored services. In other words, funds spent on developing software modules FRIENDS and BangaloreOne could have been saved to a large extent had the governments of Kerala and Karnataka thought of replicating e-Seva of Andhra Pradesh. Similarly, CARD was developed much earlier in AP in 1999, but Karnataka voted to go with entirely a new version called KAVERI.

Sound economic planning coupled with creative modules like Akshaya of Kerala can be supported for different states since the interactive module needs content generated totally at the local level and with the help of the targeted communities.

Innovation in private-public partnership is another key factor that helps in saving precious resources. KAVERI programme of Karnataka best underscores this point. Entire investment in technology came from the private partner. For the private partner the payback is over 8-9 years at current levels of user fee. For the 2006-07 fiscal, the registration department of the state spent only Rs.39.98 crore while the income was to the tune of Rs. 3415.20 crore. The expenditure incurred by the state on the programme was just over 1.5 per cent of the total income.

Transparency, accountability, responsiveness and reduction in time and costs in electronic delivery of public services that collective enhance the satisfaction levels of the users/citizens are the key factors that determine the success of any e-governance project.

As the premise of the study is on gauzing the overall satisfaction levels among users of electronic public services, a definitive methodology was worked out purely from a user perspective. It has been established theoretically and empirically that the success of any e-governance programme in a traditional and developing society like India depends largely on transparency, accountability, responsiveness and reduction in time and costs for the users that collectively enhances their levels of satisfaction. For instance, the success of e-Seva, BangaloreOne and Akshaya was largely on account of the above key factors. There is a greater demand for inclusion of more services in the current programmes with varied levels of accountability and responsibility.

However, users are highly satisfied on the time and costs front besides the 'perceived' transparency in these programmes. In the case of projects like Bhoomi, that involves greater deal of time and costs for survey and mapping of land, the issues of accountability and responsibility come into question from users as the process is totally undertaken by the revenue staff. Transparency is there, but in the form of a digital land record (RTC). Costs relating to acquiring land records have come down a little and time taken for the same is now only 30 days as compared to six months in the traditional system. The same is the case with property registration projects like the CARD and KAVERI.

Interoperability in the delivery of electronic services at all levels can lay strong foundations for e-government in its true sense.

Interoperability denotes scaling up the existing e-governance projects with effective linkages down to the grassroots level. Bhoomi and KAVERI offer a tremendous hope for interoperability of e-governance projects in the country. The sale transactions (property registration) are generated and sent on daily basis from the Registration Department to Bhoomi system electronically through the State Data Centre (SDC) and Bhoomi collects and processes them as per the business processes up to the taluk level. Bhoomi has also been linked with banks for credit and courts of law for speedy resolution of disputes.

Efforts are on to link the Palakkad DC* Suite (e-Collectorate) with taluka suites and up to the block level where Akshaya centres are offering various electronic public services. Once integration is done with, this interoperability can be model for future e-district projects across the country.

The city portals of Vijayawada and Visakhapatnam–VOICE and Saukaryam–have been integrated successfully with the wide-ranging e-Seva network for more effectiveness in service delivery.

Efforts till now in the country have demonstrated the potential of e-governance projects, though much work remains to be done in the areas of organization, policy, technology development and transition, systems architecture and engineering practice.

Though much has been said about the 'imminent' success of e-governance projects, there has been little or no contribution to evolving a coherent organizational structure, administrative policy, further research in software applications, institutional readiness for smooth transition from a PPP model to entirely state-owned one, standardization of systems architecture and developing best engineering practices. For instance, a department has to have a strong organizational structure with related administrative guidelines and best practices to run an e-governance project entirely on its own.

Technological adaptation, skill development of public employees, and hiring of technical staff (contract) are the key concerns that administrative systems face in the country.

If we take the case of KAVERI, Pune-based C-DAC provided the software for the project, while CMS Computers Ltd. and the ECIL are service providers for hardware, supporting software and maintenance. Initial investment came entirely from these companies. There is a problem of transition when the government takes over the management from the private entrepreneurs after the expiry of contract period which is five years (2008). Capacity building in technical operations (of kiosks) is a major concern for KAVERI which could have been avoided if a strong organizational structure had been put in place in the interim. Bhoomi, whose kiosks too are managed by private operators, faces a similar predicament.

Instead of spending millions of dollars on procurement of software applications for e-governance programmes from multi-national corporations like Microsoft, Sun, Oracle and Linux, the Central and State Governments would do well to come up with a policy that totally supports Free Open Source Software (FOSS). Already, the Centre has in principle approved 100 per cent open source technology. This is also the basic recommendation of the National Knowledge Commission (NKC) headed by Sam Pitroda.

> *"Because of the enormous size and scope of the e-governance effort in India and because of the availability of globally recognized software talent of Indians, we must actively encourage wherever possible open source software implementations and open standards. This will allow us to have cost-effective solutions and help develop open software products and standards. It will also help improve scaling up as well as minimize delays caused by repeat tendering."*

The best example for a successful adaptation of the free open source software policy in the country can be traced to Thiruvarur district in Tamil Nadu which developed a model DC* Suite (e-Collectorate or e-district) as early as 1999. (Only six years later, the NeGP conceived the e-district project as a pilot.) Though the project is not a part of our study, we are presenting it as a model for future e-district projects. Interestingly, Thiruvarur received no financial support from the TN Government. A non-profit organization, District Welfare Committee was floated to mobilize funds worth Rs. 2.5 crore. Four software development centres were set up in the Collector's Office employing around 30 software professionals. The district ushered in a Wi-Fi revolution by setting up the first wireless LAN (on 802.11b standard) connecting all the 20 offices in 14 different locations. In February 2001, the e-district project became fully operational.

MAJOR RECOMMENDATIONS

Though a slew of positive attributes/impacts of different e-governance projects have been observed at the grassroots level in the course of this study, a number of inhibiting factors or constraints too have come to the fore. Ideas from early experiments in e-governance have definitely contributed to technology development as well as to the improvement of government practices. There is a wealth of experience already at hand to create and deploy e-governance projects. Such an experience can be found at the local, state and central levels as well as different departments at the national level. The best practices emerging from this experience can be adopted by many or all government agencies.

From the citizen's point of view, perceptible achievements in the field of e-governance have been new means of access to government information, task-oriented cross-departmental portals (e-Seva, FRIENDS, BangaloreOne) and launch of government portals (www.apgovonline.com, www.kar.nic.in, www.kerala.gov.in) and one-stop facility for payment of utility bills (both of public and private sectors). Other illustrations include computer-based tax filing and inquiry-response services that are provided by multiple agencies, each accessed through a task-oriented web portal.

The benefits to business have also been considerable, including broader access to government data, more rapid and efficient interaction with regulatory agencies and streamlined acquisition and procurement processes. Also, administrative burdens associated with initiating and managing small and start-up businesses are being reduced through online sources.

However, much needs to be done in enhancing systems used for information management and collaboration among government officials and departments. Broadening e-government services from information access to transaction support which enable citizens, businesses and other government entities to submit information to, engage in financial transactions with, or interact with government departments. In these spheres, issues like confidentiality, data integrity, information management, and usability are the major hurdles. These issues mix technology and policy which is difficult to address without proper collaboration between technology and policy makers. There are many government departments that are experiencing difficulties in deploying new capabilities.

The following are the major recommendations that can be taken into account for effective implementation of e-governance projects at all levels in a vast country like India:

- Ensuring interoperation and integration of diverse e-governance models used by different departments and agencies with multiple stakeholders besides developing a considerable legacy base.
- Adapting institutions and personnel so as to maximize their capabilities in tune with the new technologies, which are hard to implement in public administrative systems than in the private sector. (An element of feudalism pervades public staff at all levels that inherently resists changes to existing models of governance and this needs to be defeated comprehensively through time-bound orientation programmes).
- Improving trustworthiness by providing broader access to government information and assuring information systems security, user privacy and system availability.
- Bridging considerable gaps between successful models of e-governance and experimental projects.
- Making electronic services more citizen-centric than government-centric.
- Meeting technological needs related to future government policies and programmes.
- Harnessing ICTs in governance for the benefit of marginalized sections of society, including the rural poor, women, physically and mentally challenged.
- Ensuring comprehensive and effective public-private collaboration in conceptualizing, designing and implementing e-governance projects is critical to achieving the goals of good governance.

- Effective linkages between Bhoomi, KAVERI and BangaloreOne up to panchayat level can herald in real e-government in Karnataka besides scaling up of services of each individual portal.
- Similarly, interoperability between CARD, e-Seva along with a new e-governance portal for land registration on the lines of Bhoomi can place Andhra Pradesh on a high pedestal in the field of e-governance.
- DC* Suite can be the order of day in the country in terms of district level administration. This e-district module can be successfully integrated with leading e-governance modules like Akshaya and FRIENDS in Kerala, Bhoomi and KAVERI in Karnataka and e-Seva and CARD in Andhra Pradesh. All the DC* Suites can be effectively integrated with the State Wide Area Networks of respective states.
- Integration of State Wide Area Network (SWAN) up to the panchayat level and cross-networking of SWANs with the Union Government can ultimately establish an e-government in the country in the near future. Appropriate technologies and adequate funds are the only major obstacles in achieving this goal.

Ten Recommendations for Future e-governance Projects

1. Strengthening systems for effective public service delivery.
2. Concentrating more on peoples' needs rather than administrative conveniences.
3. Compatibility of electronic services with the needs of institutional stakeholders.
4. Developing organizational structure and leadership.
5. Aiming for saturation in the provision of electronic services.
6. Leveraging existing PPPs and market funds.
7. Sensitizing public employees on technology adaptation.
8. Replicating successful e-governance modules across the country.
9. Standardizing IT architecture and best e-governance practices.
10. Overcoming digital divide with innovative and interactive programmes.

BIBLIOGRAPHY AND WEBLIOGRAPHY

BOOKS

Andhra Pradesh Government — Vision 2020, State Secretariat, Hyderabad, 1999.

Anne Mette Kjaer, *Governance*, Atlantic Publishers and Distributors, New Delhi, 2005.

Bedi, K.S., Parminder, J. Srivastava, S. *Government @ net*, Sage, New Delhi, 2000.

Bhatnagar, S. and N. Bjorn Anderson (Eds.), *Information Technology in Developing Countries*, Amsterdam, North-Holland, 1990.

Bhatnagar, S. and R. Sechware, (Eds.), *Information and Communication Technology in Development: Cases from India*, Sage Publications, New Delhi, 2000.

Christine Bellamy and Taylor John A., *Governing in the Information Age*, Open University Press, Buckingham, 1998.

Farnham, D. and Harton, S. *Managing the New Public Service*, MacMillan, London, 1996.

Garson, G.D., *Hand Book of Public Information System*, New York, USA, 2000.

Gosling, P., *Government for Digital Age*, Bowerdean, London, 1997.

Harris, Roger and Arora, Rajesh, *Empowering the Poor: Information and Communications Technology for Governance and Poverty Reduction — A Study of Rural Development Projects in India*, UNDP-APDIP, Elsevier, 2006.

Harris, Roger and Rajesh Rajora, UNDP-APDIP ICT4D Series, 2006.

Harry Bouwman, *et. al., Information and Communication Technology in Organisations,* Sage Publications, New Delhi, 2005.

Heeks Richard (Ed.), *Reinventing Government in the Information Age,* Routledge, London 1999.

Heeks, R. (Ed.), *"Reinventing Government in the Information Age: International Practice in IT-Enabled Public Sector Reform,"* Routledge, London, 1999.

Heidegger, M., "The question concerning technology," in *Basic Writings,* Routledge, London, 1978.

ICTD Case Studies, Asia-Pacific Development Information Programme, UNDP Regional Centre, Bangkok, 2006.

Joyojeet Pal, Sergiu Nedevschi, Rabin K. Patra, Eric A. Brewer, *A Multi-Disciplinary Approach to Shared Access Village Computing Initiatives: The Case of Akshaya,* 2006.

Madon, Shirin, 'IT Diffusion for Public Service Delivery: Looking for Plausible Theoretical Approaches', In *Information Systems and the Economics of Innovation.* Edited by Avgerou, C.; La Rovere, R. Edward Elgar, 2003.

Madon, Shirin, 'Evaluating e-Governance Projects in India: A focus on micro-level implementation.' In *The Handbook of Information Systems Research: Critical perspectives on information systems design, implementation and use.* Edited by Howcroft, Debra; Trauth, Eileen. Edward Elgar, 2005.

Madon, Shirin, Avgerou, C. 'Framing Information Systems Studies: Understanding the social context of information systems innovation.' In *The Social Study of Information Technology,* Edited by Avgerou, C.; Ciborra, C.; Land, F. Oxford University Press, 2004.

Madon, Shirin, Krishna, S. (Eds.), *The Digital Challenge: Information Technology in the Development Context.* Ashgate, 2003.

Osborne, D. and Gaebler, T. *Reinventing Government: How the Entrepreneurial Spirit is Transforming the Public Sector,* MA: Addison Wesley, Reading, 1992.

Prabhu CSR, *E-Governance: Concepts and Case Studies,* Prentice-Hall India Pvt. Ltd., 2004.

Ramachandrudu G. and Prasada Rao M. (Eds.), 2004, *Census 2001 and Human Development in India*, Vedam Books, New Delhi.

Snellen and Van de Donk (Ed.), *Public Administration in an Information Age*, IOS Press, Amsterdam, 1998.

Sood, A., D., *A Social Investor's Guide to ICTs for Development*, Centre for Knowledge societies and Charities Aid Foundation India, Bangalore, 2001.

Tapscott, D., *The Digital Economy*, McGraw Hill, New York, 1996.

The Working Group on E-Government in the Developing World, Pacific Council on International Policy, UNESCAP, Bangkok, April 2002.

United Nations Department of Economic and Social Affairs, "*World Public Sector Report 2003: E-Government at the Crossroads*," 2003.

Vittal, N., 'E-Development Enabling Communities to Shape their Future: The Indian Perspective', in Jayakumar, R., G. Vijayaraghavan and D.S. Sureshkumar. (Eds.), *Information Technology for Development: A Millennium Perspective*. Thiruvananthapuram: STEC, Government of Kerala, 2001.

World Public Sector Report 2003, Department of Economic and Social Affairs, United Nations, New York, 2003.

Zajtchuk, Russ *et. al.* (Ed.)., *Information Technology, Development and Policy: Theoretical Perspectives and Practical Challenges*, Aldershot, Hants, England: Brookfield, 1996.

Articles and Working Papers

"The Next Revolution – A Survey of Government and the Internet," *The Economist*, June 24, 2000.

Basu, S., "E-Government and Developing Countries: An Overview," *International Review of Law Computers & Technology*, Vol. 18, No. 1, 2004.

Bellamy, C. and J. A. Taylor. (Eds.), 'Towards the Information Polity: Public Administration in the Information Age,' *Journal of Public Administration*, 72 (1), 1994.

Bhatnagar, S., "E-Government: Lessons from Implementation in Developing Countries," *Regional Development Dialogue*, Vol. 24, UNCRD, Autumn Issue 2002.

Bouckaert, Geert and Van de Walle, Steven, Comparing measures of citizen trust and user satisfaction as indicators of good governance: difficulties in linking trust and satisfaction indicators, *International Review of Administrative Sciences,* 2003.

Cecchini, S. and Raina, M., "Electronic Government and the Rural Poor: The Case of Gyandoot," *Information Technologies and International Development,* Vol. 2, No. 2, 2004.

Centre for Electronic Governance, IIM, Ahmedabad study on 'Gyandoot: Rural Cyber Cafes on Internet', Dhar, Madhya Pradesh, Draft Report, October 2002.

Ciborra, C., "Interpreting e-government and Development Efficiency, transparency or governance at a distance?" *Information Technology & People,* Vol. 18, No. 3, 2005.

D. Dada Ho, A.T-K., "Reinventing local governments and the e-government initiative," *Public Administration Review,* Vol. 62, No. 4, 2002.

Ebrahim, Z. and Irani, Z., "E-government adoption: architecture and barriers," *Business Process Management Journal,* Vol. 11, No. 5, 2005.

E-Government Benefit Study, Commonwealth of Australia, 2003.

Heeks, R., "Information Age Reform of the Public Sector: The Potential and Problems of IT for India," Information Systems for Public Sector Management, Working Paper Series, Paper No. 6, 1998.

Heeks, R., "Information Systems and Developing Countries: Failure, Success, and Local Improvisations," *The Information Society,* Vol. 18, 2002.

Heeks, R., "Most e-Government-for-Development Projects Fail: How Can Risks be Reduced?" i-Government Working Paper Series, Paper No. 14, 2003.

Information and Communication Technologies for Development: A Comparative Analysis of Impacts and Costs from India, A report for a project funded by Department of IT & Infosys Technologies, 2004.

Information Technology Security Training Requirements: A Role- and Performance-Based Model, US Department of Commerce, Washington D.C., April 1998.

Jaeger, P.T. and Thompson, K.M., "E-government around the World:

Lessons, Challenges, and Future Directions,", *Government Information Quarterly*, 20, 2003.

Kaul. M. *et. al.*, 'New Information Technology Applications for Local Development in Asian and Pacific Countries', *Information Technology for Development*, 4 (1), 1989.

Krishna, S. and Walsham, G., "Implementing Public Information Systems in Developing Countries: Learning From a Success Story", *Information Technology for Development*, Vol. 11 (2), 2005.

Lewis, David, Madon, Shirin. 'Information Systems and Non-governmental Development Organisations: Advocacy, Organisational Learning and Accountability in a Southern NGO.' *The Information Society*, Vol. 20, No. 2, 2004.

Madon, Shirin, Beck, E.; Sahay, S. 'On the Margins of the Information Society: A comparative study of mediation.' *The Information Society*, Vol. 20, No. 4, 2004.

Madon, Shirin, 'Evaluating the Developmental Impact of E-Governance Initiatives: An Exploratory Framework,' *EJISDC*, Vol. 20, No. 5, 2005.

Madon Shirin, 'Governance Lessons from the Experience of Telecentres in Kerala', *European Journal of Information Systems*, 14, No. 4, 2005.

Madon, Shirin, Sahay S., 'An Information-based Model of NGO-mediation for the Empowerment of Slum Dwellers in Bangalore', *The Information Society*, 18, No. 1, 2002.

Madon, Shirin; Sahay, S.; Sahay, J. 'Implementing Property Tax Reforms in Bangalore: An Actor-Network Perspective.' *Information & Organization* 14, No. 4, 2004.

Moon, M.J., "The evolution of e-Government among Municipalities: Rhetoric or Reality," *Public Administration Review*, Vol. 62, No. 4, 2002.

Navarra D.D. and Cornford T., "ICT, Innovation and Public Management: Governance, Models and Alternatives for E-Government Infrastructures," in *'Proceedings of the Thirteenth European Conference on Information Systems'*, Regensburg, Germany, 2005.

Ndou, V.D., "E-Government for Developing Countries: Opportunities and Challenges," *Electronic Journal of Information Systems in*

Developing Countries, 18, 1, 2004.

Norris, P., "The Worldwide Digital Divide: Information Poverty, the Internet and Development," Paper for the Annual Meeting of the Political Studies Association of the UK, London School of Economics and Political Science, Roundtable on The Future Role of New Media in Elections, 2000.

Schware, R. and Deane, A., "Deploying e-Government programmes: The Strategic Importance of 'I' before 'E'," *Info*, Vol. 5, No. 4, 2003.

Shirin, Madon; Kiran G.R., *Information Technology for Citizen-Government Interface, A Study of Friends Project in Kerala*, 2004.

Sreekumar T. T., *Civil Society and State-led Initiatives in ICTs: The Case of Kerala*, Information Technology in Developing Countries, Vol. 12, No. 3, December 2002.

Sreekumar, T., 'Civil Society and ICT-Based Models of Rural Change: History, Rhetoric and Practice' Paper presented at the International Seminar on "*ICTS for Indian Development: Processes, Prognosis and Policies*" jointly organized by Institute of Social Studies, The Netherlands and Institute of Human Development, New Delhi, Bangalore 9-11 December 2002.

WEBLIOGRAPHY

www.unpan.org/egovernment.asp

http://www.oecd.org/department/

www.whitehouse.gov/omb/egov

www.pacificcouncil.org

http://www.unpan.org/training_egovform.asp/

www.unpan1.un.org/intradoc/groups/public/documents/UN/UNPAN012553.pdf

http://www.erg.usgs.gov/isb/pubs/gis_poster/index.html

http://www.egovindia.org/whitepapers.html

http://www.egovindia.org/whitepapers.html

http://www.aoema.org/E-Government/Definitions_and_Objectives.htm

http://www.gdrc.org/u-gov/governance-understand.html

http://www.gdrc.org/u-gov/work-def.html

http://www1.worldbank.org/mena/governance/Issues-

KeyQuestion.htm
http://www.gdrc.org/u-gov/indicators.html
http://www.iadb.org/ict4dev/governance.htm
www.iimahd.ernet.in
www.keelan.ie/uploads/documents/egovernment/Benchmark.Report.pdf www.aponline.gov.in
http://www.singaporeonline.com
www.esevaonline.com
www.aponline.com
www.esevaonline.com
www.planningcommission.gov.in
www.bhoomi.kar.nic.in
www.intech.unu.edu
www.bangaloreone.gov.in
http://www.man.ac.uk/idpm/idpm_dp.htm#ig
www.keralaitmission.org
www.kerala.gov.in
www.mlp.kerala.gov.in/gen.htm
www.friendscentre.net
www.keralaitmission.org
www.palakkad.nic.in
www.electronicgov.com
www.oii.ox.ac.uk
www.itc.napier.ac.uk
www.cira.org
www.cordis.lu/united_kingdom
www.cdt.org
www.ksg.harvard.edu/digitalcenter
www.ukonline.gov.uk
www.e-envoy.gov.uk
http://www.europa.eu.int/yourvoice

www.ipmmarkt.homestead.com

www.headstar.com/egb

www.edentool.org

http://www.unpan.org/dpepa_worldpareport.asp

http://web.worldbank.org/WBSITE/EXTERNAL/TOPICS/EXTINFORMATIONANDCOMMUNICATIONANDTECHNOLOGIES/EXTEGOVERNMENT 0, menu PK: 702592~ page PK: 149018~piPK:149093~theSitePK:702586,00.html

Index